Warman's
Star ~~Wars~~

FIELD GUIDE

Stuart W. Wells III

Values and Identification

©2005 by Stuart W. Wells III

Published by

kp books
An Imprint of F+W Publications

700 East State Street • Iola, WI 54990-0001
715-445-2214 • 888-457-2873

Our toll-free number to place an order or obtain a free catalog is
(800) 258-0929.

Library of Congress Catalog Number: 2004115464
ISBN: 0-89689-134-8

Designed by: Wendy Wendt
Edited by: Dan Brownell

Printed in U.S.A.

Contents

INTRODUCTION

The *Star Wars* phenomenon started in 1977, and after a little slump in the late 1980s, it is still going strong. Collectibles from the classic movie were available beginning in late 1976—first a poster and a book, then the comics in early 1977 and, finally, after the movie opened, a few games and puzzles. The real flood didn't start until 1978, when the action figures arrived.

This book covers *Star Wars* collectibles distributed in the United States from the beginning through the third quarter of 2004. It is both updated and condensed from my book *A Universe of Star Wars Collectibles, Identification and Price Guide,* 2nd Edition, Krause Publications 2002, ISBN 0-87349-415-6.

The first *Star Wars* collectible available to the general public was the original paperback book, which appeared a full seven months before the movie opened. *Star Wars* collectible #2 is the first issue of the comic book series from Marvel. It came out before the movie opened, and it's worth a lot more than the paperback book. Nevertheless, neither the paperback nor the comic are as valuable as any of the early action figures (the 35 cent test issue of this comic is another matter).

In *Star Wars* collecting, Kenner (now Hasbro) is king. Almost anything made by Kenner/Hasbro, and a lot of things it never actually made, is collected more intensely than anything, however attractive, made by any other company.

The amount of coverage given to any category depends on its popularity. Action figures are the most popular *Star Wars* collectible,

so they are given the most coverage, with additional sections on the vehicles, accessories and 12-inch dolls. Less popular items have been given less coverage or eliminated in this field guide.

Condition

Most *Star Wars* items are graded on a 10-point scale from C-10 (the best) down to C-1. Prices in this book are for items in their original packaging in "near mint" condition, which corresponds to about C-9 or C-9.5. The occasional extraordinary item that is actually "mint" (i.e. C-10) commands a slightly higher price. How much higher depends on how much better than an ordinary near-mint copy it actually is. The criteria for mint always remains the same, regardless of the age or type of product. Mint is not the same as "new." Most new products are not truly mint, as they have suffered from handling by store employees and by all the customers who handled the items, but did not buy them.

Pricing

A single price is given for each listed item. This represents the full retail price or asking price. Prices vary from one dealer to another and from one location to another, so prices actually fall into a range.

But even though no single price can cover all situations, a price range of $40 to $100, for example, is no more meaningful than a single price, and is even less satisfying. The single price given in this book should be used as a guideline or baseline. If you can find the item that you want to buy for 10 percent to 25 percent less than this price, you are getting a good deal. If you are paying more, but you really want the item, that's okay, too. Just shop around a little first to see if you can do better. This book is based on the author's research. The author is not a dealer in *Star Wars* collectibles and is not associated with any dealer or manufacturer, nor with Lucasfilms or its licensees.

STAR WARS: CLASSIC FIGURES (1978-1995)

STAR WARS Kenner (1977–1986)

The very first *Star Wars* action figures arrived in the mail in 1978. Of course, they only did so if you bought the famous Early Bird Package. The figures came in a white plastic tray in a white mailer box. There were four figures, along with a bag of plastic pegs for the display stand. Already there were variations. In the very earliest packages, Chewbacca had a dark green plastic rifle instead of the later black plastic, and Luke had a telescoping lightsaber. Some people call it a double telescoping lightsaber, as it not only extends out of his arm, it also telescopes out of the middle of the blade and almost reaches the floor. This version lightsaber can occasionally be found on carded Luke Skywalker and sometimes even on Darth Vader and Ben (Obi-Wan) Kenobi figures. It adds about $1,000 to the value of the Luke Skywalker figure and $2,000 to the value of the other two! It also increases the value of the loose figure, but it can be faked, even on a carded figure. For that kind of money, anything can be faked.

Early Bird "Figures" (Early 1978)
Early Bird figures R2-D2, Luke Skywalker (telescoping lightsaber),
    Princess Leia and Chewbacca (green blaster rifle), in tray and box . . . $450.00
See Carry Cases and Display Stands on page 55 for listing of
    the Early Bird Package.

Packaging Variations — Header Cards

Star Wars action figures are heavily collected, and every tiny variation in the figure or the packaging makes a difference in the price. The chief variation is the repackaging of the figures with new movie logos, first to *The Empire Strikes Back* and then to *Return of the Jedi* as each of those movies premiered. After the movies, figures were issued on Power of the Force header cards with a collectible coin as a premium.

In addition, most of the figures were available in the United States on foreign "Tri-Logo" header cards, which had *Return of the Jedi* movie logos in three languages. There are variations among Tri-Logo header cards as well, but all are lumped together for pricing purposes.

Early Bird Certificate package, back (Kenner 1977)

Early Bird Certificate package, front (Kenner 1977)

Packaging Variations — Card Backs

The most significant header card changes involve the pictures and lists on the back. Initially, just the original 12 figures are pictured, and these are called 12-backs and command the highest prices, as befits the earliest figures. Original figures on 12-back cards are scarce and desirable, so they are worth a lot more money—$75 to $100 more at current prices.

The second figure release added eight new figures, and the card back was changed to reflect this, becoming 20-backs. The 21st figure was the regular Boba Fett figure and it got a 21-back card. Most collectors treat 20- and 21-back figures as part of the same series, without distinction or price difference.

This pattern continued with *The Empire Strikes Back* and *Return of the Jedi*. Some early versions of the former contained a

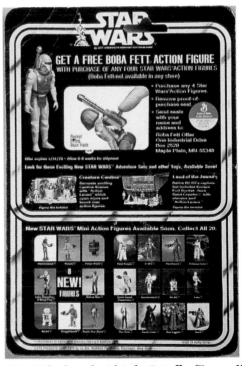

Star Wars 20-back card, with Boba Fett offer (Kenner 1978)

Revenge of the Jedi offer. These cards command a premium, as does anything that mentions this title. Within each group of 12-backs, 20-backs, etc., there are variations. There are two slightly different 12-backs, eight different 20-backs, and two or more versions of most of the others, for a total of 45 different U.S. header cards.

Figure Variations

The most significant of the figure variations was with the Jawa, where the original version had a vinyl cape. This was quickly changed to cloth, which was used for all the rest of the figures. The few vinyl-caped Jawas are the most valuable of all the *Star Wars* figures and currently sell for about $1,500, with loose figures going for $250 to $300. Care in buying is essential, because a loose Jawa in cloth cape is only worth $15 and a fake vinyl cape is not hard to make.

All *Star Wars* action-figure prices are volatile and generally increasing. This will almost certainly continue with the forthcoming release of another movie in the series.

STAR WARS (SERIES)
Kenner (1978–79)

First series, 12-back cards (1978)

Artoo-Detoo (R2-D2) (#38200)	$350.00
Ben (Obi-Wan) Kenobi (#38250) **grey hair**	700.00
Ben (Obi-Wan) Kenobi (#38250) **white hair**	800.00
Chewbacca (#38210) **black blaster rifle**	300.00
Chewbacca (#38210) **green blaster rifle**	325.00
Darth Vader (#38230)	600.00

First Series: Chewbacca, with black rifle (Kenner 1978)

Death Squad Commander (#38290) 350.00
Han Solo (#38260) **large head**, dark brown hair 1,000.00
Han Solo (#38260) **small head**, brown hair 850.00
Jawa (#38270) **vinyl cape** 3,500.00
Jawa (#38270) **cloth cape** 275.00
Luke Skywalker (#38180) **blond hair** 750.00
Princess Leia Organa (#38190) 750.00
Sand People (#38280) 400.00
See-Threepio (C-3PO) (#38220) 300.00
Stormtrooper (#38240) 400.00

Second Series, New Figures on 20-/21-back cards
Boba Fett (#39250) 1,500.00
Death Star Droid (#39080) 200.00
Greedo (#39020) 300.00
Hammerhead (#39030) 225.00
Luke Skywalker X-wing Pilot (#39060) 300.00
Power Droid (#39090) 190.00
R5-D4 (#39070) 325.00
Snaggletooth (#39040) **red** 175.00
Walrus Man (#39050) 275.00

Reissue Figures on 20-/21-back cards
Artoo-Detoo (R2-D2) (#38200) 200.00
Ben (Obi-Wan) Kenobi (#38250) **grey hair** 175.00
Ben (Obi-Wan) Kenobi (#38250) **white hair** 175.00
Chewbacca (#38210) 225.00
Darth Vader (#38230) 300.00
Death Squad Commander (#38290) 150.00
Han Solo (#38260) **large head**, dark brown hair 650.00
Han Solo (#38260) **small head**, brown hair 550.00
Jawa (#38270) **cloth cape** 200.00

Second Series: R5-D4 (Kenner 1979)

Luke Skywalker (#38180) **blond hair**	250.00
Princess Leia Organa (#38190)	275.00
Sand People (#38280)	150.00
See-Threepio (C-3PO) (#38220)	100.00
Stormtrooper (#38240)	150.00

THE EMPIRE STRIKES BACK SERIES
Kenner (1980–82)

Third Series, New Figures (1980)

Bespin Security Guard (#39810) **white**	$75.00
Bossk (Bounty Hunter) (#39760)	125.00
FX-7 (Medical Droid) (#39730)	75.00
Han Solo (Hoth Outfit) (#39790)	100.00
IG-88 (Bounty Hunter) (#39770)	150.00
Imperial Stormtrooper (Hoth Battle Gear) (#39740)	125.00
Lando Calrissian (#39800) **no teeth**	75.00
Lando Calrissian (#39800) **white teeth**	75.00
Leia Organa (Bespin Gown) (#39720) **crew neck**	200.00
Leia Organa (Bespin Gown) (#39720) **turtle neck**	200.00
Leia Organa (Bespin Gown) (#39720) **new package**	175.00
Luke Skywalker (Bespin Fatigues) (#39780)	250.00
Luke Skywalker (Bespin) (#39780) new package	150.00
Rebel Soldier (Hoth Battle Gear) (#39750)	75.00

Fourth Series, New Figures (1981)

AT-AT Driver (#39379)	90.00
Dengar (#39329)	100.00
Han Solo (Bespin Outfit) (#39339)	175.00
Imperial Commander (#39389)	90.00
Leia Organa (Hoth Outfit) (#39359)	175.00

Fourth Series: AT-AT Driver (Kenner 1981)

Lobot (#39349) 70.00
Rebel Commander (#39369) 150.00
2-1B (#39399) 100.00
Ugnaught (#39319) blue smock 80.00
Yoda (#38310) **brown snake** 325.00
Yoda (#38310) **orange snake** 225.00

Fifth Series, New Figures (1982)
Artoo-Detoo (R2-D2) (with Sensorscope) (#69590) 75.00
AT-AT Commander (#69620) 100.00
Bespin Security Guard (#69640) **black** 65.00
Cloud Car Pilot (Twin Pod) (#69630) 125.00
C-3PO (Removable Limbs) (#69600) 90.00
4-LOM (#70010) 300.00
Imperial TIE Fighter Pilot (#70030) 125.00
Luke Skywalker (Hoth Battle Gear) (#69610) 125.00
Zuckuss (#70020) 125.00

Reissue Figures on *The Empire Strikes Back* header cards
Artoo-Detoo (R2-D2) (#38200) 150.00
Ben (Obi-Wan) Kenobi (#38250) **grey hair** 125.00
Ben (Obi-Wan) Kenobi (#38250) **white hair** 125.00
Boba Fett (#39250) 400.00
Chewbacca (#38210) 125.00
Darth Vader (#38230) 125.00
Death Star Droid (#39080) 150.00
Greedo (#39020) 125.00
Hammerhead (#39030) 125.00
Han Solo (#38260) **large head**, dark brown hair 250.00
Han Solo (#38260) **small head**, brown hair 325.00
Jawa (#38270) **cloth cape** 125.00
Luke Skywalker (#38180) **blond hair** 275.00

Sixth Series: Biker Scout (Kenner 1983)

Luke Skywalker (#38180) **brown hair** 325.00
Luke Skywalker (X-wing Pilot) (#39060) 125.00
Power Droid (#39090) 125.00
Princess Leia Organa (#38190) 325.00
R5-D4 (#39070) 140.00
Sandpeople (#38280) 125.00
See-Threepio (C-3PO) (#38220) 150.00
Snaggletooth (#39040) **red** 150.00
Star Destroyer Commander (#38290) 125.00
Stormtrooper (#38240) 125.00
Walrus Man (#39050) 125.00

RETURN OF THE JEDI SERIES
Kenner (1983–84)

Sixth Series, New Figures (1983)
Admiral Ackbar (#70310) $30.00
Bib Fortuna (#70790) 30.00
Biker Scout (#70820) 35.00
Chief Chirpa (#70690) 30.00
Emperor's Royal Guard (#70680) 40.00
Gamorrean Guard (#70670) 25.00
General Madine (#70780) 30.00
Klaatu (#70730) **tan arms** or **grey arms** 30.00
Lando Calrissian (Skiff Guard) (#70830) 45.00
Logray (Ewok Medicine Man) (#70710) 30.00
Luke Skywalker (Jedi Knight) (#70650) with **green** light saber 100.00
Luke Skywalker (Jedi Knight) (#70650) with **blue** light saber 175.00
Nien Nunb (#70840) 35.00
Princess Leia Organa (Boushh Disguise) (#70660) 55.00
Rebel Commando (#70740) 30.00

Seventh Series: Klaatu, Skiff Guard (Kenner 1984)

Ree-Yees (#70800) 30.00
Squid Head (#70770) 30.00
Weequay (#70760) 35.00

Seventh Series, New Figures (1984)
AT-ST Driver (#71330) 30.00
B wing Pilot (#71280) 30.00
8D8 (#71210) 30.00
The Emperor (#71240) 75.00
Han Solo (Trench Coat) (#71300) 50.00
Klaatu (Skiff Guard) (#71290) 30.00
Lumat (#93670) 55.00
Nikto (#71190) 30.00
Paploo (#93680) 55.00
Princess Leia Organa (Combat Poncho) (#71220) 60.00
Prune Face (#71320) 40.00
Rancor Keeper (#71350) 30.00
Teebo (#71310) 45.00
Wicket W. Warrick (#71230) 50.00

Reissue Figures on *Return of the Jedi* header cards
Artoo-Detoo (R2-D2) (with Sensor Scope) (#69420) 75.00
AT-AT Commander (#69620) 60.00
AT-AT Driver (#39379) 50.00
Ben (Obi-Wan) Kenobi (#38250) **grey hair** 50.00
Ben (Obi-Wan) Kenobi (#38250) **grey hair**, new package . . 50.00
Ben (Obi-Wan) Kenobi (#38250) **white hair** 50.00
Bespin Security Guard (#39810) **white** 50.00
Bespin Security Guard (#69640) **black** 60.00
Boba Fett (#39250) 350.00
Boba Fett (#39250) new package 375.00
Bossk (Bounty Hunter) (#39760) 100.00

Reissue: Han Solo, Hoth Battle Gear (Kenner 1984)

Chewbacca (#38210) 50.00
Chewbacca (#38210) new package 45.00
Cloud Car Pilot (Twin Pod) (#69630) 60.00
Darth Vader (#38230) 50.00
Darth Vader (#38230) new package 45.00
Death Squad Commander (Star Destroyer Commander) (#38290) . . 75.00
Death Star Droid (#39080) 75.00
Dengar (#39329) 35.00
4-LOM (#70010) 50.00
FX-7 (Medical Droid) (#39730) 75.00
Greedo (#39020) 75.00
Hammerhead (#39030) 75.00
Han Solo (#38260) **large head**, dark brown hair, new package . . 185.00
Han Solo (#38260) **large head**, brown hair 175.00
Han Solo (#38260) **small head**, brown hair, new package . . 200.00
Han Solo (Bespin Outfit) (#39339) 85.00
Han Solo (Hoth Battle Gear) (#39790) 75.00
IG-88 (Bounty Hunter) (#39770) 75.00
Imperial Commander (#39389) 40.00
Imperial Stormtrooper (Hoth Battle Gear) (#39740) 50.00
Imperial TIE Fighter Pilot (#70030) 75.00
Jawa (#38270) **cloth cape** 45.00
Lando Calrissian (#39800) **white teeth** 45.00
Leia Organa (Bespin Gown) (#39720) **turtle neck** 150.00
Leia Organa (Bespin Gown) (#39720) **crew neck** 125.00
Lobot (#39349) 35.00
Luke Skywalker (#38180) **blond hair** 225.00
Luke Skywalker (#38180) **blond hair**, new package 175.00
Luke Skywalker (#38180) **brown hair** 300.00
Luke Skywalker (#38180) **brown hair**, new package 175.00
Luke Skywalker (Bespin Fatigues) (#39780) new package, yellow hair 140.00
Luke Skywalker (Bespin Fatigues) (#39780) new package, brown hair 100.00

Reissue: Walrus Man (Kenner 1984)

Luke Skywalker (Hoth Battle Gear) (#69610) 75.00
Luke Skywalker (X-wing Fighter Pilot) (#39060) 150.00
Power Droid (#39090) 55.00
Princess Leia Organa (#38190) 450.00
Princess Leia Organa (Hoth Outfit) (#39359) 100.00
Princess Leia Organa (Hoth Outfit) (#39359) new package 75.00
R5-D4 (Arfive-Defour) (#39070) 65.00
Rebel Commander (#39369) 40.00
Rebel Soldier (Hoth Gear) (#39750) 35.00
See-Threepio (C-3PO) (Removable Limbs) (#69430) 75.00
Snaggletooth (#39040) **red** 55.00
Stormtrooper (#38240) 50.00
Too-Onebee (2-1B) (#71600) 50.00
Tusken Raider (Sand People) (#38280) 75.00
Ugnaught (#39319) 35.00
Walrus Man (#39050) 60.00
Yoda (#38310) **brown snake** 100.00
Yoda **The Jedi Master**, (#38310) **brown snake** 100.00
Zuckuss (#70020) 75.00

THE POWER OF THE FORCE

The Power of the Force figures were produced after all three movies had come and gone. Kenner wanted to keep the figure series alive, so it changed the name of the series and added silver- colored aluminum coins as an in-package premium.

Without a new movie to boost sales, fewer of these figures were ordered, and many that were planned were never made. Now they are

Eighth Series: Anakin Skywalker (Kenner 1985)

among the most valuable of *Star Wars* figures. Several were released only overseas.

Thirty-seven figures came with coins. However, two of the foreign release figures (AT-AT Driver and Nikto) came with coins from other figures, so only 35 different coins came with these 37 figures. Coins were also available as a mail-in premium with a proof of purchase from some prior *The Empire Strikes Back* and *Return of the Jedi* figures, so there are actually 62 coins in the series to collect. See the *Coins* chapter of this book.

THE POWER OF THE FORCE SERIES
Kenner (1985)

Eighth Series, New Figures (1985) with silver coin

A-wing Pilot (#93830)	$100.00
Amanaman (#93740)	200.00
Anakin Skywalker (#93790) foreign release	2,750.00
Artoo-Detoo (R2-D2) Pop-up Lightsaber (#93720)	175.00
Barada (#93750)	100.00
EV-9D9 (#93800)	200.00
Han Solo (Carbonite Chamber) (#93770)	250.00
Imperial Dignitary (#93850)	100.00
Imperial Gunner (#93760)	150.00
Lando Calrissian (General Pilot) (#93820)	150.00
Luke Skywalker (Battle Poncho) (#93710)	125.00
Luke Skywalker, Stormtrooper Outfit (#93780)	450.00
Romba (#93730)	60.00
Warok (#93810)	75.00
Yak Face (#93840) foreign release	2,000.00

Reissue: Princess Leia, Combat Poncho (Kenner 1985)

Reissue Figures on Power of the Force header cards

AT-AT Driver (#39379) foreign release only 550.00
AT-ST Driver (#71330) 75.00
B-wing Pilot (#71280) 40.00
Ben (Obi-Wan) Kenobi (#38250) **white hair** 150.00
Ben (Obi-Wan) Kenobi (#38250) **grey hair** 150.00
Biker Scout (#70820) 100.00
Chewbacca (#38210) 150.00
Darth Vader (#38230) 175.00
The Emperor (#71240) 75.00
Gamorrean Guard (#70670) foreign release only 400.00
Han Solo (Trench Coat) (#71300) 550.00
Imperial Stormtrooper (#38240) 275.00
Jawa (#38270) **cloth cape** 125.00
Luke Skywalker (Jedi Knight) (#70650) with **green** lightsaber 275.00
Luke Skywalker (X-wing Fighter Pilot) (#39060) 150.00
Lumat (#93670) 60.00
Nikto (#71190) foreign release only 600.00
Paploo (#93680) 60.00
Princess Leia Organa (Combat Poncho) (#71220) 100.00
See-Threepio (C-3PO) Removable Limbs (#69430) 100.00
Teebo (#71310) 225.00
Wicket W. Warrick (#71230) 225.00
Yoda (with **brown snake**) (#38310) 400.00

TRI-LOGO (*RETURN OF THE JEDI*)

There is no series that has the words "Tri-Logo" on it. Tri-Logo is just the universally used collector's name for figures on header cards with *Return of the Jedi* logos in three languages. It is not even really

Tri-Logo: AT-AT Commander (Kenner 1985)

a single series, as there are differences among Tri-Logo header cards depending on the countries that were the intended market for these figures. Collectors generally ignore such differences, and all such cards for a given figure have the same value. Generally, a figure on a Tri-Logo card has a lower value than the same figure on any other type of card from the 1970s and 1980s.

There are foreign versions of *Star Wars* figures from many countries and some of them were distributed in quantity in this country at many stores. As the least desirable version of *Star Wars* figures and the last ones distributed, they often spent the longest time at toy stores. They were knocked onto the floor by collectors looking for scarce figures and were plastered with red-tag stickers. Consequently, Tri-Logo figures are often in worse condition than those from other series, which further reduces their value. Figures on beat-up cards are often worth little more than the corresponding loose figures.

TRI-LOGO "SERIES"
Kenner (1984–86)

Reissue Figures on Tri-Logo header card

Admiral Ackbar (#70310)	$50.00
Amanaman (#93740)	150.00
Anakin Skywalker (#93790) foreign release	125.00
Artoo-Detoo (R2-D2) (#38200)	35.00
Artoo-Detoo (R2-D2) (Sensor Scope) (#69590)	50.00
Artoo-Detoo (R2-D2) (Pop-up Lightsaber) (#93720)	150.00
AT-AT Commander (#69620)	50.00

Tri-Logo: The Emperor (Kenner 1984)

AT-AT Driver (#39379) 90.00
AT-ST Driver (#71330) 40.00
A-wing Pilot (#93830) 75.00
B-wing Pilot (#71280) 50.00
Barada (#93750) 60.00
Ben (Obi-Wan) Kenobi (#38250) **grey hair** 75.00
Ben (Obi-Wan) Kenobi (#38250) **white hair** 75.00
Bespin Security Guard (#39810) **white** 50.00
Bespin Security Guard (#69640) **black** 50.00
Bib Fortuna (#70790) 50.00
Biker Scout (#70820) 50.00
Boba Fett (#39250) 700.00
Bossk (Bounty Hunter) (#39760) 100.00
C-3PO (Removable Limbs) (#69600) 50.00
Chewbacca (#38210) 60.00
Chief Chirpa (#70690) 25.00
Cloud Car Pilot (Twin Pod) (#69630) 50.00
Darth Vader (#38230) 50.00
Death Squad Commander (#38290) 75.00
Death Star Droid (#39080) 125.00
Dengar (#39329) 50.00
8D8 (#71210) 100.00
Emperor (#71240) 60.00
Emperor's Royal Guard (#70680) 150.00
EV-9 D9 (#93800) 125.00
4-LOM (#70010) 28.00
FX-7 (Medical Droid) (#39730) 60.00
Gamorrean Guard (#70670) 50.00
General Madine (#70780) 100.00
Greedo (#39020) 125.00
Hammerhead (#39030) 75.00
Han Solo (#38260) **large head**, dark brown hair 175.00

Tri-Logo: Luke Skywalker, Bespin Fatigues (Kenner 1985)

Han Solo (#38260) **small head**, brown hair 175.00
Han Solo (Bespin Outfit) (#39339) 50.00
Han Solo (Hoth Outfit) (#39790) 40.00
Han Solo (in Carbonite Chamber) (#93770) 225.00
Han Solo (Trench Coat) (#71300) 50.00
IG-88 . . . . 175.00
Imperial Commander (#39389) 40.00
Imperial Dignitary (#93850) 50.00
Imperial Gunner (#93760) 135.00
Imperial Stormtrooper (Hoth Battle Gear) (#39740) 50.00
Imperial Stormtrooper (#38240) new package 65.00
Imperial TIE Fighter Pilot (#70030) 90.00
Jawa (#38270) **cloth cape** 75.00
Klaatu (#70730) with **tan** or **grey arms** 20.00
Klaatu (Skiff Guard Outfit) (#71290) 35.00
Lando Calrissian (#39800) 75.00
Lando Calrissian (General Pilot) (#93820) 75.00
Lando Calrissian (Skiff Guard Disguise) (#70830) 50.00
Leia Organa (Bespin Gown) (#39720) 115.00
Leia Organa (Hoth Outfit) (#39359) 100.00
Lobot (#39349) 90.00
Logray (Ewok Medicine Man) (#70710) 50.00
Luke Skywalker (#38180) **blond hair** 225.00
Luke Skywalker (#38180) **brown hair** 260.00
Luke Skywalker (Bespin) (#39780) yellow hair 125.00
Luke Skywalker (Bespin) (#39780) brown hair 125.00
Luke Skywalker (Hoth Battle Gear) (#69610) 50.00
Luke Skywalker (Battle Poncho) (#93710) 100.00
Luke Skywalker (Jedi Knight) (#70650) **blue** lightsaber (#70650) . . . 200.00
Luke Skywalker (Jedi Knight) (#70650) **green** lightsaber 125.00
Luke Skywalker (X-wing Fighter Pilot) (#39060) 100.00
Luke Skywalker (Storm Trooper Outfit) (#93780) 250.00

Tri-Logo: Yoda (Kenner 1985)

Lumat (#93670) 50.00
Nien Nunb (#70840) 60.00
Nikto (#71190) 40.00
Paploo (#93680) 65.00
Power Droid (#39090) 75.00
Princess Leia Organa (#38190) 150.00
Princess Leia Organa (Boushh Disguise) (#70660) 100.00
Princess Leia Organa (Combat Poncho) (#71220) 100.00
Prune Face (#71320) 50.00
R5-D4 (#39070) 75.00
Rancor Keeper (#71350) 60.00
Rebel Commander (#39369) 50.00
Rebel Commando (#70740) 50.00
Rebel Soldier (Hoth Battle Gear) (#39750) 25.00
Ree-Yees (#70800) 25.00
Romba (#93730) 35.00
See-Threepio (C-3PO) (#38220) 45.00
Snaggletooth (**red**) (#39040) 75.00
Squid Head (#70770) 50.00
Teebo (#71310) 50.00
Tusken Raider (Sand People) (#38280) 75.00
2-1B (#39399) 75.00
Ugnaught (#39319) 45.00
Walrus Man (#39050) 100.00
Warok (#93810) 75.00
Weequay (#70760) 40.00
Wicket W. Warrick (#71230) 50.00
Yak Face (#93840) foreign release 400.00
Yoda (with **brown snake**) (#38310) 110.00
Zuckuss (#70020) 50.00

Droids: Artoo-Detoo, R2-D2 (Kenner 1985)

(THE TV ANIMATED SERIES)
DROIDS
The Adventures of R2-D2 and C-3PO
Kenner (1985)

The real movies were gone from the theaters, but there was still money to be made, so a couple of Ewok movies (*The Ewok Adventure* and *Ewoks: The Battle For Endor*) were produced, along with both an Ewoks and a Droids animated ABC television series. The greatest interest in the Droids and Ewoks figures for the first 10 years or so was in the coins rather than the figures. Although the coins are not part of the 62-coin regular set, they do form their own sets and sell for between $10 and $15 each. Recently, however, the figures have drawn more collector interest and now command prices in the same range as Tri-Logo figures.

While interest in Droids has been relatively low, one figure—Boba Fett—has always been the exception, but only because he is a very popular figure from the previous lines and his Droids figure is very scarce. Collectors also want Vlix, a Droids figure produced only in Brazil, and not distributed in the United States. For the $5,000 or so he sells for, collectors would be better off flying to Brazil and looking for him there.

3-3/4" Figures (1985) with copper- or gold-colored coin

A-wing Pilot (#93830) reissue $175.00
Artoo-Detoo R2-D2 (#71780) with pop-up lightsaber 100.00
Boba Fett (#39260) 1,100.00

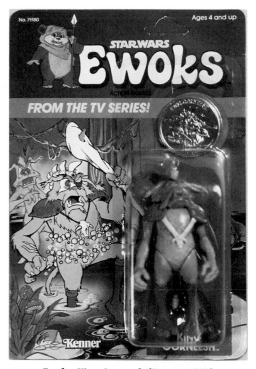

Ewoks: King Gorneesh (Kenner 1985)

Jann Tosh (#71840) 40.00
Jord Dusat (#71810) 40.00
Kea Moll (#71800) 40.00
Kez-Iban (#71850) 40.00
See-Threepio C-3PO (#71770) 125.00
Sise Fromm (#71820) 100.00
Thall Joben (#71790) 30.00
Tig Fromm (#71830) 125.00
Uncle Gundy (#71880) 40.00

EWOKS
Kenner (1985)

3-3/4" Figures (1985) with copper- or gold-colored coin
Dulok Shaman (#71150) $35.00
Dulok Scout (#71160) 35.00
Urgah Lady Gorneesh (#71170) 35.00
King Gorneesh (#71180) 35.00
Logray (Ewok medicine man) (#71260) 35.00
Wicket W. Warrick (#71250) 35.00

LOOSE FIGURES

A lot of *Star Wars* figures are collected as loose figures. This is a popular type of collecting for those whose mothers did not throw away all their *Star Wars* figures when they left home. There's nothing like finding half the figures for your collection in a box in your own attic. Usually, the challenge is finding figures in good condition and matching them with the correct weapons and accessories. The following prices are for near-mint figures complete with original weapons and accessories.

Loose figures

Admiral Ackbar, with staff	$10.00
Amanaman, with skull staff	125.00
Anakin Skywalker, no accessories, foreign release	30.00
Artoo-Detoo (R2-D2) no accessories	15.00
Artoo-Detoo (R2-D2) (with Sensor Scope)	12.50
Artoo-Detoo (R2-D2) with Pop-Up Lightsaber	100.00
Artoo-Deetoo (R2-D2) (Droids)	50.00
AT-AT Commander, with pistol	10.00
AT-AT Driver, with rifle	10.00
AT-ST Driver, with pistol	10.00
A-wing Pilot, with pistol	50.00
Barada, with staff	40.00
Ben (Obi-Wan) Kenobi **grey hair**, with lightsaber	15.00
Ben (Obi-Wan) Kenobi **white hair**, with lightsaber	15.00
Bespin Security Guard **black**, with pistol	10.00
Bespin Security Guard **white**, with pistol	10.00
Bib Fortuna, with brown cloak and staff	10.00
Biker Scout, with pistol	15.00
Boba Fett, with pistol	45.00
Bossk (Bounty Hunter) with rifle	15.00
B-wing Pilot, with pistol	10.00
Chewbacca, with black rifle	15.00
Chewbacca, with green rifle (Early Bird Figure)	35.00
Chief Chirpa, with long club	10.00
Cloud Car Pilot (Twin Pod) with pistol and light	20.00
Darth Vader, with lightsaber	12.00
Death Squad Commander, with pistol	15.00

Loose Figure: Amanaman, with skull staff

Death Star Droid, no accessories 25.00
Dengar, with rifle 10.00
Dulok Shaman 10.00
Dulok Scout 10.00
8D8, no accessories 10.00
Emperor, with cane 10.00

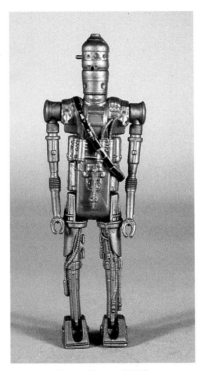

Loose Figure: IG-88

Emperor's Royal Guard, with staff 10.00
EV-9D9, no accessories 85.00
4-LOM, with weapon 15.00
FX-7 (Medical Droid) no accessories 10.00
Gamorrean Guard, with axe 10.00
General Madine, with staff 10.00
Greedo, with pistol 10.00
Hammerhead, with pistol 12.50
Han Solo with **large head**, with pistol 25.00
Han Solo with **small head**, with pistol 35.00
Han Solo (Bespin Outfit) with pistol 15.00
Han Solo (Carbonite Chamber) with carbonite sheet 110.00
Han Solo (Hoth Outfit) with pistol 15.00
Han Solo (Trench Coat) with pistol 15.00
IG-88 (Bounty Hunter) with rifle and pistol 15.00
Imperial Commander, with pistol 10.00
Imperial Dignitary, no accessories 35.00
Imperial Gunner, with pistol 100.00
Imperial Stormtrooper, with weapon 15.00
Imperial Stormtrooper (Hoth Gear) with rifle 10.00
Imperial TIE Fighter Pilot, with pistol 15.00
Jann Tosh 10.00
Jawa **vinyl cape**, with weapon 275.00
Jawa **cloth cape**, with weapon 13.00
Jord Dusat 15.00
Kea Moll 15.00
Kez-Iban 15.00
King Gorneesh 10.00
Klaatu, with **tan arms** or **grey arms**, with apron and spear 10.00
Klaatu (Skiff Guard Outfit) with weapon 10.00
Lando Calrissian **no teeth** version, with pistol 15.00
Lando Calrissian **white teeth** version, with pistol 15.00

Loose figures: Lumat and Paploo, Ewoks

Lando Calrissian (Skiff Guard Disguise) with spear 15.00
Lando Calrissian (General Pilot) with cape and pistol. 65.00
Leia Organa (Bespin Gown) **crew neck**, in cloak with pistol. 20.00
Leia Organa (Bespin Gown) **turtleneck**, in cloak with pistol. 20.00
Leia Organa (Hoth Outfit) with pistol 25.00
Lobot, with pistol 8.00
Logray (Ewok Medicine Man) with mask, staff and pouch 10.00
Logray (Ewoks) 10.00
Luke Skywalker **blond hair**, with lightsaber 65.00
Luke Skywalker **brown hair**, with lightsaber. 90.00
Luke Skywalker (in Battle Poncho) with poncho and pistol. 75.00
Luke Skywalker (Bespin Fatigues) **brown hair**, with
  pistol and lightsaber 20.00
Luke Skywalker (Bespin Fatigues) **yellow hair**,
  with pistol and lightsaber 20.00

Luke Skywalker (Hoth Gear) with rifle. 10.00
Luke Skywalker, Imperial Stormtrooper Outfit, with
  removable helmet and pistol 175.00
Luke Skywalker (Jedi Knight) with **green lightsaber**,
  cloak and pistol 50.00
Luke Skywalker (Jedi Knight) with **blue lightsaber**,
  cloak and pistol 60.00
Luke Skywalker (X-wing Pilot) with pistol. 15.00
Lumat, with bow 17.00
Nien Nunb, with pistol 10.00
Nikto, with staff 10.00
Paploo, with staff 18.00
Power Droid, no accessories 10.00
Princess Leia Organa, with pistol 45.00
Princess Leia Organa (Boushh Disguise) with helmet and weapon 15.00
Princess Leia Organa (Combat Poncho) with pistol 20.00
Prune Face, with cloak and rifle 10.00
R5-D4, no accessories 10.00
Rancor Keeper, with prod 10.00
Rebel Commander, with rifle 10.00
Rebel Commando, with rifle. 10.00
Rebel Soldier (Hoth Gear) with pistol 10.00
Ree-Yees, with weapon 10.00
Romba, with spear 25.00
See-Threepio (C-3PO) no accessories 25.00
C-3PO (Removable Limbs) with backpack. 10.00
See-Threepio (C-3PO) (Droids) 50.00
Sise Fromm 50.00
Snaggletooth (**blue**) from Cantina Adventure Set 350.00
Snaggletooth (**red**) with pistol 10.00
Squid Head, with pistol and cloak 10.00
Teebo, with club, mask and pouch 15.00

Loose figures: Ugnaught and Yoda

Thall Joben 15.00
Tig Fromm. 50.00
Tusken Raider (Sand People) with cloak and weapon 15.00
2-1B, with weapon 10.00
Ugnaught, in blue smock with case 10.00
Ugnaught, in lavender smock with case 12.50
Uncle Gundy. 15.00
Urgah Lady Gorneesh 10.00
Walrus Man, with pistol 12.50
Warok, with bow and pouch. 25.00
Weequay, with spear 20.00
Wicket W. Warrick, with spear. 15.00
Wicket W. Warrick (Ewoks) 12.00
Yak Face, with staff, foreign release. 275.00

Yoda, with **brown snake** and stick 25.00
Yoda, with **orange snake** and stick 20.00
Zuckuss, with rifle 10.00

MAIL-INS

Mail-Ins
Boba Fett with Rocket Launcher (mail-in offer) $200.00
Bossk, Boba Fett, Darth Vader, IG-88, in plastic
   bags with Kenner logo (1980) 200.00
Bossk (1980) 25.00
4-LOM (1982) 25.00
Admiral Ackbar (1983) 20.00
Nien Nunb (1983) 20.00
The Emperor (1984) 20.00
Anakin Skywalker (1985) 40.00

Mail-in Boba Fett with box and note

Sy Snootles and the Rebo Band (Kenner 1984)

CLASSIC SERIES — MULTI-PACKS
SY SNOOTLES AND THE REBO BAND

Sy Snootles and the Rebo Band (#71360, 1984)

Original *Return of the Jedi* header card $150.00
Reissue on Tri-Logo header card 100.00
Loose: each 15.00

REISSUE SETS

While no other new figures came out in multi-packs, Kenner did produce "Action Figure Sets" of three leftover figures for each of the movies. They were subtitled "Hero Set," "Villain Set," "Rebel Set," etc. They are quite scarce, and there is some uncertainty as to their value.

Two six-pack sets of figures were issued for *The Empire Strikes Back* movie. These are not as valuable as the three-packs. Last, and least, are *Return of the Jedi* two-packs. They are worth the price of the two leftover loose figures (if they have their weapons) and maybe an additional dollar or two.

Star Wars Action Figure Sets —Three-Packs

Three-pack sets, three different, each $1,000.00
Three-pack sets with backdrops, four different, each 1,250.00

The Empire Strikes Back—Three-Packs

Three-pack sets, nine different, each 900.00

The Empire Strikes Back—Six-Packs

Six-pack sets, two different, each 750.00

Return of the Jedi Two-Pack: Klaatu and Princess Leia

***Return of the Jedi*—Three-Packs**
Three-packs, four different, each 750.00

***Return of the Jedi*—Two-Packs**
Two-packs, many different, each . . . . value of loose figures, plus $1.00

CARRY CASES
AND DISPLAY STANDS

Vinyl collector's cases feature two storage trays designed to
hold 12 figures each. The backsides have foot pegs and can be used
to display figures. There were stickers for the figures so each figure
could be matched to its own slot. Later, the Darth Vader and C-3PO
head-shaped cases, along with the Laser Rifle carry case and even
the Chewbacca Bandolier Strap proved to be more popular designs,
making the rather plain Collector's Case much more common in *Star
Wars* packaging than in packaging for the later two films.

CARRY CASES
Kenner (1979–84)

Carry Cases
Collector's Case, black vinyl with illustrated cover
    Star Wars package $30.00
    The Empire Strikes Back package, *Star Wars* pictures (#39190, 1980) . . . 50.00
    Variation, with *The Empire Strikes Back* pictures 50.00
    Return of the Jedi package 100.00
Darth Vader Collector's Case, black plastic bust
    (#93630, 1980) *The Empire Strikes Back* package, without figures 40.00

Empire Strikes Back Carry Case (Kenner 1980)

With IG-88, Bossk and Boba Fett figures in
The Empire Strikes Back package (#39330) 500.00
Loose, without figures 15.00
See-Threepio Collector's Case, gold plastic bust
(#70440, 1983) *Return of the Jedi* package 30.00
Loose, without figures 15.00
Chewbacca Bandolier Strap (#70480,1983) in
16 1/4" x 9 1/4" x 1 1/2" *Return of the Jedi* box 8.00
Loose, without figures 4.00
Laser Rifle Case, rifle-shaped (#71530, 1984)
cardboard base, *Return of the Jedi* package 30.00
Loose, without figures 20.00

Laser Rifle Carry Case (Kenner 1984)

DISPLAY STANDS
Kenner (1977–83)

Early Bird Package, 19" x 9 1/2" flat envelope with
    cardboard backdrop (#38140) *Star Wars* logo $300.00
Action Display Stand for *Star Wars* Figures
    Loose, with original plain box. 50.00
    Original *Star Wars* box (#38990) 350.00
    Reissue as Special Action Display Stand in
    The Empire Strikes Back box, with six figures 550.00
    Loose, *without box* 40.00
Display Arena, mail-order premium (1981)
    Original *The Empire Strikes Back* box. 40.00
    Reissue in *Return of the Jedi* box. 35.00
    Loose 15.00

STAR WARS: NEW FIGURES (1995–2004)

THE POWER OF THE FORCE (NEW)
Kenner (1995–98)

Kenner reintroduced the *Star Wars* action figures starting in 1995—almost two years before the release of the *Star Wars* Trilogy, Special Edition. Better early than late! The first item to appear was the Classic Edition 4-Pack and, in some ways, it is the functional

Classic Edition 4-Pack (Kenner 1995)

equivalent of the Early Bird Figures from the original series—an initial four figures that are not on their own header cards.

Star Wars Power of the Force Classic Edition 4-Pack, including Luke Skywalker, Han Solo, Darth Vader and Chewbacca (#69595, 1995) $60.00

Packaging Variations

The most significant packaging changes in the new series is in the color of the header card. The 1995 and 1996 header cards have a red or orange laser blast running diagonally across them, while the 1997 cards have a green laser blast. Shadows of the Empire figures, from late 1996, are on purple laser-blast cards.

Package Printing Numbers

All of Kenner's 1995–98 action figures have a small printed number on the back, at the bottom, which can be used to distinguish earlier packages from later ones. It's the two digits after the decimal point that collectors look at. The first version of each package is

Package revision numbers ".00" and ".01"
(Kenner 1996–97)

numbered ".00." With each printing change, this number is increased, so on the third change, for example, the number will read ".03," and so on. All changes affect the value of the figure, and the earlier version is almost always the more valuable. However, this number only works for *printing* changes, not for variations in the figure itself.

Throughout this book, these numbers are reported in brackets [ ] to distinguish them from UPC codes, which are listed in parentheses ( ).

Figure Variations

In addition to packaging variations, the figures contain several important variations. The one that affects the most figures is the change from the ridiculously long early lightsabers to shorter lightsabers. This yielded variations for Darth Vader, Luke Skywalker and Ben (Obi-Wan)

Boba Fett Hand Variations, "black circle" & "half-circles" (Kenner 1996–98)

Kenobi. If short lightsabers weren't variation enough, some figures were found with short lightsabers in the plastic slots designed for long sabers. Luke Skywalker (Jedi Knight) originally came with a

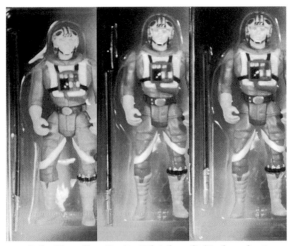

Luke Skywalker, X-wing Pilot, long lightsaber, short lightsaber in long tray, and in short tray (Kenner 1996)

brown vest, but this was switched to black, matching the rest of his costume. Boba Fett was issued with a black circle on the back of each hand. Originally he had a bar across this circle, forming two "half-circles." A very few have even been found with a black circle on only one hand, and they are very scarce and valuable. Except for these few popular variations, all of the figures were shipped (and purchased) in enormous quantity.

Red Card Series: Princess Leia Organa (Kenner 1995)

RED CARD SERIES
Kenner (1995–96)

3-3/4" Figures (1995–96)

Ben (Obi-Wan) Kenobi (#69576) head photo, long lightsaber [.00] $50.00
    Reissue, full-figure photo, long lightsaber [.01] 50.00
    Reissue, full-figure photo, short lightsaber 15.00
    Variation: short lightsaber in long tray, scarce 1,500.00
Boba Fett (#69582) half circles on hand [.00] 50.00
    Variation: half circle one hand, full circle on
    other hand, scarce 350.00
    Reissue, with full circle on both hands [.01] 15.00
Chewbacca (#69578) [.00] 10.00
C-3PO (#69573) [.00] 10.00
Darth Vader (#69572) with long lightsaber [.00]. 25.00
    Reissue, short lightsaber 15.00
    Variation: short lightsaber, long slot 45.00
Han Solo (#69577) [.00] 10.00
Han Solo in Hoth Gear (#69587) open hand [.00] 25.00
    Variation, closed hand 15.00
Han Solo in "Carbonite Freezing Chamber"
    (#69613) [.00] 12.00
    Reissue: in "Carbonite Block"(#69613) [.01] 100.00
Jedi Knight Luke Skywalker (#69596) brown vest [.00] 75.00
    Variation: black vest [.00] 12.00
Lando Calrissian (#69583) [.00] 10.00
Luke Skywalker (#69571) long lightsaber [.00] 40.00
    Reissue, short lightsaber, long slot 700.00
    Reissue, short lightsaber 15.00
Luke Skywalker in Dagobah Fatigues (#69588)
    long lightsaber [.00] 30.00

Shadows of the Empire: Dash Rendar (Kenner 1996)

Reissue, short lightsaber [.01] 18.00
Variation: short lightsaber in long slot 25.00
Luke Skywalker in X-wing Fighter Pilot Gear
  (#69581) long lightsaber [.00] 25.00
  Reissue, short lightsaber 15.00
  Variation: short lightsaber in long slot 20.00
Princess Leia Organa (#69579) three bands on belt 15.00
  Variation: two bands on belt [.00] 12.00
R2-D2 (#69574) [.00] 15.00
Stormtrooper (#69575) [.00] 12.00
TIE Fighter Pilot (#69584) warning on sticker [.00] 25.00
  Reissue, warning on card [.01] 12.00
TIE Fighter Pilot (#69673) [.02] 6.00
Yoda (#69586) [.00] 12.00
Yoda (#69672) [.01] with hologram 35.00

SHADOWS OF THE EMPIRE

Shadows of the Empire figures are based on the book series, not any of the movies. In early 1998, Princess Leia in Boushh Disguise was reissued on a purple header card that said "Collection 1." This packaging variation has proven to be extremely scarce.

PURPLE CARD SERIES
Kenner (1996)

3-3/4" Figures (1996)
Chewbacca (Bounty Hunter) (#69562) $12.00
Dash Rendar (#69561) 20.00
Luke Skywalker (Imperial Guard) (#69566) 20.00

Red Card Collection 1: Death Star Gunner (Kenner 1996)

Prince Xizor (#69594) 10.00
Princess Leia (Boushh Disguise) (#69602) [.00] 10.00
   Reissue, **Collection 1** (#69818) [.01] 300.00

POWER OF THE FORCE 1996

The fourth batch of Power of the Force figures appeared in December 1996 with the captions "Collection 1" or "Collection 2" at the top. Nobody knew what that was supposed to mean. The two collections appeared at the same time, and the earliest versions came on a header card with a red laser blast, the same color used on the other new Power of the Force figures from 1995–96.

These proved to be quite scarce, as the header cards were all quickly changed to a green laser blast design. Just as collectors were digesting these changes, holographic sticker pictures were added to the cards.

The Tatooine Stormtrooper (red-carded) and the Sandtrooper (green-carded) are identical—only the name had been changed to confuse the weary collector.

TRANSITION — RED "COLLECTION" CARDS
Kenner (1996)

Collection 1 Figures (1996)
Death Star Gunner (#69608) $15.00
Greedo (#69606) 15.00
Tatooine Stormtrooper (#69601) 15.00

Red Card Collection 2: R5-D4 (Kenner 1996)

Collection 2 Figures (1996)

Jawas (#69607) 25.00
Luke Skywalker, "Storm Trooper Disguise" (#69604) 35.00
Momaw Nadon "Hammerhead" (#69629) 25.00
R5-D4 (#69598) straight latch,
   no small parts warning 20.00
   with small parts warning 20.00
Tusken Raider (#69603) closed hand 25.00
   Variation: open hand 75.00

POWER OF THE FORCE 1997

As 1997 began, the three Collection 1 and and five Collection 2 figures were appearing on green header cards with holo pictures. Some of these early 1997 figures were shipped in staggering quantities, and figures such as Bib Fortuna, Emperor Palpatine, Lando Calrissian Skiff Guard, Bossk, 2-1B, Admiral Ackbar, 4-LOM and Grand Moff Tarkin were mind-numbingly common.

Collection Numbers

The idea of the "collection number" was to sort the action figures into groups so "Collection 1" would be the Rebel Alliance, "Collection 3" would be the Galactic Empire and "Collection 2" would be the various nonaligned aliens.

Unfortunately, there weren't equal numbers of each type, and new figures were not added at uniform rates in each group, but almost all boxes have to contain 16 figures. Except for the occasional "block case" of all one figure, Kenner doesn't ship more than three of any one figure in any assortment, and usually it's no more than two.

Green Card, Plain Picture: Tusken Raider (Kenner 1997)

The result was that a lot of figures came out in the "wrong" collection and later in the "right" collection. Overall, there were 17 collection-error figures to look for.

Holo Stickers or Plain Picture

A holo sticker picture was added to the header cards about the time the cards switched from red/orange to green. The first boxes of these green-carded figures displayed plain pictures of the characters on the front, similar to the ones used on all the red cards. Figures occasionally appear without holo stickers, and in early 1998, when the green cards were about to be phased out in favor of the Freeze Frame cards, a large number of tail-end green cards were produced without holo pictures. Initially there were price differences, but today there are none.

Figure Variations

Boba Fett occasionally comes with the same "black circle on one hand" or other scarce variations that occurred in the red cards, while Ponda Baba has been found with a grey beard instead of the normal black beard. These and a few other variations have had the most significant effect on price. However, the pants color of Han Solo's Endor Gear changed from navy blue (almost black) to brown, but this has not affected its value.

Green Card, Plain Picture: Admiral Ackbar (Kenner 1997)

GREEN CARD SERIES
Kenner (1997)

3-3/4" Figures, (1997) green card

Admiral Ackbar (#69686) Col. 2 [.00] $9.00
AT-ST Driver (#69623) Col. 2 [.00] 14.00
AT-ST Driver (#69823) Col. 3 [.02] 7.00
ASP-7 Droid (#69704) Col. 2 [.00] 9.00
Ben (Obi-Wan) Kenobi (#69576) Col. 1 [.02] 8.00
Bespin Han Solo (#69719) Col. 1 [.00] 8.00
Bib Fortuna (#69634) Col. 1 [.00] 12.00
Bib Fortuna (#69812) Col. 2 [.01] 10.00
Boba Fett (#69582) Col. 1 [.02] 30.00
Boba Fett (#69804) Col. 3 [.03] 20.00
Bossk (#69617) Col. 2 [.00 and .01] 10.00
Chewbacca (#69578) Col. 1 [.01] 10.00
C-3PO (#69573) Col. 1 [.01] 10.00
Darth Vader (#69572) Col. 1 [.01] 15.00
Darth Vader (#69802) Col. 3 [.02] 6.00
Death Star Gunner (#69608) Col. 1 [.01] 12.00
Death Star Gunner (#69809) Col. 3 [.02] 8.00
Dengar (#69687) Col. 2 [.00] 12.00
Emperor Palpatine (#69633) Col. 1 [.00] 12.00
Emperor Palpatine (#69811) Col. 3 [.01] 6.00
Emperor's Royal Guard (#69717) Col. 3 [.00] 8.00
EV-9D9 (#69722) Col. 2 [.00] 12.00
4-LOM (#69688) Col. 2 [.00] 12.00
Gamorrean Guard (#69693) Col. 2 [.00] 12.00
Garindan (Long Snout) (#69706) Col. 3 [.00] 6.00
Greedo (#69606) Col. 1 [.01] 9.00
Grand Moff Tarkin (#69702) Col. 2 [.00] 25.00

Green Card, Holo Picture: Han Solo, Carbonite
(Kenner 1997)

Grand Moff Tarkin (#69702) Col. 3 [.01] 6.00
Han Solo (#69577) Col. 1 [.01] 8.00
Han Solo in Endor Gear (#69621) Col. 1 [.00] **blue pants** 12.00
Han Solo (Endor Gear) (#69621) Col. 1 **brown pants** 15.00
Han Solo in Carbonite (#69613) Col. 2 [.02] 8.00
Han Solo in Carbonite (#69613) Col. 1 [.03] 8.00
Hoth Rebel Soldier (#69631) Col. 2 [.00] 12.00
Hoth Rebel Soldier (#69821) Col. 1 [.01] 10.00
Jawas (#69607) Col. 2 [.01] 15.00
Jedi Knight Luke Skywalker (#69816) Col. 2 [.01] 25.00
Jedi Knight Luke Skywalker (#69816) Col. 1 [.02] 10.00
Lando Calrissian as Skiff Guard (#69622) Col. 1 [.00] 10.00
Luke Skywalker (Ceremonial Outfit) (#69691) Col. 2 [.00] 40.00
Luke Skywalker (Ceremonial Outfit) (#69691) Col. 1 [.01] 8.00
Luke Skywalker (Hoth Gear) (#69619) Col. 2 [.00] 12.00
Luke Skywalker (Hoth Gear) (#69822) Col. 1 [.01] 10.00
Luke Skywalker (Stormtrooper) (#69819) Col. 2 [.01] 12.00
Luke Skywalker (Stormtrooper) (#69819) Col. 1 [.02] 12.00
Luke Skywalker (X-wing Pilot) (#69581) Col. 1 [.02] 15.00
Malakili (Rancor Keeper) (#69723) Col. 2 [.00] 10.00
Momaw Nadon "Hammerhead" (#69629) Col. 2 [.01] 12.00
Nien Nunb (#69694) Col. 2 [.00] 10.00
Ponda Baba (#69708) Col. 2 [.00] 40.00
Ponda Baba (#69708) Col. 3 [.01] 6.00
Princess Leia Organa (#69579) Col. 1 [.01] 12.00
Princess Leia (Boushh Disguise) (#69818) Col. 1 [.01 & .02] 18.00
Princess Leia Organa (Jabba's Prisoner) (#69683) Col. 1 [.00] 6.00
R2-D2 (#69574) Col. 1 [.01] 15.00
R5-D4 (#69598) Col. 2 [.01] with warning 15.00
Rebel Fleet Trooper (#69696) Col. 2 [.00] 30.00
Rebel Fleet Trooper (#69696) Col. 1 [.01] 10.00
Saelt-Marae (Yak Face) (#69721) Col. 2 [.00] 10.00

Green Card, Holo Picture: Saelt-Marae (Kenner 1997)

Sandtrooper (prev. Tatooine Stormtrooper) Col. 1 (#69601) [.01] 15.00
Sandtrooper (#69808) Col. 3 [.02] 6.00
Snowtrooper (#69632) Col. 3 [.00] 8.00
Stormtrooper (#69803) Col. 3 [.01] 10.00
TIE Fighter Pilot (#69673) Col. 2 [.03] 12.00
TIE Fighter Pilot (#69806) Col. 3 [.04] 12.00
2-1B Medic Droid (#69618) Col. 2 [.00] 10.00
Tusken Raider (#69603) Col. 2, closed hand 45.00
Tusken Raider (#69603) Col. 2 [.01] open hand 12.00
Weequay Skiff Guard (#69707) Col. 2 [.00] 20.00
Weequay Skiff Guard (#69707) Col. 3 [.01] .6.00
Yoda (#69672) Col. 2 [.02] 10.00
Yoda (#69586) Col. 1 [.03] 12.00

Special
Four-figure set of Han Solo in Endor Gear, Lando Calrissian as Skiff Guard,
AT-ST Driver and Darth Vader (J.C. Penney catalog 1997) 25.00

POWER OF THE FORCE 1998

The new header card packaging for 1998 added a 35 mm Freeze Frame Action Slide as an in-package premium. Loose figures do *not* include the 35 mm slide. In-package premiums are a separate collectible once they are removed from the package. Just about every beast, accessory and vehicle issued in 1998 came with an exclusive figure.

The first batch of Freeze Frame Action Slide Collection 1 figures all had a printing error, but corrected versions, with new printing numbers, arrived quickly. The error is on the back of the header card,

Freeze Frame: Biggs Darklighter (Kenner 1998)

in the list that follows the words "Collect all these *Star Wars* Action Figures." "Saelt-Marae" is misspelled as "Sealt-Marie"—two errors in just 10 letters. The error is the same on all packages, and the corrected version has the higher printing number: ".01" versus ".00" for the new figures and other numbers on the reissues.

GREEN CARD — FREEZE FRAME SERIES
Kenner (1998)

3-3/4" Figures (1998) with Freeze Frame Action Slides

8D8 (#69834) Col. 2 [.00]	$10.00
Admiral Ackbar (#69686) Col. 2 [.01]	12.00
AT-ST Driver (#69623) Col. 3 [.03] scarce	75.00
Ben (Obi-Wan) Kenobi *renamed Obi-Wan (Ben) Kenobi*	10.00
Biggs Darklighter (#69758) Col. 2 [.00]	20.00
Boba Fett (#69804) Col. 3 [.04]	35.00
Variations, **black circle** on one hand, or **no circle**, or	
no emblem on chest, or **no skull** on shoulder.	500.00
C-3PO (Pull-Apart Feature) (#69832) Col. 1 [.00]	10.00
Captain Piett (#69757) Col. 3 [.00] name plate error	30.00
Reissue with Blaster Pistol and Baton [.00]	100.00
Chewbacca as Boushh's Bounty (#69882) Col. 1 [.00]	15.00
Darth Vader (Removable Cape) (#69802) Col. 3 [.03]	12.00
Darth Vader (Removable Helmet, Detachable Hand) (#69836) Col. 3 [.00] . .	40.00
Death Star Trooper (#69838) Col. 3 [.00]	15.00
Emperor Palpatine (#69811) Col. 3 [.02]	10.00
Emperor's Royal Guard (#69717) Col. 3 [.01]	25.00
Endor Rebel Soldier (#69716) Col. 1 [.00] error	15.00
Reissue, "Saelt-Marae" corrected [.01].	8.00

Freeze Frame: Ishi Tib (Kenner 1998)

EV-9D9 (#69722) Col. 2 [.01] 15.00
Ewoks: Wicket & Logray (#69711) Col. 2 [.00] 18.00
Gamorrean Guard (#69693) Col. 2 [.01] 15.00
Garindan (#69706) Col. 3 [.01] 30.00
Grand Moff Tarkin (#69702) Col. 3 [.02] 10.00
Han Solo (#69577) Col. 1 [.02] 10.00
Han Solo in Carbonite (#69817) Col. 1 [.04] misspelling 20.00
    Reissue, "Saelt-Marae" corrected [.05] 10.00
Bespin Han Solo with (#69719) Col. 1 [.01] misspelling 20.00
    Reissue, "Saelt-Marae" corrected [.02] 10.00
    Reissue, "Unbeknownst" corrected [.03] 15.00
Han Solo in Endor Gear (#69621) Col. 1 [.01] misspelling 20.00
    Reissue, "Saelt-Marae" corrected [.02] 12.00
Hoth Rebel Soldier (#69821) Col. 1 [.02] misspelling 20.00
    Reissue, "Saelt-Marae" corrected [.03] 10.00
Ishi Tib (#69754) Col. 3 [.00] 20.00
Lak Sivrak (#69753) Col. 2 [.00] 20.00
Lando Calrissian as Skiff Guard (#69622) Col. 1 [.01] misspelling . . . 15.00
    Reissue, "Saelt-Marae" corrected [.02] 8.00
Lando Calrissian in General's Gear (#69756) Col. 1 [.00] misspelling 20.00
    Reissue, "Saelt-Marae" corrected [.01] 10.00
Lobot (#69856) Col. 1 [.00] 15.00
Bespin Luke Skywalker with Detachable Hand and with Lightsaber
    and Blaster Pistol (#69713) Col. 1 [.00] with misspelling 30.00
    Reissue, "Saelt-Marae" corrected [.01] 10.00
Luke Skywalker in Ceremonial Outfit (#69691) Col. 1 [.01] 12.00
Luke Skywalker in Stormtrooper Disguise (#69819) Col. 1 [.03]
    misspelling 20.00
    Reissue, "Saelt-Marae" corrected [.04] 10.00
Luke Skywalker (New Likeness, Blast Shield Helmet) (#69691) Col. 1
    [.00] 10.00
Malakili (Rancor Keeper) (#69723) Col. 2 [.01] 15.00

Freeze Frame: Malakili (Kenner 1998)

Mon Mothma (#69859) Col. 1 [.00] 15.00
Nien Nunb (#69694) Col. 2 [.01] 20.00
Obi-Wan (Ben) Kenobi (#69576) Col. 1 [.03] misspelling 25.00
   Reissue, "Saelt-Marae" corrected [.04] 20.00
Orrimaarko (Prune Face) (#69858) Col. 1 [.00] 15.00
Princess Leia Organa (New Likeness) (#69824) Col. 1 [.00] 10.00
Princess Leia Organa (Ewok Celebration Outfit)
   (#69714) Col. 1 [.00] misspelling 20.00
   Reissue, "Saelt-Marae" corrected [.01] 10.00
Princess Leia Organa as Jabba's Prisoner (#69683) Col. 1 [.01]
   misspelling 15.00
   Reissue, "Saelt-Marae" corrected [.02] 10.00
Rebel Fleet Trooper (#69696) Col. 1 [.01] misspelling 25.00
   Reissue (#69696) Col. 1 [.01 sticker] 20.00
   Reissue, "Saelt-Marae" corrected [.02] 18.00
Ree-Yees (#69839) Col. 3 [.00] 25.00
R2-D2 with Pop-Up Scanner (#69831) Col. 1 [.00] 15.00
   Variation, "Imperial trash compactor" on slide 50.00
Saelt-Marae (Yak Face) (#69721) Col. 2 [.01] 15.00
Sandtrooper (#69808) Col. 3 [.03] scarce 125.00
Snowtrooper (#69632) Col. 3 [.02] 20.00
Stormtrooper (#69803) Col. 3 [.02] 15.00
TIE Fighter Pilot (#69806) Col. 3 [.05] 50.00
Ugnaught (#69837) Col. 2 [.00] 12.00
Weequay Skiff Guard (#69707) [.02] scarce 350.00
Zuckuss (#69747) [.00] 30.00

Fan Club exclusives (early 1999) sold in sets of two
AT-AT Driver (#69864) [.0000] 25.00
Death Star Droid (#69862) [.00] 25.00
Pote Snitkin (#69863) [.00] 25.00
Princess Leia Organa in Hoth Gear (#84143) [.0000] 25.00

Expanded Universe 3-D: Dark Trooper (Kenner 1998)

3-D PLAYSCENE
(Expanded Universe)
Kenner (1998)

These figures are from the comics, video games and novels figures, not from the movies. They were released in November 1998, and include Mara Jade and Grand Admiral Thrawn, from *Heir to the Empire*, and Kyle Katarn, from *Dark Forces*. They are very popular with collectors. No one has reported finding figures with ".00" revision numbers, and the numbers listed are the earliest known.

Expanded Universe, 3-D PlayScene figures

Dark Empire comics

Clone Emperor Palpatine (#69886) [.02] $20.00
Imperial Sentinel (#69887) [.01]. 20.00
Luke Skywalker (Black Cloak) (#69883) [.01] 20.00
Princess Leia (Black Cloak) (#69884) [.03]. 20.00

Heir to the Empire novels

Grand Admiral Thrawn (#69888) [.02] 20.00
Mara Jade (#69891) [.03] 25.00
Spacetrooper (#69892) [.03] 25.00

Dark Forces video game

Dark Trooper (#69894) [.01] 30.00
Kyle Katarn (#69893) [.02] 25.00

Flashback Photo: Princess Leia Ceremonial (Kenner 1998)

FLASHBACK PHOTO
Kenner (1998–99)

Flashback Photo figures came with a detachable pull-down photo that showed the figure from the original movies and, when pulled down, showed the same or related figure from the then forthcoming Episode I movie. These revealed some essential plot points for that movie, such as that Queen Amidala is Luke and Leia's mother. Even the Flashback Photos have variations. The earlier ones have a down-arrow on the front and back of the pull-tab, while later ones have an up-arrow and a down-arrow on the front but no arrow on the back.

3-3/4" Figures (1998–99) with Flashback Photos

Anakin Skywalker (#84047) [.0000] $12.00
Aunt Beru (#84049) [.0000] 15.00
Ben (Obi-Wan) Kenobi (#84037) [.00] 10.00
C-3PO (#84041) [.0000] 10.00
Darth Vader (#84046) [.00] 10.00
Emperor Palpatine (#84042) [.00] 15.00
Hoth Chewbacca (#84051) [.00] 10.00
Luke Skywalker (#84036) [.00] 10.00
Princess Leia in Ceremonial Dress (#84038) [.01]
    with Celebration Gown photo (incorrect) 10.00
    with Freedom Fighter outfit (correct) 10.00
R2-D2 (#84043) [.01]
    Lightsaber packed left side. 10.00
    Lightsaber packed right side. 100.00
Yoda (#84039) [.00] 15.00

COMMtech Chip: Greedo (Hasbro 1999)

COMMTECH CHIP
Hasbro (1999)

COMMTech Chip Figures appeared with a new batch of *Star Wars* figures in 1999. These are the same types of chips used on the Episode I figures listed below. Hasbro had not given up on selling the classic characters just because it had a whole new movie to work with. The chips had either a chrome or a white background.

3-3/4" Figures (Hasbro 1999) with COMMTech Chips

Admiral Motti (#84366) [.00]	$25.00
Darth Vader (#84203) [.00]	12.00
Greedo (#84201) [.0000]	8.00
Han Solo (#84202) [.0000]	8.00
Jawa with Gonk Droid (#84198) [.0000]	
with two foot holes	8.00
with no foot holes	50.00
with one foot hole	60.00
Luke Skywalker (#84211) [.0000]	8.00
Princess Leia (#84361) [.0000]	25.00
R2-D2 with "Holographic" Princess Leia (#84199)	45.00
with foot peg on side of foot	300.00
Stormtrooper with "Battle Damage" (#84209) [.0000]	15.00
Wuher (#84389) [.0100]	25.00

Episode 1 Sneak Preview: STAP and Battle Droid
(Hasbro 1999)

STAR WARS: EPISODE I FIGURES

STAR WARS EPISODE I — *THE PHANTOM MENACE*
Hasbro (1999–2000)

The Phantom Menace toy avalanche began on May 3, 1999, and most stores opened just after midnight to lines of eager collectors. Stock was adequate, and most of the figures were still available the following morning and for a few days. The Battle Droids came in four different design patterns and collectors naturally wanted one of each color. This turned out to be a good move, as packaging changes made the earliest versions of the figures—with revision numbers ending in ".00"—fairly scarce. Many stores only got "Collection 1" figures such as Battle Droids with revision numbers ending in ".0100." Even these proved to be worthwhile investments, as package revision ".0200" was on the shelves within a month.

There were 16 additional figures added to the mix over the next year or so. Common versions of all these figures were produced in huge quantities and remained on retailers' racks for years. This glut of unsold figures greatly reduced the production and distribution of the final 13 figures, and they remained quite scarce.

Episode I: Boss Nass (Kenner 1999)

Sneak Previews (1998–99) boxed

STAP and Battle Droid (#84069) $35.00
Mace Windu (#84138) mail order 30.00

3-3/4" Figures (Hasbro 1999) with COMMTech Chips

Early Figures: (1999)

Anakin Skywalker (Tatooine) (#84074) [.00] $15.00
Battle Droid (#84092)
   Brown [.00] 20.00
   Reissue Brown [.0100] 15.00
   Tan [.00] 20.00
   Reissue Tan [.0100] 15.00
   Lightsaber slashed [.00] 20.00
   Reissue Lightsaber slashed [.0100] 15.00
   Blaster Battle scars [.00] 20.00
   Reissue Blaster Battle scars [.0100] 15.00
Boss Nass (#84119) [.0000] 8.00
C-3PO (#84106) [.00] 10.00
Chancellor Valorum (#84132) [.0000] small parts warning . . . 12.00
   Variation: [.0000] black sticker over warning 10.00
Darth Maul (Jedi Duel) (#84088) [.00] 18.00
   Reissue [.0000] 20.00
   Variation: with Black Vest, scarce 500.00
Darth Sideous (#84087) [.00] 12.00
Gasgano with Pit Droid (#84116) [.0000] 7.00
Jar Jar Binks (#84077) [.00] 20.00
   Reissue [.0100] 12.00
Ki-Adi-Mundi (#84123) Col. 3 [.0000] 10.00
Mace Windu (#84084) Col. 3 [.0000] 12.00
Obi-Wan Kenobi (Jedi Duel) (#84073) [.00] 10.00

Episode I: OOM-9, binoculars upper left (Hasbro 1999)

Padmé Naberrie (#84076) [.00] 10.00
Queen Amidala (Naboo) (#84078) [.00] 10.00
Qui-Gon Jinn (Jedi Duel) (#84072) [.00] 8.00
Ric Olie (#84109) [.00] 8.00
Senator Palpatine (#84082) [.00] 12.00
Watto (#84093) [.00] 10.00
All other reissues of above figures, each 7.00

Later Figures
Adi Gallia (#84124) $10.00
Anakin Skywalker (Naboo) (#84112) 7.00
Captain Panaka (#84108) 12.00
Captain Tarpals (#84121) 12.00
Darth Maul (Tatooine) (#84134) 7.00
    Variation: with Black Vest 500.00
Destroyer Droid (#84181) 7.00
Naboo Royal Security (#84079) 7.00
Nute Gunray (#84089) 6.00
Obi-Wan Kenobi (Naboo) (#84114) 7.00
Ody Mandrell (#84117) 7.00
OOM-9 (#84127) Binoculars packed upper left 30.00
    Binoculars packed over left hand 7.00
Queen Amidala (Coruscant) (#84111) 15.00
Qui-Gon Jinn (Naboo) (#84113) 7.00
R2-D2 (#84104) 7.00
Rune Haako (#84091) [.0000] 6.00
Yoda (#84086) [.0000] 7.00
    Without "Episode I" on card 30.00

Final Figures (2000)
Anakin Skywalker (Naboo Pilot) (#84246) $15.00
Darth Maul (Sith Lord) (#84247) 18.00

Episode I: R2-B1 Astromech Droid (Hasbro 2000)

Darth Sidious (Holograph) (#84081) 30.00
Destroyer Droid (Battle Damaged) (#84126) 20.00
Jar Jar Binks (Naboo Swamp) (#84252) 30.00
Naboo Royal Guard (#84083) 20.00
Obi-Wan Kenobi (Jedi Knight) (#84244) 20.00
Pit Droids (2-pack) (#84129) 25.00
Queen Amidala (Battle) (#84273) 30.00
Qui-Gon Jinn (Jedi Master) (#84107) 15.00
R2-B1 Astromech Droid (#84128) 25.00
Sio Bibble (#84257) 30.00
TC-14 Protocol Droid (#84276) 35.00

POWER OF THE JEDI
Hasbro (2000–2002)

Power of the Jedi figures include characters from all four movies. They come with a "Jedi Force File," which is an eight-page foldout. The card revision number was still present, but the only revisions are to the names and photos of the other available figures, listed on the back. Most of the figures are available on two or more different header cards, but are not necessarily in sequence. A given figure may well appear on a ".0100" and on a ".0400" card, but not on a ".0200" or ".0300" card.

3-3/4" Figures (Hasbro 2000–01) with Jedi Force File

Anakin Skywalker, Mechanic (#84254) [.0000] $12.00
Aurra Sing, Bounty Hunter (#84584) [.0300] 15.00
Battle Droid, Boomer Damage (#84563) [.0100] 15.00
    Reissue [.0300] 10.00
Battle Droid, Security (#84249) [.0000] 12.00

Power of the Jedi: Aurra Sing (Hasbro 2000)

Ben (Obi-Wan) Kenobi, Jedi Knight (#84362) [.0100] 12.00
Bespin Guard, Cloud City Security (#84638) [.0400]. 10.00
Boss Nass, Gungan Sacred Place (#84473) [.0000]. 15.00
    Reissue [.0100] 10.00
Chewbacca, Dejarik Champion (#84363) [.0000] 15.00
Chewbacca, Millennium Falcon Mechanic (#84577) [.0300] 12.00
Coruscant Guard (#84277) [.0000] 15.00
    Reissue [.0100] 12.00
    Reissue [.0300] 12.00
Darth Maul, Final Duel (#84506) with
    break-apart battle damage [.0000 with sticker] 15.00
Darth Maul, Sith Apprentice (#84561) [.0300] 20.00
    Reissue [.0400] 10.00
Darth Vader, Emperor's Wrath (#84637) [.0400] 10.00
Darth Vader, Dagobah (#84472) [.0100]. 15.00
Ellorrs Madak, Duros (#84647) (Fan Choice Figure #1) [.0400] 8.00
Fode and Beed, Podrace Announcer (#84474) Col. 2 [.0100] 20.00
Gungan Warrior (#84274) [.0000] 25.00
    Reissue [.0100] 20.00
    Reissue [.0400] 10.00
Han Solo, Bespin Capture (#84564) [.0100] 20.00
    Reissue [.0300] 15.00
    Reissue [.0400] 10.00
Han Solo, Death Star Escape (#84626) [.0400]. 10.00
IG-88, Bounty Hunter (#84587) [.0100] 15.00
    Reissue [.0300] 10.00
Jar Jar Binks, Tatooine (#84267) [.0300] 13.00
    Reissue [.0400] 10.00
Jek Porkins, X-wing Pilot (#84457) [.0000] 15.00
    Reissue [.0100] 12.00

Power of the Jedi: Sabé, Queen's Decoy (Hasbro 2001)

Reissue [.0300] 10.00
K-3PO, Echo Base Protocol Droid (#84643) [.0100] 15.00
Reissue [.0400] 10.00
Ketwol (#84634) [.0400] 10.00
Lando Calrissian, Bespin Escape (#84589) [.0300] 15.00
Leia Organa, General (#84642) Col.1 [.0000] 12.00
Leia Organa, Bespin Escape (#84588) [.0300] 12.00
Luke Skywalker X-wing Pilot (#84571) [.0400] 8.00
Mas Amedda (#84136) [.0000] 15.00
Reissue [.0100] 12.00
Reissue [.0300] 12.00
Mon Calamari Officer (#84644) [.0100] 15.00
Reissue [.0300] 12.00
Obi-Wan Kenobi, Jedi (#84251) [.0000] 12.00
Obi-Wan Kenobi, Cold Weather (#84573) [.0300] 15.00
Obi-Wan Kenobi, Jedi Training Gear (#84651) [.0300] 15.00
Plo Koon, Jedi Master (#84568) [.0100] 15.00
Reissue [.0300] 12.00
Queen Amidala, Theed Invasion (#84567) [.0100] 15.00
Reissue [.0300] 15.00
Qui-Gon Jinn, Mos Espa Disguise (#84253) [.0000] 12.00
Qui-Gon Jinn, Jedi Training Gear (#84559) [.0400] 12.00
R2-D2, Naboo Escape (#84259) [.0000] 15.00
Reissue [.0100] 8.00
R2-Q5, Imperial Astromech Droid (#84629) [.0400] 15.00
Sabé, Queen's Decoy (#84137) [.0400] 12.00
Saesse Tiin (#84569) [.0300] 12.00
Sandtrooper, Tatooine Patrol (#84579) [.0400] 8.00
Scout Trooper Imperial Pilot (white) (#84586) [.0100] 12.00
Scout Trooper Imperial Pilot (dirty) (#84586) [.0400] 10.00
Sebulba, Bonta Eve Challenge (#84266) [.0100] 12.00
Shmi Skywalker (#84271) [.0400] .8.00

Power of the Jedi, transition: Eeth Koth (Hasbro 2002)

Tessek (#84639) [.0300] 12.00
Tusken Raider, Desert Sniper (#84248) [.0000] 15.00
   Reissue [.0100] 15.00
   Reissue [.0300] 12.00
All other reissues of above figures, each 8.00

POWER OF THE JEDI (TRANSITION)

Starting in 2002, Hasbro dropped the "Jedi Force File" foldout and printed the character's name on the front. The back was changed to contain the character biographical information. For lack of a better name, these are called "Transition" header cards. Since the cards are no longer generic, the package revision number no longer works the same as on earlier figures in the Power of the Jedi lineup. The decimal point has been dropped, and the last four digits now represent distinct character numbers.

3-3/4" Figures (Hasbro 2002) Transition

Eeth Koth, Jedi Master (#84662) 8.00
FX-7, Medical Droid (#84656) 8.00
Imperial Officer (#84659) Col. 2 . . . . 8.00
Queen Amidala, Royal Decoy (#84657) 8.00
Rebel Trooper, *Tantive IV* Defender (#84658) 8.00
Zutton, Snaggletooth (#84661) 8.00

ATTACK OF THE CLONES
Hasbro (2002)

Attack of the Clones figures are numbered on the back with the last two digits of the year (02) and a two-digit figure number. Fifty-

Attack of the Clones: Kit Fisto, with insert (Hasbro 2002)

seven such figures were issued, along with four Sneak Preview figures. Vast numbers were issued, and only a couple have proved to be scarce.

Sneak Preview Figures, Green Card

Clone Trooper (#84680)	7.00
Jango Fett (#84678)	7.00
R3-T7 (#84679)	7.00
Zam Wesell (#84677)	7.00

The first 16 *Attack of the Clones* figures originally came with a background insert behind the figure. Later the insert was omitted. If the insert is present, add $2 to the value listed below. Except for Ephant Mon (Figure 02-43), all of these figures were produced in vast numbers and can still be found in many stores in abundance.

3-3/4" Figures, "02" Prefix, Blue Card

01 Anakin Skywalker, Outland Peasant Disguise (#84852)	6.00
02 Padmé Amidala, Arena Escape (#84855)	6.00
03 Obi-Wan Kenobi, Coruscant Chase (#84854)	6.00
04 C-3PO, Protocol Droid (#84856)	6.00
05 Kit Fisto, Jedi Master (#84858)	6.00
06 Super Battle Droid (#84853)	6.00
07 Boba Fett, Kamino Escape (#84863)	6.00
08 Tusken Raider Female with Child (#84864)	6.00
09 Captain Typho (#84862)	6.00
10 Shaak Ti, Jedi Master (#84872)	6.00
11 Battle Droid, Arena Battle (#84865)	6.00
12 Plo Koon, Arena Battle (#84868)	6.00
13 Jango Fett, Kamino Escape (#84857)	6.00
14 R2-D2, Coruscant Sentry (#84865)	6.00

Attack of the Clones: Djas Puhr (Hasbro 2002)

15 Geonosian Warrior (#84867) 6.00
16 Dexter Jettster, Coruscant Informant (#84866) 6.00
17 Clone Trooper (#84635) 6.00
18 Zam Wesell, Bounty Hunter (#84655) 6.00
19 Royal Guard, Coruscant Security (#84831) 6.00
20 Saesee Tinn, Jedi Master (#84832) 6.00
21 Nikto, Jedi Knight (#84823) 6.00
22 Anakin Skywalker, Hangar Duel (#84605) 6.00
23 Yoda, Jedi Maser (#84615) 6.00
24 Jar Jar Binks, Gungan Senator (#84821) .6.00
25 Taun We, Kamino Cloner (#84822) 6.00
26 Luminara Uduh, Jedi Master (#84833) 6.00
27 Count Dooku, Dark Lord (#84889) 6.00
28 Mace Windu, Geonosian Rescue (#84515) 6.00
29 Luke Skywalker, Bespin Duel (#84525)
    Bloody stump 20.00
    Clean stump, plastic or metal 6.00
30 Darth Vader, Bespin Duel (#84580) 6.00
31 Jango Fett, Final Battle (#84505) 6.00
32 Qui-Gon Jinn, Jedi Master (#84801) 6.00
33 Endor Rebel Soldier (#84802) facial hair or clean shaven 6.00
34 Massiff (#84803) 6.00
35 Orn Free Taa (#84804) 6.00
36 Obi-Wan Kenobi, Jedi Starfighter Pilot (#84860) 6.00
37 Han Solo, Endor Raid (#84880) 6.00
38 Chewbacca, Cloud City Capture (#84890) .6.00
39 Supreme Chancellor Palpatine (#84808) .6.00
40 Djas Puhr, Alien Bounty Hunter (#84809) 6.00
41 Padmé Amidala, Coruscant Attack (#84809) 6.00
42 Darth Maul, Sith Training (#84580) 6.00
43 Anakin Skywalker, Tatooine Attack (#84906) 6.00
44 Ki-Adi-Mundi, Jedi Master (#84912) 6.00

Attack of the Clones: Aayla Secura, blue card (Hasbro 2003)

45 Ephant Mon (#84812) 25.00
46 Teemto Pagalies, Pod Racer (#84813) .6.00
47 Jango Fett, *Slave I* Pilot (#84909) 6.00
48 Destroyer Droid, Geonosis Battle (#84910) 6.00
49 Clone Trooper, Republic Gunship Pilot (#84911) 6.00
50 Watto, Mos Espa Junk Dealer (#84260) 6.00
51 Lott Dod Neimoidian Senator (#84913) 6.00
52 Tusken Raider, with Massiff (#84914) .6.00
53 Yoda, Jedi High Council (#84968) 6.00

ATTACK OF THE CLONES/ CLONE WARS
Hasbro (2003)

Distribution of 2003 figures was spotty, at best, and many are hard to find. They were numbered with an "03" prefix and had a slightly different nameplate style. The early figures originally came on a blue card that was just like the 2002 figures' card. This was changed to a card with a gold stripe along the left side for the later figures, and, eventually, a number of the early figures were reissued on this style of card. This has not affected the price yet. *Clone Wars* figures (#42 through #51) were issued on cards with a blue stripe and light background color.

3-3/4" Figures, "03" Prefix, Blue Card, Later Gold-Stripe Card
01 Obi-Wan Kenobi, Acklay Battle (#84870) 10.00
02 Mace Windu, Arena Confrontation (#84918) 10.00
03 Darth Tyranus, Geonosian Escape (#84919) 15.00
04 Padmé Amidala, Droid Factory Chase (#84923) 7.00

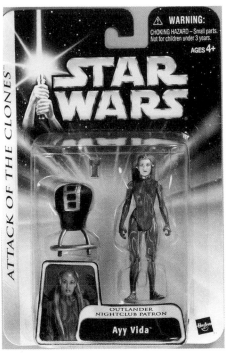

Attack of the Clones: Ayy Vida, gold-stripe card
(Hasbro 2003)

05 SP-4 & JN-66 Research Droids (#84924) 8.00
06 Tusken Raider (#84921) 8.00
07 Anakin Skywalker, Secret Ceremony, blue card 8.00
    Gold-stripe card (#85014) 8.00
08 Boba Fett, Pit of Carkoon, blue card 15.00
    Gold-stripe card (#85013) .15.00
09 R2-D2 Droid Factory Flight (#84922) 8.00
10 Lama Su with Clone Youth (#84925) 9.00
11 Aayla Secura
    (#84928) Jedi Knight, blue card 8.00
    (#85015) Battle of Geonosis, gold-stripe card 8.00
12 Barriss Offee
    (#84926) Luminara Unduli's Padawan, blue card 10.00
    (#85025) Battle of Geonosis, gold stripe card 10.00
13 Han Solo, Hoth Rescue, blue card 8.00
    Gold-stripe card (#85012) 8.00
14 Chewbacca, Mynock Hunt (#84960) 10.00
15 Yoda & Chian
    (#84969) Padawan Lightsaber Training, blue card 8.00
    (#85029) Jedi Temple, gold-stripe card 8.00
16 Ashla & Jempa, Jedi Padawans (#84970) blue card 8.00
    Gold-stripe card (#85030) 8.00

3-3/4" Figures, "03" prefix, Gold-Stripe Card
17 Luke Skywalker, Throne Room Duel (#84977) &
    (#85008) gloved right hand 12.00
18 Darth Vader, Throne Room Duel (#85009) 10.00
19 Snowtrooper, The Battle of Hoth (#84979) & (#85011) . . .10.00
20 Jango Fett, Kamino Escape .10.00
21 C-3PO Tatooine Ambush (#84705) 10.00
22 Padmé Amidala, Secret Ceremony (#84989) 15.00
23 Wat Tambor, Geonosis War Room (#84990) 15.00

Clone Wars: ARC Trooper (Hasbro 2003)

24 Coleman Trebor, Battle of Geonosis (#84991) 15.00
25 Darth Maul, Theed Hangar Duel (#84706) 10.00
26 Princess Leia Organa, Imperial Captive (#84707) 12.00
27 Han Solo, Flight to Alderaan (#84708) 10.00
28 WA-7, Dexter's Diner (#84817) 10.00
29 Lt. Dannl Faytonni, Coruscant Outlander Club (#84818) 10.00
30 The Emperor, Throne Room (#84820) 8.00
31 Luke Skywalker, Tatooine Encounter (#84709) 8.00
32 Darth Vader, Death Star Clash (#84710) .8.00
33 Bail Organa (#84830) 10.00
34 McQuarrie Concept Stormtrooper (#84829) 25.00
35 Imperial Dignitary Janus Greejatus (#84842) 8.00
36 Padmé Amidala, Lars Homestead (#84843) 10.00
37 Achk Med-Beq, Coruscant Outlander Club (#84742) 8.00
38 Ayy Vida, Outlander Nightclub Patron (#84723) 10.00
39 Obi-Wan Kenobi, Outlander Nightclub (#84717) 8.00
40 Elan Sleazebaggano, Outlander Nightclub Encounter (#84718) . . .8.00
41 Imperial Dignitary Kren Blista-Vanee (#84769) 8.00

3-3/4" Clone Wars Figures, "03" Prefix, Blue-Stripe Card

42 Anakin Skywalker (#84814) 8.00
43 ARC Trooper (#84815) 8.00
44 Yoda (#84828) 8.00
45 Obi-Wan Kenobi, General of the Republic Army (#84826) 8.00
46 Durge, Commander of the Separatist Forces (#84816) 8.00
47 Asajj Ventress, Sith Apprentice (#84827) .8.00
48 Mace Windu, General of the Republic Army (#84848) 8.00
49 Kit Fisto (#84849) 8.00
50 Clone Trooper (#84724) 10.00
51 Saesee Tiin (#84722) 8.00

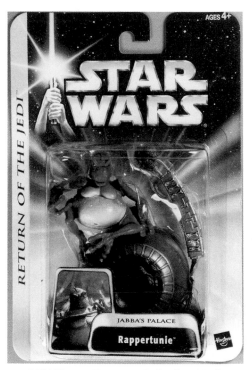

2004 Figures: Rappertunie (Hasbro 2004)

CLASSIC FIGURES &
ORIGINAL TRILOGY COLLECTION
Hasbro (2004)

Hasbro's 2004 figures were much the same as the 2003 figures, except that you could find them more easily. Many stores had some 2004 figures, lots of leftover 2002 figures, but no 2003 figures available. Then the fun started, as figures appeared without the year number. These are called "Classic figures" below.

3-3/4" Figures, "04" Prefix, Gold-Stripe Card

01 Hoth Trooper, Hoth Evacuation (#84725) 8.00
02 R-3PO, Hoth Evacuation (#84726) 8.00
03 Luke Skywalker, Hoth Attack (#84727) .8.00
04 Luke Skywalker, Jabba's Palace (#84731) 8.00
05 R2-D2, Jabba's Sail Barge (#84719) 8.00
06 R1-G4, Tatooine Transaction (#84721) .8.00
07 Lando Calrissian, Jabba's Sail Barge (#84743) 8.00
08 Rappertunie, Jabba's Palace (#84746) .8.00
09 J'Quille, Jabba's Sail Barge (#84744) .8.00
10 Tanus Spijek, Jabba's Sail Barge (#84747) 8.00
11 Holographic Luke Skywalker, Jabba's Palace (#84745) 8.00
12 General Jan Dodonna, Battle of Yavin (#84766) 8.00
13 Dutch Vander, Gold Leader, Battle of Yavin (#84764) 8.00
14 TIE Fighter Pilot, Battle of Yavin (#84765) 8.00
15 Captain Antilles, *Tantive IV* Invasion (#84767) 8.00
16 Admiral Ozzel, *Executor* Assault (#84770) 8.00
17 Dengar, *Executor* Meeting (#84771) 8.00
18 Bossk, *Executor* Meeting (#84772) 8.00

Vintage: Han Solo (Hasbro 2004)

3-3/4" Classic Figures, (2004), Gold-Stripe Card

Anakin Skywalker, Geonosis Hangar Duel (#84793) 8.00
C-3PO, Death Star Rescue (#84791) 8.00
Chewbacca, Escape from Hoth (#84789) .8.00
Darth Maul, Theed Hangar Duel (#85090) 8.00
Darth Vader, Death Star Clash (#85156) .8.00
Han Solo, Flight to Alderaan (#85154) 8.00
Luke Skywalker, Tatooine Encounter (#85155) 8.00
Obi-Wan Kenobi, Coruscant Chase (#84792) 8.00
Princess Leia, Death Star Captive (#85110) 8.00
R2-D2, Tatooine Mission (#84790) 8.00
Stormtrooper, Death Star Chase (#84794) 8.00
Yoda, Battle of Geonosis (#84795) 8.00

2004 VINTAGE FIGURES

The vintage figures are part of the "Original Trilogy Collection" but are a separate series of replicas of the original 1978 83 figures on replica cards, inside a plastic outer-hanging box. The box lists the initial 12 figures, but not all had been seen at press time.

3-3/4" *Star Wars* vintage figures (2004)

Ben (Obi-Wan) Kenobi (#85215) 10.00
Han Solo (#85224) 10.00
Princess Leia (#85225) 10.00
Luke Skywalker (#85214) 10.00

3-3/4" *The Empire Strikes Back* vintage figures (2004)

C-3PO (#85236) 10.00
Darth Vader (#85235) 10.00
Lando Calrissian (#85238) 10.00
Yoda (#85237) 10.00

Original Trilogy Collection: IG-88 (Hasbro 2004)

3-3/4" *Return of the Jedi* vintage figures (2004)

Chewbacca (#85191) 10.00
R2-D2 (#85199) 10.00
Boba Fett (#85271) 10.00
Stormtrooper (#85272) 10.00

ORIGINAL TRILOGY COLLECTION

The original trilogy collection figures come on black header cards similar to the 1978 design. They are numbered on the back, as on 2002–04 figures, but the prefix is "OTC," and the card has the symbol of the Evil Empire or the Rebel Alliance, depending on the allegiance of the character. Not all were seen at press time.

3-3/4" Original Trilogy figures (2004) black *"Star Wars"* card

01 Luke Skywalker (#84778) 8.00
02 Yoda (#84779) 8.00
03 Spirit Obi-Wan (#84780) 8.00
04 R2-D2 (#84781) 8.00
05 Luke Skywalker, X-wing pilot (#85184) 8.00
06 Luke Skywalker, Jedi (#85185) 8.00
07 Han Solo (#85190) 8.00
08 Chewbacca (#85191) 8.00
09 Princess Leia (#85192) 8.00
10 Darth Vader (#85193) 8.00
11 Scout Trooper (#85198) 8.00
12 R2-D2 (#85199) 8.00
13 C-3PO (#85248) 8.00
14 Boba Fett (#85249) 8.00
15 Obi-Wan Kenobi (#85259) 8.00
16 Stormtrooper (#85262) 8.00

17 Wicket (#85263) 8.00
18 Princess Leia, Bespin (#84837) 8.00
19 Cloud Car Pilot (#85054) 8.00
20 Lobot (#85060) 8.00
21 TIE Fighter Pilot (#85371) 8.00
22 Greedo (#85372) 8.00
23 Tusken Raider (#00202) 8.00
24 Jawas (#00204) 8.00
25 Snowtrooper (#85375) 8.00
26 Luke Skywalker, Bespin (#85376) 8.00
27 IG-88 (#00209) (#85377) 8.00
28 Bossk (#00210) (#85378) 8.00
29 Darth Vader, Hoth (#85379) (#00337) .8.00
30 Gamorrean Guard (#85380) (#00338) 8.00
31 Bib Fortuna (#00210) (#85381) (#00339) 8.00
32 Lando Calrissian, Skiff Guard (#85382) (#00340) 8.00
33 Princess Leia, Slave (#85383) (#00341) .8.00
34 Darth Vader (#85193) (#00342) 8.00
35 Han Solo, AT-ST Driver (#85385) (#00728) 8.00
36 General Madine (#85386) (#00729) 8.00
37 Lando Calrissian, General (#85387) (#00730) 8.00
38 Imperial Trooper (#85447) (#02822) 8.00

LOOSE FIGURES
Kenner/Hasbro (1995–2004)

Only a few exotic variations, and some scarce recent figures, have attained any collector value as "loose figures." Exotic variations are so rare that no accepted market price is known. The merely "scarce" figures are listed below. All the other common figures sell for about $3. All loose figure prices include the original weapons and accessories.

Loose New Power of the Force Figures, scarce

Admiral Motti	$15.00
AT-AT Driver	12.50
Ben (Obi-Wan) Kenobi, with long lightsaber	12.50
Boba Fett, with half circle on hand	10.00
Captain Piett	10.00
Clone Emperor Palpatine	10.00
Dark Trooper	10.00
Darth Vader, with long lightsaber	12.50
Darth Vader, removeable helmet	15.00
Death Star Droid, with mouse droid	12.50
Death Star Trooper	12.50
Grand Admiral Thrawn	10.00
Han Solo in Hoth Gear, with open hand	10.00
Imperial Sentinel	10.00
Jedi Knight Luke Skywalker, with brown vest	30.00
Kyle Katarn	10.00
Luke Skywalker, with long lightsaber	17.50
Luke Skywalker in Dagobah Fatigues, with long lightsaber	17.50
Luke Skywalker (Black Cloak) Expanded Universe	10.00

AT-AT Driver and Commander, from AT-AT (Kenner 1997)

Luke Skywalker in X-wing Fighter Pilot Gear, with long lightsaber 12.50
Mara Jade 10.00
Mon Mothma 7.00
Ponda Baba, grey beard 20.00
Pote Snitkin 12.50
Princess Leia in Hoth Gear 12.50
Princess Leia (Black Cloak) Expanded Universe 10.00

Ree-Yees	12.50
R2-D2 with holographic Princess Leia	15.00
Spacetrooper	10.00

Loose Episode I figures, scarce

Darth Sidious (Holographic)	.9.00
Destroyer Droid (Battle Damaged)	8.00
Jar Jar Binks (Naboo Swamp)	10.00
Queen Amidala (Battle)	15.00
R2-B1 Astromech Droid	10.00
Sio Bibble	15.00
TC-14	15.00

LOOSE FIGURES FROM VEHICLES, CREATURES & PLAYSETS

Many of the new Power of the Force vehicles came with exclusive figures. Starting in 1998, it was hard to find a vehicle without one. The most interesting of these exclusives is the Wedge Antilles error figure. The first batches of the *Millennium Falcon* carry case came with a Wedge Antilles with a white stripe down each arm. This was clearly visible, as the figure can be seen in the gun turret of the ship. Later batches of these carry cases corrected the figure.

Loose Figures from new Power of the Force vehicles

Wedge Antilles, from *Millennium Falcon* carry case, with white stripes down arms, error figure	$10.00
Correct figure, no white stripes	.8.00
Almost all other figures, each	$5.00

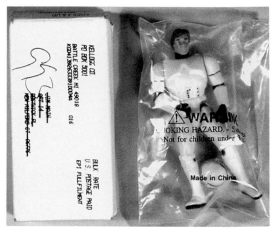

Mail-in Han Solo Stormtrooper Disguise (Kenner 1995)

Loose Figures from Episode I vehicles

Gungan Warrior from Femba creature/vehicle 10.00

Qui-Gon Jinn from Eopie creature 20.00

R2 Unit (Red) from Naboo Royal Starship vehicle 10.00

Loose Figures from other vehicles and games

Rorworr, Wookiee Scout from Invasion of Theed RPG Game 8.00

On mini-card, as issued 15.00

Almost all other figures, each 5.00

MAIL-IN EXCLUSIVE FIGURES

Mail-in figures

Mail-in Han Solo in Stormtrooper disguise, in plastic bag,
(Froot Loops offer) with mailer box $35.00

Spirit of Obi-Wan Kenobi, with box (Frito-Lay offer, 1997) 15.00

Cantina Band Member, Official *Star Wars* Fan Club
exclusive, in plastic bag, with five musical
instruments (#69734, 1997) in white mailer box 15.00

Cantina Band Set, five figures: (All five figures are
the same as above. Only the instruments are
different.) Official *Star Wars* Fan Club 50.00

Loose: Doikk N'ats with Fizzz Instrument 10.00

Loose: Figrin D'an with Kloo Horn Instrument 10.00

Loose: Ickabel with Fanfars Instrument 10.00

Loose: Nalan with Bandfill Instrument 10.00

Loose: Techn with Omnibox Instrument 10.00

B'Omarr Monk, Hasbro Internet Web site offer, in plastic bag,
with instruction sheet (#69718, 1997–98) in white mailer box 15.00

Oola and Salacious Crumb, Official *Star Wars* Fan Club exclusive
(#69871, 1998) in window box 20.00

Kabe and Muftak, Internet exclusive (#84071) in window box 20.00

Theater giveaway figure (1997)

Jedi Knight Luke Skywalker, *Star Wars* Trilogy Edition, carded 75.00

DELUXE FIGURES

Deluxe figures follow the basic concept behind the Mini-Rigs
from the original series. One- and two-man weapons, radar and
communication stations, loading dock, cargo handling, refueling and

repair droids and other equipment that fit in with the ones featured in the film and could be envisioned as "just off camera." Later, Kenner added major characters to this lineup, with accessories that are actually seen in the movies, such as Gunner Stations from the *Millennium Falcon*, and later a Bacta Tank (with Luke) and a Sail Barge Cannon (with Leia). The packages for the figures do not say "Deluxe" anywhere, but they follow the same basic concept of a figure plus a large accessory.

DELUXE FIGURES
Kenner (1996–2004)

First Wave (1996) red Power of the Force header card
Crowd Control Stormtrooper (#69609)
    with two warning stickers [.00] $35.00
    Variation, with one warning sticker. 15.00
    Reissue, printed warnings [.01] 7.00
    Loose, with all parts 4.00
Luke Skywalker's Desert Sport Skiff (#69611) 10.00
    Loose, with complete Sport Skiff 4.00
Han Solo with Smuggler Flight Pack (#69612) 10.00
    Loose, with complete Flight Pack 4.00

Second Wave (1997) green Power of the Force header card
Boba Fett with Wing-Blast Rocketpack and Overhead Cannon (#69638)
    on card [.00] that says "Weaponry: Photon Torpedo" 15.00
    Variation [.01] says "Weaponry: Proton Torpedo" 12.00
    Loose, with complete Rocketpack 4.00
Note: Scarce variations: Circle on one hand, or no
    emblem on chest, or no skull on shoulder, each 500.00

Deluxe Han Solo with Smuggler Flight Pack (Kenner 1996)

Millennium Minted Coin Collection:
Princess Leia, Endor Gear (Kenner 1998)

Probe Droid (#69677) on green card [.00] with red-
  color-scheme back picturing figures 25.00
  Variation [.01] 10.00
  Variation [.02] green-color-scheme back 8.00
  Loose, complete 4.00

Third Wave (1997) green Power of the Force header card
Hoth Rebel Soldier with Anti-Vehicle Laser Cannon (#69744) 10.00
  Loose, with complete Laser Cannon .4.00
Snowtrooper with E-Web Heavy Repeating Blaster (#69724) [.00] 10.00
  Loose, with complete Blaster. 4.00

GUNNER STATIONS

Gunner Stations (1998) green Power of the Force card
Millennium Falcon with Luke Skywalker (#69848)
  [.00] with warning sticker. $12.00
  with printed warning [.01] 10.00
Millennium Falcon with Han Solo (#69766)
  [.00] with warning sticker 12.00
  with printed warning [.01] 10.00
TIE Fighter with Darth Vader (#69847) 30.00

MILLENNIUM
MINTED COIN COLLECTION

Each figure in the series comes with a gold-colored coin
mounted on a display pedestal. The combination costs about $10, or
about $4 more than the figure alone.

Episode I Light-Up Qui-Gon Jinn (Hasbro 2000)

3-3/4" Figures with Gold Coin (1998) in window box (Toys "R" Us exclusive)

Bespin Han Solo (#84022) [.00] with text	$25.00
with variant coin	30.00
Chewbacca (#84023) [.00] with text	25.00
C-3PO (#84024) [.00]	10.00
Luke Skywalker, Endor Gear (#84026) [.00] with text	25.00
Princess Leia, Endor Gear (#84027) [.00] with text	25.00
Snowtrooper (#84028) [.00] with text	25.00
Emperor Palpatine (#84029) [.00]	10.00
Reissues of any of above [.01] no text, each	10.00

EPISODE I

Episode I Deluxe (1999) with Lightsaber Handle

Deluxe Darth Maul (#84144) [.0000]	$7.00
Deluxe Obi-Wan Kenobi (#84152) [.0000]	7.00
Deluxe Qui-Gon Jinn (#84148) [.0000]	7.00

Trophy Assortment

Darth Maul with Sith Infiltrator (#84409) [.0000]	10.00

EPISODE I LIGHT-UP FIGURES

These figures are designed to portray the holographic communications seen in Episode I by having a clear plastic figure with a base that projects a light through them. They are Wal-Mart stores exclusives.

Episode I Light-Up figures (Wal-Mart exclusives 2000)

Light-up Darth Maul figure as holograph (#84372)	$15.00
Light-up Qui-Gon Jinn figure as holograph (#84371)	15.00

*Power of the Jedi Deluxe: Princess Leia
with Sail Barge Cannon (Hasbro 2001)*

POWER OF THE JEDI

Power of the Jedi Deluxe (2001)

Darth Maul with Sith Attack Droid (#84654) $10.00

Luke Skywalker in Echo Base Bacta Tank (#84652) 10.00

Princess Leia with Sail Barge Cannon (#84653) 10.00

Boba Fett special 300th Figure (#84566) [.0100] 25.00

    Reissue: [.0200] 15.00

ATTACK OF THE CLONES

***Attack of the Clones* Deluxe (2002–03) blue card**

Darth Tyranus, Force Flipping Attack (#84879) $10.00

Jango Fett, with Electronic Jetpack (#84877) 10.00

Mace Windu, Force Power Attack (#84876 . . . . 10.00

Obi-Wan Kenobi, Force Flipping Attack (#84878) 10.00

Anakin Skywalker, Force Flipping Attack (#84901) 10.00

Second Batch, blue card

Anakin Skywalker, Lightsaber Slashing (#84882) 10.00

Nexu (#84885) 10.00

C-3PO with Droid Factory Assembly Line (#84899) 10.00

Yoda with Force Powers (#84900) 10.00

Flying Geonosian (#84902) 10.00

***The Empire Strikes Back* Deluxe, gold-stripe card**

General Rieekan, Hoth Evacuation (#84713) 12.00

C-3PO with Escape Pod (#84714) 10.00

Wampa with Hoth Cave (#84712) 15.00

***Return of the Jedi*, gold-stripe card**

Jabba's Palace Court Denizens (#84741) 12.00

Jabba the Hutt, Jabba's Palace (#84740) 12.00

Deluxe Momaw Nadon, Cantina Bar (Hasbro 2003)

Attack of the Clones, **gold-stripe card**
Jango Fett, Kamino Confrontation (#85158) 12.00
Obi-Wan Kenobi, Kamino Confrontation (#85157). 12.00

CLONE WARS

Clone Wars (2003) **blue-stripe card**
Destroyer Droid Battle Launcher (#84988) $10.00
Spider Droid (#85051) 10.00
Durge, with Swoop Bike (#84844) 10.00
Clone Trooper with Speeder Bike (#84846) 10.00

CANTINA ALIENS

Cantina Bar (2003) Wal-Mart exclusive
Greedo (#32542) $15.00
Momaw Nadon (#32544) 15.00
Ponda Boba (#32543) 20.00

ELECTRONIC FIGURES

With electronic figures you can add "bells and whistles" to your action figure—literally. The only figure that features both sound and lights is the Electronic Power F/X R2-D2. The others just add lights.

ELECTRONIC POWER F/X
Kenner (1997)

There are five Electronic Power F/X figures and all of them, except R2-D2, come with a light-up feature and an action feature controlled by hidden buttons and levers. The packages have diorama scenes that can be cut out, and the first two figures, Ben and Darth, interconnect to allow a simulated duel. Luke can also connect with Darth for a duel, but not with the Emperor, who is facing the wrong way.

Electronic Power F/X: Ben (Obi-Wan) Kenobi
(Hasbro 1997)

Electronic Power F/X (1997) green header cards

Ben (Obi-Wan) Kenobi (#69643) [.00] $10.00
Darth Vader (#69644) [.00] 10.00
Luke Skywalker (#69746) [.00] 10.00
R2-D2 (Artoo-Detoo) (#69646) [.00] 10.00
    Variation [.01] blue UPC code bars 10.00
    Variation [.02] black UPC code bars 8.00
Emperor Palpatine (#69726) [.00] energy bolts pictured pointing up 12.00
    Variation [.01] energy bolts pointing down 10.00
Loose on stand, with backdrop cut-out, each .4.00

LARGER FIGURES

EPIC FORCE

These 5-inch figures were introduced at the 1998 Toy Fair. Other than the size, the gimmick is the rotating base, which lets the collector see all sides of the figure without removing it from the package.

5" Epic Force Figures with in-package rotating base

Darth Vader [.00] $10.00
Bespin Luke Skywalker [.00] 10.00
Boba Fett [.00] 10.00
C-3PO [.00] 10.00
Princess Leia Organa [.00] 10.00
Stormtrooper [.00] 10.00

Epic Force Three-pack, boxed (FAO Schwarz)

Three-pack of Chewbacca, Han Solo and Obi-Wan Kenobi (#84281) 65.00

Mega Action: Obi-Wan Kenobi (Hasbro 2000)

Episode I 5" Epic Force Figures (1999)

Darth Maul 15.00
Obi-Wan Kenobi 15.00
Qui-Gon Jinn 15.00

MEGA ACTION

Hasbro produced these 6-inch figures in 2000. They have levers and other devices so you can activate their action moves by hand.

Power of the Jedi 6" Mega Action Figures

Obi-Wan Kenobi $13.00
Darth Maul 13.00
Destroyer Droid 15.00

STAR WARS UNLEASHED
Hasbro (2003–04)

While these are packaged like larger action figures, they are really dramatically posed sculptures and are released in groups of two or three.

Darth Vader, no helmet (#84945) $35.00
Obi-Wan Kenobi (#84946) 15.00
Darth Sidious (#84948) 15.00
Darth Tyranus (#84915) 15.00
Mace Windu (#84916) 25.00
Count Dooku 25.00
Darth Vader (#84897) 30.00
Padmé Amidala (#84898) 25.00

Star Wars Unleashed: Princess Leia (Hasbro 2004)

Anakin Skywalker (#84805) 15.00
Darth Maul (#84807) 25.00
Jango & Boba Fett (#84806) 15.00
Boba Fett (#84985) 20.00
Han Solo (#84984) 15.00
Yoda (#84983) 15.00
Princess Leia, Slave Girl (#84796) 30.00
Darth Sidious (#84799) 20.00
Luke Skywalker, Jedi (#84797) 25.00
Chewbacca (#84733) 15.00
Luke Skywalker, Pilot (#84734) 15.00
Clone Trooper (#84735) 15.00
Aayla Secura (#84786) 15.00
Bossk (#84788) 15.00
Tusken Raider (#84787) 15.00

MULTI-PACKS

There are two different ways to create a Multi-Pack. The first is to put two or more figures in the same package, and the second is to put two or three regular carded figures in an outer package. Kenner/ Hasbro has tried both methods, with mixed results. The most popular to date are the "Cinema Scenes" three-packs.

"CINEMA SCENES" THREE-PACKS
Kenner (1997–2000)

The "Cinema Scenes" three-packs first appeared in 1997 with the Death Star Escape group. Kenner calls them "Cinema Scenes" packs, and the back of the package contains a scene from the movie, with

Cinema Scenes: Cantina Showdown (Kenner 1997)

sprocket holes down each side to look like a piece of 70 mm film. They are collected, in part, because each one contains at least one figure that is not otherwise available.

Three-packs are produced in much smaller quantities than carded figures, contain from one to three exclusive figures and retail for the same price as three separate figures, making them a pretty good deal.

Cinema Scenes Three-Packs in green window boxes

Death Star Escape [.00] or [.01] $45.00
   Loose, three figures with backdrop 18.00
Cantina Showdown [.00] 20.00
   Variation [.01] box lists assortment (#69650) 18.00

Variation, Dr. Evazan with black hair	25.00
Loose, three figures with backdrop	12.00

Second Batch (1998)

Final Jedi Duel [.00] or [.01]	28.00
Loose, three figures with backdrop	12.00
Jabba The Hutt's Dancers [.00]	15.00
Loose, three figures with backdrop	10.00
Mynock Hunt [.00]	50.00
Loose, three figures with backdrop	25.00
Purchase of the Droids [.00]	20.00
Variation [.01] box	15.00
Loose, three figures with backdrop	9.00

Later Batches (1999) in revised green window boxes

Jedi Spirits with deceased Anakin Skywalker, Yoda and Obi-Wan Kenobi, clear figures	15.00
Cantina Aliens with Labria, Takeel and Nabrun Leeds	15.00
Jabba's Skiff Guards with Klaatu, Barada and Nikto	15.00
Rebel Pilots with Ten Numb, Wedge Antilles and Arvel Crynyd	15.00
Loose, three figures with backdrop, any series	8.00

EPISODE I CINEMA SCENES

Episode I (Asst #84115, 1999–2000) with COMMTech chip

Mos Espa Encounter with Sebulba, Jar Jar Binks and Anakin Skywalker	$20.00
Watto's Box with Watto, Graxol Kelvyyn and Shakka	30.00
Tatooine Showdown with Qui-Gon Jinn, Darth Maul and Anakin Skywalker	20.00
Loose, three figures with backdrop, any series	10.00

Clone Wars three-pack: Jedi Knight Army (Hasbro 2004)

OTHER THREE-PACKS

EPISODE II THREE-PACKS

Attack of the Clones (2004) window box

Geonosian War Room #1 (#84980) $20.00
Geonosian War Room #2 (#84711) 20.00
Jedi Council #1 (#84981) 20.00
Jedi Council #2 (#84701) 20.00

CLONE WARS THREE-PACKS

Clone Wars (2004)

Clone Trooper Army (#84987)

   Blue: One trooper has blue stripes $20.00
   Red: One trooper has red stripes 20.00
   White: None have stripes 15.00
   Yellow: One trooper has yellow stripes 20.00

Droid Army (#84992) 15.00
Jedi Knight Army (#84836) 20.00

TRILOGY DVD COLLECTION

Commemorative Trilogy DVD Collection (2004)

Star Wars: Luke Skywalker, Obi-Wan Kenobi, R2-D2, and C-3PO (#34525) . . . 15.00
The Empire Strikes Back: Han Solo, Princess Leia, and Chewbacca (#34524) 15.00
Return of the Jedi: Darth Vader, Emperor Palpatine
   and Stormtrooper (#34523) 15.00

Max Rebo Band: Joh Yowza & Sy Snootles (Kenner 1998)

TWO-PACKS

SHADOWS OF THE EMPIRE

One package variation showed up in the Shadows of the Empire two-packs. Boba Fett vs. IG-88 packages with printing code ".01" stated on the back that Boba Fett's "Vehicle of Choice" was the "*Slave I.*" This was the final line in his description, after "Weapon of Choice." Earlier packages, with printing code ".00" omitted the phrase "Vehicle of Choice:" but did include the words "*Slave I.*"

Two-Packs (Kenner 1996) on purple header card

Darth Vader vs. Prince Xizor (1996) $25.00
Boba Fett vs. IG-88 (1996) [.00]
   without "Vehicle of Choice" on data card 30.00
   with "Vehicle of Choice: *Slave I*" [.01] 25.00

PRINCESS LEIA COLLECTION

With four new outfits and four new hairstyles, the Princess could launch her own signature clothing collection. The only difference between the ".00" and ".01" package backs is the color of the names on the file card: black on the ".00" and red on the ".01" figures.

Princess Leia Collection (Kenner 1998) green header card

Princess Leia and R2-D2 [.00] $25.00
Princess Leia (Medal Ceremony) and Luke Skywalker [.00] 25.00
Princess Leia (Bespin) and Han Solo [.00] 25.00
Princess Leia (Endor Celebration) and Wicket the Ewok [.00] 30.00
Reissues of above figures [.01], each. 10.00

MAX REBO BAND

Max Rebo Band Pairs (Wal-Mart) (Kenner 1998)

Joh Yowza and Sy Snootles $35.00
Barquin D'an and Droopy McCool 35.00
Max Rebo and Doda Bodonawieedo 38.00

OTHER TWO-PACKS

Episode I Two-Pack (Hasbro 2002)

The Final Lightsaber Duel, Darth Maul vs. Obi-Wan Kenobi,
    with break-apart Darth Maul $15.00

Power of the Jedi Two-Pack

Darth Maul & Darth Vader, Masters of the Dark Side. 20.00

Silver Anniversary Two-Packs (2002)

Han Solo and Chewbacca Death Star Escape 16.00
Luke Skywalker & Princess Leia Organa Swing to Freedom 16.00
Obi-Wan Kenobi and Darth Vader Final Duel 16.00

Trash Compactor (2004)

Death Star Trash Compactor #1 (#84931) 15.00
Death Star Trash Compactor #2 (#84930) 15.00

CLONE WARS

Clone Wars **(Hasbro 2003) side-by-side value pack**

Yoda and Clone Trooper Commander (#84754) 15.00
Anakin Skywalker and Clone Trooper Lieutenant (#84752) 15.00
ARC Trooper and Clone Trooper (#84753). 15.00

Four-Pack: Skirmish at Carkoon (Hasbro 2004)

FOUR-PACKS

Four-Packs (2003–04)

Skirmish at Carkoon (#34511)	20.00
Jedi Warriors (#26720)	20.00
Imperial Forces (#26798)	20.00
Ultimate Bounty (#32132)	20.00
The Battle of Hoth (#26703)	20.00
Endor Ambush (#34515)	20.00
Naboo Final Combat (#34514)	20.00

Wholesale Club 3-Pack: Empire Strikes Back (Kenner 1997)

WHOLESALE CLUB PACKS

These are three figures, in original packages, with an outer corrugated cardboard package with holes so the original packages show through. They are sold to various "wholesale club" stores. There was little collector interest in them because the included figures are all common. The one exception is the group two-pack, which contains a reissue Lando Calrissian on a green header card. This scarce version was never sold separately.

Wholesale Club Three-Packs

Group One (1996) all figures are on red header cards

Set One: Han Solo, Chewbacca and Lando Calrissian $40.00

Set Two: R2-D2, Stormtrooper and C-3PO 35.00

Set Three: Luke Skywalker, Obi-Wan Kenobi and Darth Vader 40.00

Group Two (1997) all figures are on green header cards

Star Wars: Luke Skywalker in Stormtrooper Disguise,
   Tusken Raider and Obi-Wan Kenobi [.00] (#69851) 30.00
The Empire Strikes Back: Lando Calrissian, Luke Skywalker
   in Dagobah Fatigues and TIE Fighter Pilot [.00] (69852) 75.00
Return of the Jedi: Jedi Knight Luke Skywalker, AT-ST Driver
   and Princess Leia in Boushh Disguise [.00] (69853) 30.00

Wholesale Club Episode I Two-Packs (1999)
COMMTech two-pack with COMMTech Reader, and
   Anakin Skywalker (Tatooine) 20.00
   Darth Maul Jedi Duel (#84379) 20.00
   Obi-Wan Kenobi Jedi Duel (#84374) 20.00
   Qui-Gon Jinn Jedi Duel (#84373) 20.00
   Jar Jar Binks (#84378) 20.00

Two-packs
Padmé Naberrie and Obi-Wan Kenobi (Jedi Duel) (#84286) 20.00
Anakin Skywalker (Naboo) and Obi-Wan Kenobi (Naboo) 20.00
Darth Maul (Jedi Duel) and Anakin Skywalker (Tatooine) (#84392) 25.00
Jar Jar Binks and Qui-Gon Jinn (Naboo) 20.00
Queen Amidala (Naboo) and Qui-Gon Jinn (Jedi Duel) (#84391) 20.00

CARRY CASES
Kenner/Hasbro (1995–2004)

Carry Cases (1995–99)
Electronic Talking C-3PO Carry Case (1996) $20.00
Millennium Falcon Carry Case with exclusive
   Wedge Antilles figure (1997) with white arm stripes (error) 50.00
   Reissue, figure with no stripe on arm (1998) 25.00

R2-D2 Carryall Playset (Hasbro 2001)

Reissue with **Imperial Scanning Crew** figure 60.00
Darth Vader Official Collector Case box-shaped carry case 20.00
R2-D2 Carry all Playset with **Destroyer Droid** 20.00
Darth Vader Carry Case, plastic bust with **Boba Fett**
    and **Stormtrooper** figures (#01234, 2004) 25.00
C-3PO Carry Case, plastic bust with **Chewbacca** and
    Han Solo figures (#01233, 2004) 25.00

DISPLAY STANDS

Display 3-D Diorama (Kenner 1998)
Cantina at Mos Eisley with two figures (#84063) $20.00
    Fan Club exclusive 25.00
Jabba's Palace, with Han Solo in Carbonite (#84068) 20.00
    Variation, different bio card 15.00

Display Stand: Cantina at Mos Eisley (Kenner 1997)

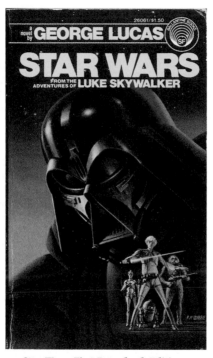

Star Wars, First Paperback Edition
(Ballantine-Del Rey 1976)

BOOKS

Star Wars mass market Collectible #1, the very first mass market *Star Wars* item produced, was the movie's novelization in paperback form, which appeared in late November 1976, seven months before the movie opened. It can be identified by the words "First Edition: December 1976" at the bottom of the copyright page. As the movie became a hit, the paperback was reprinted many times, with huge print runs—3.5 million copies in the first year. None of these reprintings is scarce, and none is valuable.

The novel appeared in hardcover in the fall of 1977. The trade hardcover is scarce and valuable. While the first paperback edition and the hardcover edition enjoy crossover collector interest from people who are not primarily *Star Wars* fans, book club editions have no collector following whatever apart from die-hard *Star Wars* fans and thus are not valuable. The one exception might be the very first printing of the book club edition of *Star Wars*. This can be identified by the printing code "S27" in the gutter on page 183. It appeared before the trade hardcover, making it the first hardcover edition of the book.

Each of the other movies was novelized in turn, and other original novels followed for a few years. In mid-1991, *Star Wars* novels returned with Timothy Zahn's *Heir to the Empire*. This book made it to the top of the *New York Times* bestseller lists. Lucasfilms licensing has insisted on overall continuity in the storylines for both the books and the comics, so that they constitute a consistent

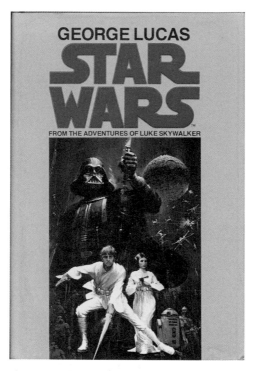

Star Wars, First Hardcover Edition (Del Rey 1977)

"expanded universe." This makes these novels important in the *Star Wars* universe because there are only about 10 hours of actual films.

FICTION
MOVIE NOVELIZATIONS

Star Wars, by Alan Dean Foster, uncredited ghost writer,
  from screenplay by George Lucas
  1st PB: Ballantine #26061, 1976 . . . . $90.00
  2nd PB: Ballantine-Del Rey #26079, 1977 . . . . 10.00
  1st SFBC: 1977, printing code S27 . . . . 20.00
  Later SFBC: later printing codes. 5.00
  1st HC: Del Rey 1977 . . . . 100.00

The Empire Strikes Back, by Donald F. Glut, from story by George Lucas
  and screenplay by Lawrence Kasdan and Leigh Brackett
  1st PB: Ballantine-Del Rey 28392, 1980 . . . . 15.00
  Later PB: Ballantine-Del Rey #29209, 1980 . . . . 5.00
  1st SFBC: 1980, printing code K29 . . . . 25.00
  Later SFBC: later printing codes. 5.00
  Later PB: Ballantine-Del Rey #32022, 1980s 3.00

Return of the Jedi, by James Kahn, from screenplay
  by Lawrence Kasdan and George Lucas
  1st PB: Ballantine-Del Rey #30767-4, 1983 . . . . 10.00
  SFBC: 1983, printing code N31 . . . . 20.00
  HC: Ballantine-Del Rey 1994 . . . . 16.00

Movie Novelizations: Illustrated Editions
The Empire Strikes Back: The Illustrated Edition,
  by Donald F. Glut, Del Rey #28831, 1980. . . . . 10.00

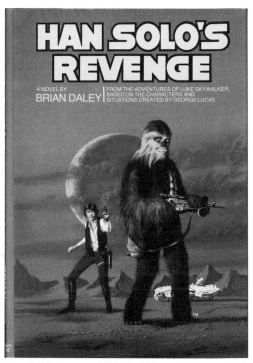

Han Solo's Revenge, First Hardcover (Del Rey 1979)

Return of the Jedi Illustrated Edition, by James Kahn,
  Del Rey #30960, 1983 . . . . 10.00

Episode I
Star Wars Episode I: The Phantom Menace, by Terry Brooks
  1st HC: Del Rey 1999 . . . . 25.00
  Lim. Ed. signed, slipcase, foil embossed Darth
  Maul cover with Qui-Gon Jinn pin 85.00

NOVELS (1978–89)

Splinter of the Mind's Eye, by Alan Dean Foster
  1st HC: Del Rey 1978 . . . . 35.00
  1st PB: Ballantine-Del Rey #26062, 1978. . . . . 20.00
  SFBC: 1978 . . . . 5.00

Han Solo Series, by Brian Daley
Han Solo at Stars' End
  HC: Del Rey #28251-5, 1979 . . . . 30.00
  SFBC: 1979. . . . . 5.00
  1st PB: Ballantine-Del Rey #29664, 1979. . . . . 5.00
Han Solo's Revenge
  1st HC: Del Rey 1979 . . . . 35.00
  SFBC: 1980. . . . . 5.00
  1st PB: Ballantine-Del Rey #28840, 1980. . . . . 5.00
Han Solo and the Lost Legacy
  1st PB: Ballantine-Del Rey #28710, 1980. . . . . 10.00
  SFBC: printing code K42, 1980 . . . . 20.00
Combined edition: ***The Han Solo Adventures***
  1st PB: 576 pgs., Del Rey #37980-2, 1992 . . . . 6.00

Lando Calrissian Series, by L. Neil Smith
Lando Calrissian and the Mindharp of Sharu
  1st PB: Ballantine-Del Rey #31158, 1983. . . . . 15.00

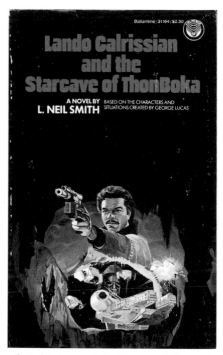

Lando Calrissian and the Starcave of ThonBoka
(Ballantine-Del Rey 1983)

1st SFBC: 1984. . . . . 5.00
Lando Calrissian and the Flame Wind of Oseon
   1st PB: Ballantine-Del Rey #31163, 1983. . . . . 15.00
   1st SFBC: 1984. . . . . 5.00
Lando Calrissian and the Star Cave of ThonBoka
   1st PB: Ballantine-Del Rey #31164, 1983. . . . . 15.00
   SFBC: none
all out of print, but combined as:
Classic Star Wars: The Lando Calrissian Adventures
   1st combined PB: Del Rey #39110, 1994 . . . . .6.00
   Current TPB: Del Rey #39443, 1995 . . . . 10.00

Novels 1990–2004 . . . . Cover price, or less

ART OF...

The Art of Star Wars, edited by Carol Titelman, script by George Lucas,
   includes sketches, blueprints, costumes, production paintings and photos.
   1st HC: Ballantine, 1979 . . . . $25.00
   TPB or SFBC versions. 15.00
   with material from the special edition 19.00
The Art of the Empire Strikes Back, edited by Deborah Call,
   with text by Valerie Hoffman and Vick Bullock
   1st HC: Del Rey, 1980 . . . . 25.00
   TPB or SFBC versions. 15.00
   SFBC: $17.50, Del Rey 5579-8, Feb. 1981. . . . . 15.00
The Art of Return of the Jedi, including the film script
   1st HC: Del Rey, 1983 . . . . 25.00
The Art of Star Wars Episode I, The Phantom Menace
   by Jonathan Bresman
   1st HC: Del Rey, 1999 . . . . 40.00
The Art of Star Wars Galaxy, edited by Gary Cerani
   TPB: Topps, 1993 . . . . 20.00

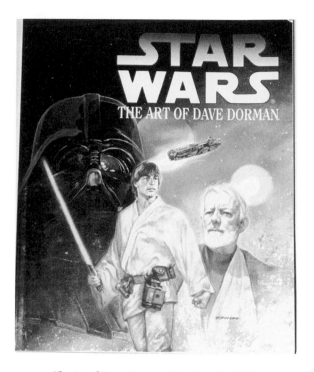

The Art of Dave Dorman (Friedlander 1996)

HC: $150, Underwood Miller March 1994,
limited to 1,000 copies, boxed, signed 150.00
The Art of Star Wars Galaxy, Volume Two
by C. Cerani and Gary Cerani
TPB: Topps, 1994, Boris Valejo cover 20.00
Star Wars: The Art of the Brothers Hildebrandt,
by Bob Woods, TPB: Ballantine #42301, 1997 . . . . 25.00
Star Wars: The Art of Dave Dorman
HC: Friedlander 1996, signed, 2,500 copies 75.00
TPB: Friedlander #37-5, 1996 . . . . 25.00
Industrial Light & Magic: The Art of Special Effects,
by Thomas G. Smith, 1st HC, Del Rey, 1986 . . . . 25.00

Other Non-Fiction Books . . . . Cover price or less

JUVENILE BOOKS
COLORING BOOKS

The Empire Strikes Back Coloring Book (Kenner 1980)
Cast $5.00
Darth Vader and Stormtroopers 5.00
Chewbacca and Leia 5.00
Chewbacca, Han, Leia and Lando 5.00
Chewbacca and C-3PO 5.00
Luke Skywalker 5.00
R2-D2 . . . . 5.00
Yoda 5.00
Return of the Jedi Coloring Books (Kenner 1983)
Lando fighting skiff guard 4.00
Lando in *Falcon* cockpit 4.00
Luke Skywalker 4.00
Max Rebo 4.00

The Star Wars Storybook (Scholastic 1977)

Ewoks Wicket on vine. 3.00
Ewoks Wicket, Kneesa and Logray 3.00
Ewoks Wicket and Kneesa on hang gliders. 3.00

MOVIE STORY BOOKS

The Star Wars Storybook, by Geraldine Richelson,
   with color photos (Random House 1977) $12.50
   TPB: Scholastic Book Service 7.50
Star Wars: A Storybook (Scholastic 1996) 6.00
The Empire Strikes Back Storybook
   (Random House 1980) 10.00
   TPB: (Scholastic Book Service) 5.00
The Empire Strikes Back Storybook (Scholastic 1996) 5.00
Return of the Jedi Storybook (Random House 1983) 12.50
   TPB: (Scholastic Book Service) 4.00
Return of the Jedi Storybook (Scholastic 1996) 6.00
Star Wars Episode I The Phantom Menace, Movie Storybook
   (1999) Anakin Skywalker cover 8.00

STORY BOOKS

The Wookiee Storybook (Random House 1979) **$7.50**
The Mystery of the Rebellious Robot (Random House 1979) 6.00
The Maverick Moon (Random House 1979) 6.00
The Droid Dilemma (Random House 1979) 6.00

Droid Story Books (Random House 1985–86)
   Four different, each. 5.00

Ewoks Story Books (Random House 1984–86)
   Twelve different, each. 5.00
Recent Juvenile novels and other books . . . . .Cover price

Yoda Ceramic Bank (Sigma 1982)

CERAMICS

BANKS

The Roman Ceramics Company was the first to manufacture ceramic banks. These, like all 1977 collectibles, appeared before the action figures, but many collectors passed them up at the time, and they were available at retail for several years. Each bank came in a white box and was hand painted. Sigma made three ceramic banks for the later movies.

Ceramic Banks (1977–82):

C-3PO Ceramic Bank, 8" tall, waist up, metallic gold
    (Roman Ceramics Corp. 1977) boxed $75.00
Darth Vader Ceramic Bank, 7" tall, head
    (Roman Ceramics Corp. 1977) boxed 85.00
R2-D2 Ceramic Bank, 8" tall, full figure
    (Roman Ceramics Corp. 1977) boxed 75.00
Chewbacca Ceramic Bank, 10 1/2" tall, kneeling with gun
    (Sigma 1982) 45.00
Jabba the Hutt Ceramic Bank, 6" tall, figural
    (Sigma 1982) 45.00
Yoda Ceramic Bank, 8" tall, figural (Sigma 1982) 45.00

COOKIE JARS

Ceramic cookie jars were another early collectible from Roman Ceramics. R2-D2 is just the right shape to hold a lot of cookies.

Chewbacca Cookie Jar (Star Jars 1998)

Cookie Jars (1977–82)

C-3PO, 10 3/4", gold metallic glaze
  (Roman Ceramics Corp. 1977) $175.00
Darth Vader (Roman Ceramics Corp. 1977). 175.00
R2-D2, 13" tall, in white cardboard box with blue
  printing (Roman Ceramics Corp. 1977) 190.00
C-3PO/Darth Vader/R2-D2 Hexagon Cookie Jar
  (Sigma 1982) 130.00

Cookie Jars by Star Jars, limited editions of 1,000 jars
First Batch, First Quarter 1998
Obi-Wan Kenobi (Star Jars #026, 1998) 200.00
Jabba the Hutt (Star Jars #027, 1998) 200.00
Chewbacca (Star Jars #028, 1998) 200.00

Second Batch, Second Quarter 1998
C-3PO (Star Jars #029, Sept. 1998) 200.00
Princess Leia (Star Jars 1998). 200.00
Boba Fett (Star Jars 1998) 200.00

FIGURES

Sigma produced a dozen seven-inch ceramic bisque figures in 1983. The faces of the human figures are somewhat juvenile; the non-humans are better sculpted.

Return of the Jedi, bisque figures
Bib Fortuna (Sigma 1983) $50.00
Boba Fett (Sigma 1983) 65.00
C-3PO and R2-D2 (Sigma 1983) 60.00
Darth Vader (Sigma 1983) 60.00
Galactic Emperor, seated (Sigma 1983) 65.00
Gamorrean Guard (Sigma 1983) 60.00
Han Solo (Sigma 1983) 50.00
Klaatu (Sigma 1983). 50.00
Lando Calrissian (Sigma 1983). 50.00
Luke Skywalker, Jedi Knight (Sigma 1983) 50.00
Princess Leia, Boushh disguise (Sigma 1983). 65.00
Wicket W. Warrick (Sigma 1983) 50.00

HOUSEHOLD AND OFFICE ITEMS

Ceramic Figural Items

Chewbacca and Darth Vader bookends (Sigma 1983) $90.00
C-3PO pencil tray (Sigma 1983) 60.00
C-3PO, seated figural tape dispenser (Sigma 1983) 60.00
C-3PO, in pieces, "Help" picture frame (Sigma 1983) 45.00
Darth Vader picture frame (Sigma 1983) 60.00
Darth Vader mirror (Sigma 1983) 60.00
Ewok music box radio (Sigma 1983) 45.00
Gun Turret with C-3PO music box (Sigma 1983). 60.00
Landspeeder soap dish, with C-3PO and Obi-Wan (Sigma 1983) 60.00
Luke (Hoth Gear) and Tauntaun teapot set (Sigma 1983) 150.00
R2-D2 picture frame (Sigma 1983) 75.00
R2-D2 and R5-D4 figural salt and pepper shakers (Sigma 1983) 125.00
R2-D2 figural string dispenser, with scissors (Sigma 1983) 60.00
Rebel Snowspeeder toothbrush holder (Sigma 1983) 60.00
Sy Snootles & Rebo Band music box (Sigma 1983) 150.00
Wicket and Kneesa music box (Sigma 1983) 90.00
Yoda pencil cup (Sigma 1983) 50.00
Yoda figural salt and pepper shakers (Sigma 1983) 50.00
Yoda and tree figural vase (Sigma 1983) 50.00
Yoda in backpack box (Sigma 1983) 30.00

MUGS — FIGURAL

Ceramic Drinking Mugs
First Batch (Sigma 1983) in white corrugated box

C-3PO $40.00
Chewbacca. 40.00
Darth Vader 40.00

Gamorrean Guard mug (Sigma 1983)

Han Solo 40.00
Princess Leia 40.00
Luke Skywalker, X-wing Pilot 40.00
Yoda 40.00

Boba Fett and Darth Vader mugs (Applause 1995)

Second Batch (Sigma 1983) in *Return of the Jedi* photo box

Biker Scout 40.00
Gamorrean Guard 40.00
Klaatu 40.00
Lando Calrissian 40.00
Stormtrooper 40.00
Wicket W. Warrick 40.00

Ceramic Mugs (Rawcliffe 1995)

Star Wars 15.00
The Empire Strikes Back 15.00
Return of the Jedi 15.00
Shadows of the Empire 15.00
Rebel Logo 15.00

Darth Vader 15.00
Obi-Wan Kenobi 15.00
Yoda 15.00
AT-AT 15.00
AT-ST 15.00
Shuttle *Tyderium* 15.00
TIE Fighter 15.00

14 oz. Figural Mugs, (Applause 1995) boxed
Darth Vader (#46044) 15.00
Boba Fett (#46045) 15.00
Stormtrooper (#46046) 15.00
C-3PO (gold) (#46047) 15.00

Second batch (Applause 1996)
Bib Fortuna (#46225) 15.00
Gamorrean Guard (#46226) 15.00
Han Solo (#46227) 15.00
Tusken Raider (#46228) 15.00
Emperor Palpatine (#46235) 15.00

Third batch (Applause 1997)
Chewbacca (#42679) 15.00
Luke Skywalker (#42680) 15.00
Obi-Wan Kenobi (#42681) 15.00
Princess Leia Organa (#42682) 15.00
Metalized Darth Vader (#42692) 15.00

15" Decal Mugs (Applause 1998)
Darth Vader (#42983) 9.00
Boba Fett (#42984) 9.00
Galactic Empire (#42985) 9.00
Jedi Knights (#42986) 9.00

**Star Wars, *featuring Luke,
X-wing Pilot, plate (Hamilton 1993)***

Episode I Figural Mugs (Applause 1999)
Darth Maul Ceramic Mug, 15 oz. (#43067) 18.00
R2-D2 Ceramic Mug, 15 oz. (#43050) 15.00
Jar Jar Binks Ceramic Mug, 15 oz. (#43068) 16.00

PLATES

The first *Star Wars* collector plates were made by the Hamilton Collection in the late 1980s. There were eight plates, plus a larger 10th anniversary plate in 1987. The plates were issued in styrofoam sandwich boxes.

8-1/4" Plates, First Series (1985–87)
Han Solo, pictured seated in Mos Eisley Cantina $50.00
Princess Leia, pictured holding blaster. 50.00
Luke Skywalker and Darth Vader, pictured fighting with lightsabers. 60.00
Five heroes, in the *Millennium Falcon* cockpit 50.00
Luke and Yoda, seated on ground in swamp 50.00
R2-D2 and Wicket the Ewok. 50.00
AT-ATs, pictured shooting 50.00
X-wings and TIE Fighters in front of Death Star 50.00

10th Anniversary commemorative plate
1977–87 Commemorative, picturing Han, Luke, Leia and Darth's heads in
   foreground with robots, Chewbacca & Obi-Wan in background. 60.00

Second Series, *Star Wars* Trilogy, 8-1/4" art by
   Morgan Weistling (Hamilton Collection 1993)
Star Wars, featuring Luke Skywalker in
   X-wing Pilot outfit in foreground. 40.00

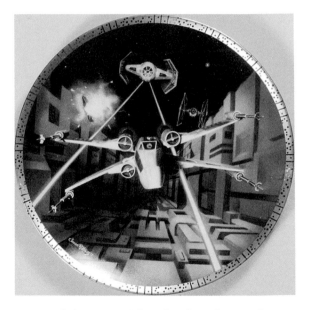

Red Five X-wing Fighter plate (Hamilton 1995)

The Empire Strikes Back, featuring Luke Skywalker with Yoda on his back at top,
    Han Solo and Leia kissing underneath 40.00
Return of the Jedi, featuring Luke Skywalker and
    Leia in Jabba's prisoner outfit swinging on rope 40.00

Third Series: Space Vehicles 8-1/4", art by Sonia Hillios
    (Hamilton Collection 1995–96) 23 K gold border
Millennium Falcon (EW1MF, 1995) $35.00
Imperial Shuttle *Tyderium* and landing pad 35.00
TIE Fighters in front of Cloud City 35.00
Red Five X-wing Fighter pursued by TIE fighter in Death Star trench 35.00
Imperial Star Destroyer orbiting planet (EW5MF) 35.00
Rebel Snowspeeder circling AT-AT feet (EW6MF) 35.00
B-wing (EW7MF) 35.00
Slave-I (1996) 35.00

Fourth Series: Space Vehicles, 9", art by Sonia Hillios
    (Hamilton Collection 1997–98) 24 K gold border
Medical Frigate (#13609) 35.00
Jabba's Sail Barge (#13602) 35.00
Y-wing Fighter (#13604) 35.00

***Star Wars* Heroes and Villains**, 8-1/4" art by Keith Birdsong
    (1997–98) bordered in 24 K gold
Luke Skywalker 35.00
Han Solo (#13661) 35.00
Darth Vader (#13662) 35.00
Princess Leia (#13663) 35.00
Obi-Wan Kenobi (#13664) 35.00
Emperor Palpatine (#13665) 35.00
Boba Fett (#13667) 35.00
Yoda (#13666) 35.00

Star Wars Stoneware Stein (Dram Tree 1995)

STEINS

Lidded Steins 6" (Metallic Impressions 1995) with solid pewter lid

Star Wars: A New Hope $34.00
Star Wars: The Empire Strikes Back 34.00
Star Wars: Return of the Jedi 34.00

Deep Relief Stoneware (Dram Tree 1995) boxed

Star Wars, heroes picture 25.00
Star Wars: The Empire Strikes Back 25.00
Star Wars: Return of the Jedi 25.00

Lidded Steins 9-1/2" (Dram Tree 1997–98)

Unique Darth Vader Stein, solid pewter lid with figure 85.00
Unique Yoda Stein, solid pewter and lid 80.00
Unique Boba Fett Stein, solid pewter and lid 85.00

TANKARDS

Ceramic "Toby" Tankard (California Originals 1977)

Chewbacca, 6-3/4" tall, 36 oz., brown $60.00
Darth Vader, 7-1/4" tall, 52 oz., glossy black 60.00
Obi-Wan Kenobi, 6-3/4" tall, 36 oz., brown 60.00

COINS

A premium is a secondary collectible issued in a package with a toy, such as an action figure, to enhance its value. When removed from the package, the premium becomes a separate collectible. By far the most valuable premiums are the Power of the Force coins, which came with the action figures in the classic series of that name. Some of the newer action figure series also included coins and others came with Freeze Frame slides and with COMMTech chips. Some of those action figure series were produced in large numbers, making most of the figures, and their premiums, quite cheap to collect.

POWER OF THE FORCE COINS

There were two ways to get one of the classic Kenner Power of the Force coins—with a figure, or by mailing in a proof of purchase. The figures came with a coin that related to the figure, but when you mailed in a proof of purchase, you got a random coin. Consequently, the coins that came with a figure are a lot more common than the ones that did not. There are a total of 37 Power of the Force figures, but only 35 coins. The AT-AT Driver and Nikto had Warok coins.

Kenner planned to issue Power of the Force figures for Chief Chirpa, Emperor's Royal Guard, Luke, Lograyand TIE Fighter Pilot, but did not. The coins for these figures were commonly used to fulfill the mail-in requests.

The most valuable coins were rarely used to fulfill the mail-in offer. They mostly got on the market from sources within Kenner. There was one other way, however, to get them all. Collectors who pestered Kenner about the missing coins were eventually given the right to buy a whole set, for $29! The offer was never made to the public. It turned out to be one of the better purchases of all time.

Star Wars Coins, Silver Color Set (Kenner 1985) $3,000.00
Amanaman 15.00
Anakin Skywalker, Jedi 125.00
AT-AT, *Star Wars*, mail-in, scarce 100.00
AT-ST Driver, Empire 20.00
A-wing Pilot, Rebel 10.00

Six Power of the Force coins (Kenner 1985)

Barada, Skiff Sentry 10.00
Bib Fortuna, Major Domo, mail-in, very scarce 125.00
Biker Scout, Empire 25.00
Boba Fett, Bounty Hunter 250.00
B-wing Pilot, Rebel 15.00
Chewbacca, Wookiee 25.00
Chief Chirpa, Ewok Leader, mail-in 40.00
Creatures, *Star Wars*, "at local cantinas" 90.00
    Variation "at local cafes" 125.00
C-3PO, Protocol Droid 15.00
Darth Vader, Lord of the Sith 25.00
Droids, *Star Wars*, mail-in, scarce 100.00
Emperor, Galactic Ruler 25.00
Emperor's Royal Guard, Empire, mail-in 100.00

Six Luke Skywalker Coins (Kenner 1985)

EV-9D9, Torture Droid 10.00
FX-7, Medical Droid, mail-in, very scarce 125.00
Gamorrean Guard, Palace Sentry 30.00
Greedo, Bounty Hunter, mail-in, very scarce 125.00
Han Solo, Carbon Freeze 10.00
Han Solo, Rebel 25.00
    Variation, "Hans Solo" 75.00
Han Solo, Rebel Fighter 15.00
Han Solo, Rebel Hero (Hoth gear) mail-in, scarce 100.00
Hoth Stormtrooper, Empire, mail-in, very scarce 250.00
Imperial Commander, Empire, mail-in, scarce 75.00
Imperial Dignitary, Empire 10.00
Imperial Gunner, Empire 10.00
Jawas, Desert Scavengers 25.00
Lando Calrissian, Rebel General (with *Millennium Falcon*) 10.00
Lando Calrissian, Rebel General (with Cloud City) mail-in, scarce 90.00
Logray, Ewok, mail-in 40.00
Luke Skywalker, Rebel Leader, mail-in 25.00
Luke Skywalker, Rebel Leader (on Tauntaun) mail-in, scarce 125.00
Luke Skywalker, Rebel Leader (with landspeeder) 50.00
Luke Skywalker, Rebel Leader (on scout bike) 12.00
Luke Skywalker, Jedi (with X-wing) 25.00
Luke Skywalker, Jedi Knight (head) 25.00
Luke Skywalker, Jedi Knight (bust, on Dagobah) mail-in, very scarce 150.00
Lumat, Ewok Warrior 10.00
Millennium Falcon, Star Wars, mail-in, scarce 125.00
Obi-Wan Kenobi, Jedi Master 25.00
Paploo, Ewok 10.00
Princess Leia, Boushh, mail-in, very scarce 125.00
Princess Leia, Rebel Leader (in Endor outfit) 20.00
Princess Leia, Rebel Leader (head, with R2-D2) 125.00
Romba, Ewok 10.00

Han Solo coin, front and back (Kenner 1985)

R2-D2, Rebel Droid 10.00
Sail Skiff, *Star Wars*, mail-in, very scarce 175.00
    Variation, does not say "Star Wars" 350.00
Star Destroyer Commander, Empire, mail-in, scarce 100.00
Stormtrooper, Empire 25.00
Teebo, Ewok 25.00
TIE Fighter Pilot, Empire, mail-in 65.00
Too-One Bee, Medical Droid, mail-in, very scarce 150.00
Tusken Raider, Sand People, mail-in, very scarce 150.00
Warok, Ewok 10.00
Wicket The Ewok 25.00
Yak Face, Bounty Hunter 125.00
Yoda, The Jedi Master 30.00
Zuckuss, Bounty Hunter, mail-in, very scarce 150.00

DROIDS COINS

Droids Coins, Gold Color (Kenner 1985)
Kea Moll, Freedom Fighter 10.00
Thall Joben, Speeder Racer 10.00
Jann Tosh, Adventurer 10.00
A-wing Pilot, Rebel 60.00
C-3PO, Protocol Droid 20.00
    Variation, C-3PO, Droids 20.00
Boba Fett, Bounty Hunter 200.00
Tig Fromm, Techno Villain 15.00
Jord Dusat, Thrill Seeker 10.00
Kez-Iban, Lost Prince 10.00
Sise Fromm, Gang Leader 20.00
R2-D2, Droids 20.00
Uncle Gundy, Prospector 10.00

EWOKS COINS

Ewoks Coins, Bronze Color (Kenner 1985)

Dulok, Scout. 10.00

King Gorneesh, Dulok 10.00

Dulok Shaman 10.00

Logray, Ewok Shaman 10.00

Wicket, Ewok Scout. 15.00

Urgah (Lady Gorneesh) Dulok 10.00

Droids and Ewoks Coins (Kenner 1985)

COMICS

Star Wars collectible #2 is the comic book adaptation of the movie, which appeared just prior to the movie premiere. There were two versions of the first issue of the comic book. The more common version displays the 30-cent price in a white box, while the rare version shows the 35-cent price in a white diamond.

There were no comics from 1987, when the Marvel series ended, until December 1991 when Dark Horse Comics started the current explosion with the publication of *Star Wars Dark Empire*. The *Shadows of the Empire* book and comic storyline has generated its own supply of action figures. Since there were no movies from 1983 until 1999, it was up to the comics and books to supply much needed additional material for the *Star Wars* saga.

CLASSIC *STAR WARS*
Dark Horse Comics (1992–94)

The events in this series take place between those in the first film *Star Wars: A New Hope* and the second film *The Empire Strikes Back*. The material was originally published from 1981 to 1984 in newspaper strips.

1 Luke and Leia on a scouting mission. $6.00
2 through 8, each. 4.00
9 and 10, each 3.50
11 through 19, each 3.00
20, final issue 4.00

Star Wars #1 (Marvel 1977)

CLASSIC *STAR WARS:*...
Dark Horse Comics

A NEW HOPE

1 reprint (1994) $4.25
2 reprint 3.95

DEVILWORLDS

1 Four Stories (1996) $2.50
2 Three Stories 2.50

THE EARLY ADVENTURES

1 *Gambler's World* (1994–95) $3.00
2 through 8, each 3.00

THE EMPIRE STRIKES BACK

1 Movie Adaptation (1994) $4.00
2 . . . . 4.00

HAN SOLO AT STAR'S END

1 through 3 (1997), each $3.50

A LONG TIME AGO

1 (of 6) reprint, Marvel, B & W (1999) $12.95
2 through 6 reprint, Marvel, each 10.00

RETURN OF THE JEDI

1 Movie Adaptation (1994) $4.00
2 Movie Adaptation 3.50

VANDELHELM MISSION

1 Han Solo, Lando and Nien Nunb (1995) $3.95

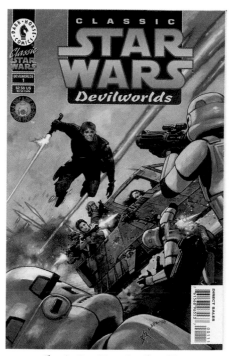

Classic Star Wars: Devilworlds #1
(Dark Horse Comics 1996)

DARK HORSE CLASSICS:
STAR WARS — DARK EMPIRE
Dark Horse Comics (1997)

1 Reprint. $2.95
2 through 6 Reprint, each 2.95

DROIDS
Star/Marvel Comics (1986–87)

1 through 8, each. $3.00

EWOKS
Star/Marvel Comics (1985–87)

1 Based on TV Series $18.00
2 through 15, each 15.00

MARVEL MOVIE SHOWCASE
FEATURING *STAR WARS*

1 Reprint, *Stars Wars* #1-6 (1982) $4.00
2 December, 1982. . . . . .4.00

MARVEL SPECIAL EDITION
FEATURING *STAR WARS*

1 Reprint of *Star Wars* #1 through #3 (1977). $10.00
2 Reprint of *Star Wars* #4 through #6 (1978). 8.00
3 Reprint of *Star Wars* #1 through #6 (1978). 10.00
Volume 2
2 *The Empire Strikes Back* (1980) reprint of Marvel Super Special #16 . . . . .7.50

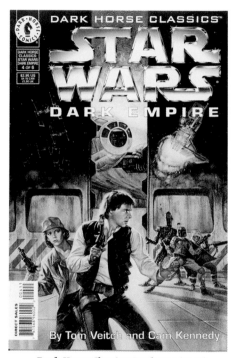

Dark Horse Classics: Dark Empire #4
(Dark Horse Comics 1997)

MARVEL SUPER SPECIALS

16 *The Empire Strikes Back* (1980) $10.00
27 *Return of the Jedi* (1983) 10.00

RETURN OF THE JEDI
Marvel Comics (1983–84)

1 . . . . $3.00
2 through 3, each 3.00

STAR WARS
Marvel Comics (July, 1977)

Although dated July 1977, the first comics actually appeared before the movie opened. The first six issues adapted the movie based on a "rough cut." This has led to considerable wonder about the "missing scenes" where, at the beginning of the movie, Luke goes to see his Tatooine pal, Biggs Darklighter, who tells him that he is going to join the Rebel forces. This scene was cut from the final version of the movie.

The most valuable comic in the Marvel series is the 35-cent version of issue Number 1. Only a very few were printed, as a price increase test. The test must have been successful, because the price has increased over a thousandfold since then.

1 30 cent, begin: movie adaptation. $65.00
1a 35 cent (square box). 600.00
1b Reprint 7.50
2 *Six Against the Galaxy* 25.00
3 *Death Star* 25.00

Star Wars #5 (Marvel Comics 1977)

4 *In Battle With Darth Vader*. 22.00
2a through 4a Reprint, each 4.00
5 *Lo, the Moons of Yavin!*. 22.00
6 end: movie adaptation 22.00
7 through 9, each. 20.00
5a through 9a Reprint, each 3.00
10 *Behemoth From The World Below* 20.00
11 through 21, each 18.00
22 through 38, each 15.00
39 through 44 *The Empire Strikes Back*, each 25.00
45 through 50, each 20.00
51 through 67, each 15.00
68 through 99, each 20.00
100 *First Strike*, Painted cover, double-size 20.00
101 through 106, each 15.00
107 last issue. 50.00
Ann. #1 *The Long Hunt*, 48 pgs.. . . . . 10.00
Ann. #2 *Shade Shine*, 48 pgs.. . . . . 10.00
Ann. #3 *The Apprentice*, 48 pgs.. . . . . 10.00

STAR WARS
Dark Horse Comics (1998–2002)

1 pt. 1 *Featuring: Ki-Adi-Mundi* $5.00
2 and 3 *Prelude to Rebellion*, pt. 2 through pt. 3, each 3.50
4 through 6 *Prelude to Rebellion*, pt. 4 through pt. 6, each 3.00
7 pt. 1 *Featuring Ki-Adi-Mundi* 3.00
8 through 12 *Outlander*, pt. 2 through pt. 6, each. 3.00
13 pt. 1 *Featuring the Jedi Council* 3.00
14 through 18 *Emissaries to Malastare*, pt. 2 through pt. 6, each 3.00
19 pt. 1 *Featuring Quinlan Vos* 3.00
20 through 22 *Twilight*, pt. 2 through pt. 4, each. 3.00
23 pt. 1 *Featuring Quinlan Vos* 3.00

Star Wars #100 (Marvel Comics 1985)

24 through 26 *Infinity's End*, pt. 2 through pt. 4, each 3.00
27 *Star Crash* 3.00
28 *The Hunt for Aurra Sing*, pt. 1 . . . . 3.00
29 through 31 *The Hunt for Aurra Sing*, pt. 2 through pt. 4, each 3.00
32 pt. 1 *Featuring Quinlan Vos* 3.00
33 through 35 *Darkness*, pt. 2 through pt. 4, each 3.00
36 pt. 1 *Featuring Iaco Stark, Plo Koon* 3.00
37 through 39 *Stark Hyperspace War*, pt. 2 through pt. 4, each 3.00
40 *The Devaronian Version*, pt. 1 . . . . 3.00
41 *The Devaronian Version*, pt. 2 . . . . 3.00
42 through 45 *Rite of Passage*, each 3.00
46 through 49 *Republic*, each 3.00
50 64-page *Republic* 6.00
51 through 64 *Republic*, each 3.00
65 and 66 *Mace Windu, Unleashed*, each 3.00
67 *Clone Army* 3.00
68 *Armor* 3.00
69 and 70 *Dreadnaughts of Rendili*, each 3.00

STAR WARS IN 3-D
Blackthorne Publishing (1987–88)

1 . . . . $3.50
2 through 7, each 3.00

STAR WARS:...
Dark Horse Comics

A NEW HOPE
THE SPECIAL EDITION

1 (1997) $6.00
2 through 4, each 5.00

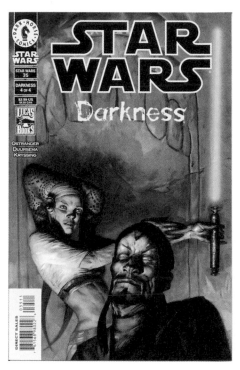

Star Wars #35–Darkness #4 (Dark Horse Comics 2000)

BATTLE OF THE
BOUNTY HUNTERS

Pop-up comic (1996) $17.95

STAR WARS: BOBA FETT —
Dark Horse Comics

One-shot *Agent of Doom* (2000) $3.00
One-shot *Bounty on Bar-Kooda*, 48 pgs. (1995) 11.00
One-shot *Murder Most Foul* (1997) 7.00
One-shot *Twin Engines of Destruction*, 32 pgs. (1997) 6.00
One-shot *When the Fat Lady Swings* (1996) 7.00

ENEMY OF THE EMPIRE

1 (of 4) *Vs. The Dark Lord of the Sith* (1999) $3.00
2 through 4, each 3.00

STAR WARS:...
Dark Horse Comics

BOUNTY HUNTERS, THE

One-shot *Aurra Sing*, by Timothy Truman (1999) $3.00
One-shot *Kenix Kil*, by Randy Stradley 3.00
One-shot *Scoundrel's Wages*, by Mark Schultz 3.00

CHEWBACCA

1 stories narrated *Mallatobuck and Attichitcuk* (2000) $4.00
1a gold foil cover 13.00
2 through 4, each 3.50

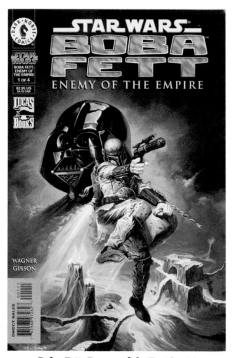

Boba Fett, Enemy of the Empire #1
(Dark Horse Comics 1999)

CRIMSON EMPIRE

1 (1997–98)	$10.00
2	8.00
3 through 6, each	5.00

COUNCIL OF BLOOD

1 (1998–99)	$4.00
2 through 6	3.00

DARK EMPIRE

1 *Destiny of a Jedi* (1991–92)	$14.00
1a 2nd Printing	5.00
1b Gold edition	15.00
2 *World Destroyer*, very low print run	12.00
2a 2nd Printing	5.00
2b Gold edition	15.00
3 *Battle for Planet Calamari*	8.00
3a 2nd Printing	4.00
4 through 6, each	5.00
3 through 6 Gold editions, each	10.00
Gold editions, embossed foil logo, set	50.00
Platinum editions, embossed foil logo, set	100.00

DARK EMPIRE II

1 2nd chapter (1994–95)	$6.00
2 through 6, each	5.00
Platinum editions, embossed foil logo, set	50.00

DARK FORCE RISING

1 (1997)	$5.00
2 through 6, each	5.00

Crimson Empire II, Council of Blood #2
(Dark Horse Comics 1998)

DARTH MAUL

1 The bad guys vs. the really bad guys (2000–01) $3.00
1a photo cover 5.00
2 through 4 . . . . @3.00
2a through 4a photo cover . . . . @3.00

DROIDS

1 Featuring C-3PO and R2-D2 (1994) $5.00
2 Interplanetary thieves steal our droids. .3.00
3 Adroid battle arena the Hosk moon 3.00
4 Leased to Jace Forno 3.00
5 A meeting with model Edroids 3.00
6 A power core rupture. 3.00
Spec. #1 Introducing Olag Greck, reprint DHC #17–#19 . . . . .3.00

DROIDS, Series 2

1 *Deputized Droids* (1995) 3.00
2 through 8, each. 3.00
One-shot *Droids–The Protocol Offensive* (1997) 4.95

EMPIRE

1 (2002) 3.00
2 through 26, each. 3.00

EMPIRE'S END

1 *Return of Emperor Palpatine* (1995). $3.50
2 conclusion. 3.50

EPISODE I
THE PHANTOM MENACE

1 (1999) $3.00
2 through 4, each. 3.00

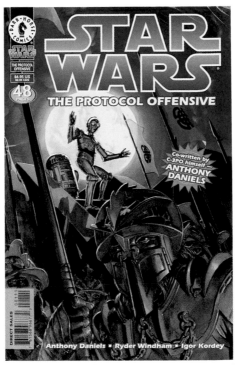

Droids: The Protocol Offensive (Dark Horse Comics 1997)

1a through 4a, newsstand editions, photo cover, each 3.00

Special tie-ins (1999)
Spec. Anakin Skywalker, direct or newsstand 3.00
Spec. Obi-Wan Kenobi, direct or newsstand 3.00
Spec. Queen Amidala, direct or newsstand 3.00
Spec. Qui-Gon Jinn, direct or newsstand 3.00

EPISODE I
1 B & W, manga (1999–2000) $9.95
2 . . . . 9.95

EPISODE II: *ATTACK OF THE CLONES*
1, 48 pgs. (2002–05) 4.00
2 through 4, 48 pgs., each 4.00
1A through 4A photo (c), each 4.00

HANDBOOKS
1 *X-wing Rogue Squadron* (1998) $3.50
2 *Crimson Empire* (1999) 3.00
3 *Dark Empire* (2000) 3.00

HEIR TO THE EMPIRE
1 *I: Grand Admiral Thrawn* (1995–96) $4.00
2 through 6, each 3.50

INFINITIES — A NEW HOPE
1 (2001) $3.00
1a gold foil cover 13.00
2 through 4, each 3.00

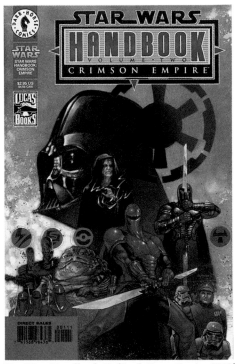

Star Wars Handbook #2 (Dark Horse Comics 1999)

INFINITIES — THE EMPIRE STRIKES BACK

1 (2002) 3.00
2 through 4, each 3.00

INFINITIES — RETURN OF THE JEDI

1 through 4 (2002), each $3.00

JABBA THE HUTT —

One-shot *The Garr Suppoon Hit* $3.00
One-shot *The Hunger of Princess Nampi*. 3.00
One-shot *The Dynasty Trap* 3.00
One-shot *Betrayal* 3.00
One-shot *The Jabba Tape* (1998) 3.00

JANGO FETT

Jango Fett, 64 pgs., graphic novel (2001) $9.95

JANGO FETT–OPEN SEASONS

1 through 4 (2002) $3.00

JEDI

Spec. *Mace Windu*, 48 pgs. (2003) $5.00
Spec. *Shaak Ti*, 48 pgs. 5.00
Spec. *Aayla Secura*, 48 pgs. 5.00
Spec. *Dooku*, 48 pgs. 5.00
Spec. *Yoda*, 48 pgs. 5.00

JEDI ACADEMY — LEVIATHAN

1 (of 4) (1998) $3.00
2 through 4 . . . . 3.00

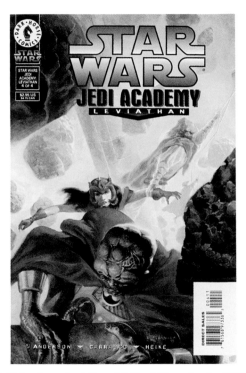

Jedi Academy–Leviathan #4 (Dark Horse Comics 1998)

JEDI COUNCIL — ACTS OF WAR

1 (of 4) *Trouble* (2000) $3.00
1a gold foil cover 10.00
2 through 4, each 3.00

JEDI QUEST

1 (of 4) An escort mission (2001) $3.00
1a ruby red foil cover 13.00
2 through 4, each 3.00

JEDI VS. SITH

1 (of 6) (2001) $3.00
1a gold foil cover, limited edition 10.00
2 through 6, each 3.00

THE LAST COMMAND

1 (1997–98) $3.50
2 through 6, each 3.50

MARA JADE—
BY THE EMPEROR'S HAND

1 (of 6) Assigned to destroy Black Sun (1998) $5.00
2 Infiltrates Black Nebula headquarters 4.00
3 Mara Jade captured 4.00
4 Escape from the Imperial Center 4.00
5 Mara's payback list 4.00
6 Her final mission for the dead Emperor 4.00

THE PROTOCOL OFFENSIVE

One-shot (1997) $4.95

Shadows of the Empire #3 (Dark Horse Comics 1997)

QUI-GON AND OBI-WAN — LAST STAND ON ORD MANTELL

1 (of 3) Investigation (2000–01) $3.00
1a through 3a photo covers, each 3.00
1b variant cover. 3.00
2 and 3. . . . . 3.00

QUI-GON AND OBI-WAN — THE AURORIENT EXPRESS

1 and 2 (2002), each. $3.00

RIVER OF CHAOS

1 The Emperor sends spies (1995) $3.00
2 through 4, each. 3.00

SHADOWS OF THE EMPIRE

1 The Emperor hires the criminal underworld (1996). $3.50
2 through 6, each 3.50

SHADOWS OF THE EMPIRE — EVOLUTION

1 through 5 (1998), each $3.50

SHADOW STALKER

One-shot (1997) $3.50

SPLINTER OF THE MIND'S EYE

1 through 4 (1995–96), each $3.50

STARFIGHTER – CROSSBONES

1 through 3 (2001–02), each $3.00

Star Wars: Tales of the Jedi #4 (Dark Horse Comics 1994)

TAG AND BINK ARE DEAD

1 Humorous adventures on the Death Star (2001) $3.00
2 After the Death Star blows up 3.00

TALES

1 (1999–2002) $4.95
2 through 04, each 4.95
5 through 21 painted, or photo covers, each 6.00

TALES FROM MOS EISLEY

1-shot, from *Star Wars Galaxy Mag.* #2–#4 (1996) $3.50

STAR WARS: TALES OF THE JEDI
Dark Horse Comics

1 (1993–94) $6.00
2 and 3, each 5.00
4 and 5, each 4.00

THE FREEDON NADD UPRISING

1 (1994) $2.75
2 . . . . 2.50

DARK LORDS OF THE SITH

1 (1994–95) $3.00
2 through 6 . . . . 3.00

THE SITH WAR

1 Exar Kun and Ulic Qel-Droma's plans (1995–96) $3.00
2 through 6 . . . . 3.00

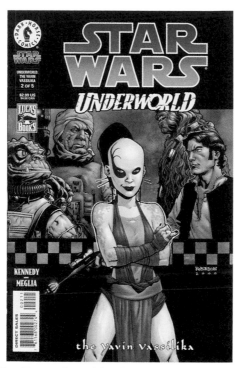

Star Wars Underworld #2 (Dark Horse Comics 1999)

THE GOLDEN AGE OF THE SITH

00 The golden age (1996–97). $2.00
1 Gavand Jori Daragon. 3.50
2 through 5, each. 3.50

THE FALL OF THE SITH EMPIRE

1 through 5 (1997), each $3.50

THE REDEMPTION OF ULIC QEL-DROMA

1 (of 5) Ten years after the Sith War (1998) $3.50
2 through 5, each. 3.50

STAR WARS:...

UNDERWORLD

1 (of 5) *The Yavin Vassilika* (2000–01). $3.00
2 through 5, each. 3.00
1a through 5a photo covers, each 3.00

UNION

1 The wedding plans (1999) $3.50
1a gold foil cover 10.00
2 through 4, each 3.00

VADER'S QUEST

1 The quest begins (1999) $3.00
2 through 4, each. 3.00

A VALENTINE STORY

One-shot (2003) $3.50

X-wing Rogue Squadron #22 (Dark Horse Comics 1997)

X-WING ROGUE SQUADRON
Dark Horse Comics (1995–1998)

0 1/5 *Wizard* limited exclusive $6.00
1 *The Rebel Opposition*, pt. 1 . . . . .5.00
2 through 4 *Rebel Opposition*, pt. 2 through pt. 4, each. 3.50
5 *The Phantom Affair*, pt. 1 . . . . .3.50
6 through 8 *The Phantom Affair*, pt. 2 through pt. 4, each 3.50
9 *Battleground Tatooine*, pt. 1 . . . . .3.50
10 through 12 *Battleground Tatooine*, pt. 2 through pt. 4, each. 3.50
13 *The Warrior Princess*, pt. 1 . . . . .3.50
14 through 16 *The Warrior Princess*, pt. 2 through pt. 4, each. 3.50
17 *Requiem for a Rogue*, pt. 1 . . . . .3.50
18 through 20 *Requiem for a Rogue*, pt. 2 through pt. 4, each 3.50
21 *In the Empire's Service*, pt. 1 . . . . .3.50
22 through 24 *In the Empire's Service*, pt. 2 through pt. 4, each 3.50
25 *The Making of Baron Fel* 5.00
26 and 27 *Family Ties*, pt. 1 and pt. 2, each. 3.50
28 *Masquerade*, pt. 1 . . . . .3.50
29 through 31 *Masquerade*, pt. 2 through pt. 4, each 3.50
32 *Mandatory Retirement*, pt. 1 . . . . .3.50
33 through 35 *Mandatory Retirement*, pt. 2 through pt. 4, each 3.50

COMIC STRIP REPRINTS

Star Wars, hardcovers, three volumes, (Russ Cochran 1991) boxed set . . . $150.00

TRADE PAPERBACKS

Many of the comic book series were reprinted in trade paperback format. These are worth the cover price if they are still in nice condition.

Twin-Pod Cloud Car (Kenner 1979)

DIE-CAST FIGURES AND SHIPS

Die-cast figures and ships are their own collecting category. They are generally not scaled to fit the characters in the same line nor each other. Typically a die-cast Death Star, Star Destroyer and X-wing are all about the same size.

DIE-CAST SHIPS
Kenner (1978–80)

Kenner issued die-cast ships on header cards, and in open boxes, which are much more valuable. Several of the boxed ships also came with backgrounds. They are marked "Special Offer" in an oval on the sides of the package.

Ships (Carded)

Darth Vader TIE Fighter (#39160) (removable figure of Darth Vader) $50.00
    Loose 25.00
    Variation, small wings, scarce 500.00
Imperial TIE Fighter (#38590) 45.00
    Loose 15.00
Landspeeder (#38570) (Luke and C-3PO in cockpit) 90.00
    Loose 35.00
Rebel Armored Snowspeeder (#39680) 125.00
    Loose 45.00
Slave I (#39670) 90.00
    Loose 35.00
Twin-Pod Cloud Car (#39660) 95.00
    Loose 35.00

Y-wing Fighter Die-Cast Ship (Kenner 1979)

X-wing Fighter (#38680) wings and cockpit open 75.00
    Loose 25.00

Ships (Boxed)
Millennium Falcon (#39210) 150.00
    Loose 50.00
    Reissue, with background 500.00
Imperial Cruiser (#39230) 200.00
    Loose 65.00
    Reissue, with background 500.00
Y-wing Fighter (#39220) 175.00
    Loose 50.00
    Reissue, with background 500.00
TIE Bomber (#39260) test market figure, scarce 800.00
    Loose 275.00

Metal Figurines (Heritage 1977)
Bantha Set, Bantha with two Sand people 45.00
C-3PO 15.00
Chewbacca 20.00
Darth Vader 20.00
Han Solo 15.00
Jawa 15.00
Luke Skywalker 20.00
Obi-Wan Kenobi 20.00
Leia 20.00
R2-D2 . . . . 20.00
Sand Person, different from Bantha set 15.00
Snitch 15.00
Stormtrooper 20.00

Darth Vader Action Master Die-Cast (Kenner 1994)

ACTION MASTERS
Kenner (1994–96)

Kenner's Action Masters figures were issued on a header card with an exclusive trading card. A Predator, two Terminators, four Aliens and several DC Superheroes were also available in the Action Masters series. A gold C-3PO was available as a free mail-in for six proof-of-purchase points. I mailed in but never received the figure, which is one reason you won't find a picture of it here.

Die-Cast Figures (1994–95)

Darth Vader Action Masters figure, with card $10.00
Luke Skywalker Action Masters figure, with card 10.00
C-3PO Action Masters figure, gold, with card 10.00
R2-D2 Action Masters figure, with card 10.00
Stormtrooper Action Masters figure, with card 10.00
Chewbacca Action Masters figure, with card. 10.00
Snowtrooper Action Masters figure, with card. 10.00
Special Edition Action Masters "Gold" C-3PO mail-in figure 25.00
Star Wars Action Masters Collectors Set (4 Pack):
    C-3PO, Princess Leia Organa, R2-D2 and
    Obi-Wan Kenobi, with four trading cards 30.00
Star Wars Action Masters Collectors Set (6 Pack):
    Han Solo, Chewbacca, Stormtrooper, Boba Fett, Darth Vader
    and Luke Skywalker, with six trading cards 45.00
Star Wars The Power of the Force 6 Pack set: Han
    Solo, Chewbacca, Stormtrooper, Boba Fett, Darth Vader and
    Luke Skywalker, with six trading cards 45.00

TIE Bomber Micro Machine Die-Cast (Galoob 1997)

MICRO MACHINE DIE-CAST
Galoob (1996–98)

The original packaging for these figures was an oval-shaped header card. The packaging was changed in 1997 to a rectangular card with stripes, similar in design to the action fleet packages (see Micro Machines). The Jawa Sandcrawler was discontinued; however, sufficient stock remained available and, in early 1998, I was able to purchase a Sandcrawler at a local Toys "R" Us store for $1.98. Die-cast figures have interested collectors over the years, and these figures, particularly on the original header cards, might turn out to be a good buy at current prices.

First Batch (1996)

X-wing Starfighter (#66261)	$6.00
Millennium Falcon (#66262)	6.00
Imperial Star Destroyer (#66263)	6.00
TIE Fighter (#66264)	6.00
Y-wing Starfighter (#66265)	6.00
Jawa Sandcrawler (#66266) original card only	9.00
Reissues, on striped card, each	5.00

Second Batch (1997)

Death Star	6.00
Executor with Star Destroyer	6.00
Landspeeder	6.00
Millennium Falcon	6.00
Slave I	6.00
Snowspeeder	6.00
TIE Bomber	6.00
Y-wing Starfighter	6.00

Episode I Gian Speeder (Galoob 1999)

Episode I Podracers (Galoob 1999)

Episode I Die-cast Vehicles (Galoob 1999)

Trade Federation Droid Starfighter 5.00
Gian Speeder 5.00
Trade Federation Battleship 5.00
Royal Starship 6.00
Republic Cruiser 5.00
Trade Federation Tanx 5.00
Sebulba's Podracer 5.00

Episode I Podracers (Galoob 1999)

Podracer Pack I Boles Roor and Neva Kee 5.00
Podracer Pack II Dud Bold and Mars Guo 5.00
Podracer Pack III Anakin Skywalker & Ratts Tyerell 5.00
Podracer Pack IV Sebulba & Clegg Holdfast 5.00
Build Your Own Podracer packs, each 8.00

PEWTER FIGURES
Rawcliffe (1993–95)

Star Wars Characters

Admiral Ackbar (#RF969) $16.00
C-3PO 16.00
Chewbacca (#RF963) 22.00
Lando Calrissian 16.00
Princess Leia (#RF958) 14.00
Luke Skywalker (#RF959) 14.00
Obi-Wan Kenobi (#RF961) 22.00
R2-D2 (#RF957) 14.00
Han Solo (#RF960) 14.00
Ewok-Wicket 10.00
Yoda (#RF955) 10.00

Build Your Own Podracer Pack (Galoob 1999)

Characters, Darkside

Bib Fortuna (#RF970)	16.00
Boba Fett (#RF966)	16.00
Emperor Palpatine (#RF968)	16.00
Gamorrean Guard (#RF971)	16.00
Stormtrooper (#RF965)	16.00
Darth Vader (#RF962)	24.00

PEWTER VEHICLES
Rawcliffe (1993–95)

Star Wars Vehicles

A-wing (#RF953)	$32.00
B-wing (#RF954)	32.00
Millennium Falcon	30.00
Outrider	36.00
Snowspeeder (#RF972)	30.00
X-wing, 3" tall (#RF975)	36.00
Y-wing (#RF973)	36.00

Vehicles, Darkside

Sail Barge	34.00
Star Destroyer (#RF964)	60.00
Slave I	28.00
TIE Fighter (#RF974)	32.00
Shuttle *Tydirium* (#RF967)	36.00
TIE Bomber	36.00

Vehicles, Special Limited Edition, with base

Death Star	160.00
Millennium Falcon (#RF951, 1993)	140.00
TIE Interceptor	75.00
Vader's Custom TIE Fighter (#RF950, 1993)	108.00
X-wing (#RF952, 1993)	76.00

 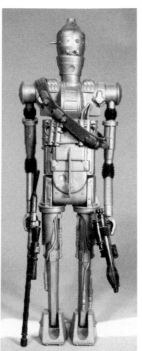

Boba Fett and IG-88 Dolls (Kenner 1979–80)

DOLLS

Between 1979 and 1980, Kenner produced a dozen Large Size Action Figures (i.e. dolls) in window boxes with a flap. All the figures were made to the same 12" scale, but R2-D2 and the Jawa were small characters, so their dolls are about 8" tall, while Chewbacca, Darth Vader and IG-88 were about 15" tall. These are highly prized collectibles, both in and out of box (loose). The Radio Controlled R2-D2, listed in the "Electronic Toys" section of the *Miscellaneous* chapter, was made to the same scale as the listed figures.

DOLLS (CLASSIC)
Kenner (1979–80)

Dolls, *Star Wars* logo box (1979)

Princess Leia Organa (#38070) 11-1/2" tall. $275.00
   Loose 125.00
Luke Skywalker (#38080) 11-3/4" tall 425.00
   Loose 200.00
Chewbacca (#38600) 15" tall 200.00
   Loose 90.00
Darth Vader (#38610) 15" tall 250.00
   Loose 100.00
See-Threepio (C-3PO) (#38620) 12" tall. 150.00
   Loose 50.00
Artoo-Detoo (R2-D2) (#38630) 7-1/2" tall 275.00
   Loose 50.00
Han Solo (#39170) 11-3/4" tall. 650.00
   Loose 275.00

C-3PO Doll (Kenner 1979)

Stormtrooper (#39180) 12" tall. 325.00
   Loose 130.00
Ben (Obi-Wan) Kenobi (#39340) 12" tall 425.00
   Loose 175.00
Jawa (#39350) 8" tall 300.00
   Loose 75.00
Boba Fett (#39140) 13" tall 1,000.00
   In *The Empire Strikes Back* box 1,100.00
   Loose 200.00

Large Figure, *The Empire Strikes Back* logo (1980)
IG-88 (Bounty Hunter) (#39960) 15" tall 800.00
   Loose 350.00

STAR WARS:
COLLECTOR SERIES
Kenner (1996–98)

Kenner began issuing Collector Series 12" dolls in 1996. The first
series of dolls had a dark blue background card inside the package.
Later, light blue cards appeared. Chewbacca is pictured on the back
of the boxes, but he was not included in the initial series. He did not
actually arrive until the fourth series. Instead of Chewbacca, the
second series had two Tusken Raiders, with different weapons—one
with a blaster and one with a more authentic Gaderffii Stick. Lando
Calrissian from this batch did not sell out as quickly as the other dolls
and could still be found almost six years after it first appeared.

Luke Skywalker Doll (Box Flap Open) (Kenner 1996)

12" Dolls (1996) in window box with flap cover
Luke Skywalker (#27724)
    On original dark blue package card,
    binoculars on belt, black lightsaber handle $60.00
    Reissue, binoculars on card 35.00
    Reissue, on light blue package card 25.00
    Reissue, black and silver lightsaber handle 20.00
    Loose 12.50
Han Solo (#27725)
    On original dark blue package card 35.00
    Reissue, on light blue package card, painted or unpainted belt pouch 20.00
    Loose 12.50
Darth Vader (#27726)
    On original dark blue package card, black lightsaber handle 30.00
    Reissue, on light blue package card, black lightsaber handle 25.00
    Reissue, black and silver lightsaber handle 20.00
    Loose 10.00
Obi-Wan Kenobi (#27719)
    On original dark blue package card,
    black lightsaber handle and silver belt buckle 60.00
    Reissue, light blue package card, silver buckle,
    black or black and silver lightsaber handle 45.00
    Reissue, gold buckle 55.00
    Loose 25.00

Second Batch (1997)
Lando Calrissian (#27755) 12.00
    Loose 6.00
Luke Skywalker in Bespin Fatigues (#27757) 25.00
    Loose 10.00
Tusken Raider (with Rifle) (#27758, 1997) 35.00
    Loose 15.00

Princess Leia Doll (Box Flap Open) (Kenner 1997)

Tusken Raider (with Gaderffii Stick) (#27758) 40.00
  Loose 15.00

Third Batch (1996 i.e. 1997)
Stormtrooper (#27689) 40.00
  Loose 12.00
Princess Leia (#27691). 45.00
  Variation: Packed with hood up 50.00
  Loose 15.00
Luke Skywalker in X-wing Gear (#27692) 35.00
  Loose 12.00
Boba Fett (#27693) 75.00
  Loose 25.00

Chewbacca did not appear until fall 1997, in the fourth batch. The package back depicts the three figures in the earlier assortment (plus Chewbacca) and is unlike the other packages in this assortment, which picture six figures. When Chewbacca did arrive, he was very short-packed in the assortment, only 12" tall, and not to scale.

Fourth Batch (1997)
TIE Fighter Pilot (#27864) 35.00
  Loose 12.00
C-3PO (#27865) 35.00
  Loose 10.00
Admiral Ackbar (#27866) 40.00
  Loose 12.00
Chewbacca (#27756). 80.00
  Loose 30.00
Chewbacca (#27756) 1996 box 500.00

Grand Moff Tarkin Doll (Kenner 1998)

Fifth Batch, *Star Wars* Trilogy (1998) window box, no flap

R2-D2, 6" (#27742) with retractable leg. 15.00
    Loose 7.50
Yoda, 6" (#27743) 45.00
    Loose 12.50
Jawa, 6" (#27744) with light-up eyes. 15.00
    Loose 7.50

Sixth Batch, *A New Hope* (1998) window box, no flap

Greedo (#27904) 25.00
    Loose 12.00
Grand Moff Tarkin with Interrogation Droid (#27905) 30.00
    Loose 15.00
Sandtrooper with Imperial Droid (#27906) 20.00
    Loose 9.00
Luke Skywalker in Ceremonial Gear (#27907) 20.00
    Loose 9.00

Seventh Batch, *The Empire Strikes Back* (1998)
    window box, no flap

Han Solo in Hoth Gear (#27916). 20.00
    Loose 10.00
Luke Skywalker in Hoth Gear (#27917) 20.00
    Loose 10.00
AT-AT Driver (#27918) 20.00
    Loose 10.00
Snowtrooper (#27919) 20.00
    Variation: Blue plate, center of chest 150.00
    Loose 10.00
    Loose, blue-plate variation. 50.00

Eighth Batch, *Return of the Jedi* (1998)

Barquin D'an (#28026) 20.00
    Loose 12.00

Chewbacca in Chains Doll (Kenner 1998)

Chewbacca in Chains (#28027) 50.00
    Loose 20.00
Emperor Palpatine (#28029) 15.00
    Loose 9.00
Luke Skywalker in Jedi Gear (#28028) 20.00
    Loose 10.00

In 1999, Collector Series Dolls had to compete with Episode I figures for shelf space and collector dollars. For the first time, significant numbers were available at discount. Emperor Palpatine from the eighth series and especially Chewbacca "over 13" tall" from the tenth series remained in stores much too long. Earlier versions of Chewbacca had something resembling hair or fur, but this one is all plastic.

Ninth Batch, Power of the Force (1999)
Luke Skywalker with Dianoga Tentacle (#57113) 25.00
    Loose 12.00
Obi-Wan Kenobi with Training Droid (#57112) 25.00
    Loose 12.00
Ponda Baba with Removable Arm (#57114) 25.00
    Loose 12.00

Tenth Batch, Power of the Force (1999)
Chewbacca, over 13" tall (#53136) 15.00
    Loose 7.00
Han Solo with Magnetic Detonators (#57138) 50.00
    Loose 25.00
Princess Leia, slave outfit (#57137) 20.00
    Loose 10.00

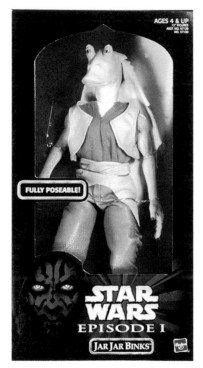

Episode I Jar Jar Binks Doll (Hasbro 1999)

EPISODE I DOLLS

The first Episode I dolls were available at midnight, on May 3, 1999. Within minutes, all the Darth Maul dolls were gone. I never saw one on the shelf, then or later. Most of the other waves sold well, exception Watto. The fifth wave figures are quite scarce.

12" Dolls (Hasbro 1999)

Jar Jar Binks (#57130) $25.00
    Loose 10.00
Qui-Gon Jinn with Lightsaber (#57131)
    "Trade Fedration" error box 30.00
    "Trade Federation" corrected 25.00
    Loose 12.00
Darth Maul with Lightsaber (#57132) 40.00
    Loose 15.00

Second Wave (1999)

Anakin Skywalker, 6" (#26229) 20.00
    Loose 7.00
Pit Droids, 6" (#26228) 20.00
    Loose 7.00
R2-A6, 6" (#26230) 20.00
    Loose 7.00

Third Wave (1999)

Obi-Wan Kenobi (#26232) 25.00
    Loose 12.00
Watto (#26233) 15.00
    Loose 5.00
Battle Droid (#26234) 20.00
    Loose 10.00

Episode I Battle Droid Commander Doll (Kenner 1999)

Fourth Wave (1999)

Battle Droid Commander (#26284) 20.00

    Loose 10.00

Mace Windu (#26280) 35.00

    Loose 20.00

Qui-Gon Jinn with "Tatooine Poncho" (#26465) 20.00

    Loose 10.00

Fifth Wave (2000)

Anakin Skywalker with Theed Hangar Droid (#28283) 50.00

    Loose 25.00

Boss Nass (#29279) 45.00

    Loose 20.00

Sebulba (#28454) 40.00

    Loose 20.00

POWER OF THE JEDI
Hasbro (2001–02)

The Power of the Jedi line of figures and dolls covers the classic movies. Hasbro has produced more than 100 dolls, and collectors continue to have trouble finding them, as distribution has been uneven, at best.

12" Dolls (2001)

Bossk (#26472) $40.00

    Loose 15.00

IG-88 (#26471) 40.00

    Loose 15.00

4-LOM (#26473) 40.00

    Loose 15.00

Luke Skywalker and Yoda Doll (Hasbro 2001)

Second Batch (2001)

Han Solo in Stormtrooper Disguise (#32489) 30.00
   Loose 12.00
Death Star Trooper (#32490) 30.00
   Loose 12.00
Death Star Droid with Mouse Droid (#32491) 30.00
   Loose 12.00

Special

Luke Skywalker & Yoda (#32486) 30.00
   Loose 15.00

ATTACK OF THE CLONES

First Batch (2002)

Anakin Skywalker (#32495) 25.00
Clone Trooper (#32494) 25.00
Obi-Wan Kenobi (#32496) 25.00
Mace Windu (#32510) 25.00
Count Dooku (#32499) 25.00

Second Batch (2002)

Zam Wesell (#32527) 25.00
Super Battle Droid (#32500) 25.00
Jango Fett (Collector's) (#32509) 30.00

Third Batch (2003)

Anakin Skywalker (#84938) 20.00
Padmé Amidala (#84937) 20.00
Geonosian Warrior (#84939) 20.00

Boba Fett, Original Trilogy Collection Doll (Hasbro 2004)

STAR WARS SAGA

First Batch (2002)

Dengar (#26474) 25.00
Imperial Officer (#26485) 25.00
Zuckuss (#26475) 25.00

Second Batch (2003)

AT-ST Driver (#84973) 30.00
Han Solo, quick draw action (#84971) 20.00
Lando Calrissian, Skiff disguise (#84972) 20.00

Third Batch (2003)

Biker Scout, Battle of Endor (#84999) 40.00
Yoda (#84998) 30.00
Luke Skywalker, Jedi Knight 20.00

Star Wars, A New Hope (square window box)

Jawas, Tatooine Scavengers (#84728) 30.00
Ewoks, Battle of Endor (#84839) 30.00
Garindan, Mos Eisley Cantina (#84729) 25.00
Obi-Wan Kenobi, Tatooine Encounter (#84730) 20.00

ORIGINAL TRILOGY COLLECTION

First Batch (2004)

Boba Fett (#85232) $30.00
Luke Skywalker (#85231) 30.00
Stormtrooper (#85233) 30.00

Electronic TC-14 Doll (Hasbro 2001)

ELECTRONIC DOLLS

New Power of the Force Electronic Dolls

Electronic Boba Fett, 14" (#57100) Kay-Bee Toy Exclusive $50.00

Darth Vader 14" Electronic Figure, with removable helmet that reveals
    Anakin Skywalker face, says four phrases (Kenner #27729, 1998) 35.00

Electronic Power F/X Obi-Wan Kenobi vs. Darth Vader with eight authentic
    recordings for each figure, battery powered, J.C. Penney stores,
    Collector Series (#27661, 1997) 40.00

Electronic Emperor Palpatine and Royal Guard, Target stores 50.00

Electronic C-3PO & R2-D2 (#57108, 1998) Toys "R" Us stores 50.00

Interactive Yoda with lightsaber, in pentagonal
    window box (Hasbro/Tiger #01248, 2001) 30.00

Episode I Electronic Talking Dolls (2000–01)

Electronic Talking Jar Jar Binks (#84166) 25.00

Electronic Talking Darth Maul (#84162) 25.00

Electronic Talking Qui-Gon Jinn (#84163) 25.00

Electronic Talking C-3PO (#84197) 30.00

Electronic TC-14 doll (#26293) Kay-Bee Toys special 25.00

Episode II Electronic Battling Dolls (2002)

Electronic Battling Obi-Wan Kenobi (#84892) 30.00

Electronic Battling Jango Fett (#84893) 30.00

COLLECTOR SERIES — EXCLUSIVES

While all the collectors were looking for the first Chewbacca,
some of them were lucky enough to find one or more of the 1997
store exclusives. Many of these had store shelf-lives of less than one

Doikk Na'ts Doll, Cantina Band (Hasbro 1997)

day. The first to appear was the Han and Luke Stormtrooper two-pack at Kay-Bee stores. Target stores got an exclusive Luke Skywalker and Wampa, while Toys "R" Us offered Han Solo mounted on a Tauntaun. The demand for each figure is different, depending on which stores are nearby. In any given area, exclusive figures from out-of-town stores are usually more in demand, because few, if any, local collectors have one.

12" Special or Exclusive Dolls

Cantina Band (1997) in window box with flap cover, Wal-Mart stores
    Doikk Na'ts, with Fizzz (#27953) $45.00
    Figrin D'an with Kloo Horn 50.00
    Ickabel with Fanfar 45.00
    Nalan with Bandfill 45.00
    Tech with Omni Box 45.00
    Tedn with Fanfar 45.00
Greedo (#27976, 1997) in window box with flap cover, J.C. Penney stores . . . 70.00
    Loose 35.00
Sandtrooper (#27928, 1997) in window box
    with flap cover, Diamond Distribution 60.00
    Loose 25.00
AT-AT Driver (#27977, 1997) in window box
    with flap cover, Service Merchandise stores 60.00
    Loose 25.00
R2-D2 with Detachable Utility Arms (#27801, 1998) Wal-Mart stores 15.00
R5-D4 (#27802, 1998) Wal-Mart stores 15.00
Wicket the Ewok (#27800, 1998) Wal-Mart stores 15.00
Princess Leia in Hoth Gear (#57110, 1998)
    in window box, Service Merchandise stores 30.00
Luke Skywalker (100th Figure) (#32437) 75.00
    Loose 30.00

*Chancellor Valorum & Coruscant Guard Dolls
(Hasbro 1998)*

Special or Exclusive Doll Multi-Packs

Han Solo & Luke Skywalker in Stormtrooper Gear
   (Kay-Bee Limited Edition of 20,000) (#27867, 1997)
     in window box with flap cover. 175.00
     Loose 15.00

Grand Moff Tarkin & Imperial Gunner with Interrogator Droid
   (#27923, 1997) in window box with flap cover, FAO Schwarz stores 150.00
     Loose, each 25.00

Jedi Luke Skywalker & Bib Fortuna (#27924, Nov. 1997)
     in window box with flap cover, FAO Schwarz stores. 140.00
     Loose, each 35.00

Han Solo as Prisoner and Carbonite Block with
   Frozen Han Solo (#30018, 1998) Target stores 50.00

Luke Skywalker in Tatooine Gear, Princess Leia in Boushh Disguise and
   Han Solo in Bespin Gear (#57101, 1998) Kay-Bee stores. 100.00

Luke Skywalker in Hoth Gear, Han Solo in Hoth Gear, Snowtrooper and
   AT-AT Driver (#57109, 1998) 4-pack in window box, J.C. Penney stores . . . 50.00

Wedge Antilles and Biggs Darklighter (#57106, 1998)
   in window box with flap cover, FAO Schwarz 75.00

Princess Leia Organa and R2-D2 as Jabba's Prisoners (#61777, 1998)
   in window box with flap cover, FAO Schwarz stores. 80.00

Qui-Gon Ginn and Queen Amidala (Defense of Naboo)
   Entertainment Earth distribution. 100.00

Chancellor Valorum & Coruscant Guard (#26477)
   Fan Club, later Kay-Bee stores 75.00

Sith Lords: Darth Vader and Darth Maul (#32438) 40.00

Luke and Yoda (#32486) Wal-Mart stores 30.00

Doll and Beast

Luke Skywalker vs. Wampa (#27947, 1997)
   Target stores 125.00
   Loose, pair 35.00

Dewback & Sandtrooper Dolls (Hasbro 1999)

Han Solo & Tauntaun (#27834, 1997) Toys "R" Us stores 75.00
    Loose, pair 40.00
Dewback and Stormtrooper (#26246) Toys "R" Us stores 100.00
Captain Tarpals & Kaadu, Target stores 60.00

Doll and Speeder
Darth Maul & Sith Speeder (#26294, 2001) Wal-Mart stores 90.00
Speeder Bike with Scout Trooper (#26495, 2000) Target stores 150.00
Speeder Bike with Luke Skywalker (in Endor Gear)
    (#26295, 2001) Target stores 50.00

Book Stores Masterpiece 12" Doll and Book
Anakin Skywalker, Masterpiece doll and
    book in trapezoidal box with flap (ISBN 0-8118-2158-7) 75.00
Aurra Sing, Masterpiece doll and book in
    trapezoidal box with flap (ISBN 0-8118-2904-9) 115.00

C-3PO with Removeable Limbs, Masterpiece doll
and book in trapezoidal box with flap (ISBN 0-8118-2487-X) 75.00

Exclusives (2003–04)
Clone Trooper, red (#26777) Kay-Bee 35.00
Clone Commander, yellow (#26776) Kay-Bee 35.00
Gamorrean Guard (#32502) Kay-Bee 25.00
Han Solo in Carbonite, with Leia in Boushh Disguise (#26789) (TRU) 30.00
Ki-Adi Mundi (Web site) 20.00
Luke & Tauntaun (#32516) (TRU) 60.00
Leia with Speeder Bike (Target) 50.00
Luke with Speeder Bike (TRU) 18.00
Plo Koon (Web site) 90.00

Darth Maul & Sith Speeder Doll (Hasbro 2001)

Princess Leia Fashion Doll (Hasbro 1999)

FASHION DOLLS
Hasbro (1999–2000)

The "Portrait Edition" dolls are very attractive, in the best Barbie tradition, which may be why they haven't sold all that well to *Star Wars* collectors. Then, the initial $50 price tag may also have had something to do with it. Since far too many were produced, they have all been available at discount for the last few years. Some still are. The quality may be the reason those same collectors change their mind in the future. If so, the discounted price of about $20 will be the starting price, not the original high price. The "Queen Amidala Collection" dolls are like entry level Barbie dolls. All of them were discounted too.

Star Wars Portrait Edition Doll (Hasbro 1999)
Princess Leia in Ceremonial Gown 1999 Portrait Edition
(#61772) number 1 in series $25.00

Episode I Portrait Edition Dolls (Hasbro 1999–2000)
Queen Amidala in Black Travel Gown, 1999 Portrait Edition
(#61773) number 2 in series 25.00
Queen Amidala in Red Senate Gown, 1999 Portrait Edition, in red velvet robe
adorned with embossed rosettes and golden, triple-braided soutache
(#61774) number 3 in series 25.00
Queen Amidala Return to Naboo, 2000 Portrait Edition, in deep-purple,
full-length gown, velour cloak inscribed with her royal crest, sheer lavender
veil and gold-finished crown (#61781) number 4 in series 30.00

Beautiful Braids Padmé Doll (Hasbro 1999)

Queen Amidala Collection 12" Dolls (Hasbro 1999)

Hidden Majesty Queen Amidala (#61776) 10.00
Ultimate Hair Queen Amidala (#61778) 10.00
Royal Elegance Queen Amidala (#61779) 10.00
Beautiful Braids Padmé (#61780) 25.00

OTHER FIGURES

BEND-EMS
Just Toys (1993–96)

The Just Toys *Star Wars* Galaxy Bend-Ems were originally
shipped in August 1993 and, by early 1994, they were fairly hot items,
since the new action figures had not yet been produced. Trading cards
were also popular at that time.

The popularity of Bend-Ems declined as the action figures
appeared and they received little retail rack space. The trading cards
are a separate collectible once the package has been opened. They are
listed in the *Trading Cards* chapter.

First Batch (1993) with matching *Star Wars* Galaxy card

Darth Vader (#12361) 8-back header card $10.00
   Reissue, no Trading Card 9.00
   Reissue, random Trading Card 9.00
C-3PO (#12362) 8-back header card 8.00
   Reissue, no Trading Card 7.00
   Reissue, random Trading Card 7.00
R2-D2 (#12363) 8-back header card 8.00
   Reissue, no Trading Card 7.00

Luke Skywalker Bend-Ems Figure (Just Toys 1993)

Reissue, random Trading Card 9.00
Stormtrooper (#12364) 8-back header card 9.00
   Reissue, no Trading Card 8.00
   Reissue, random Trading Card 8.00
Yoda, the Jedi Master (#12415) 8-back header card 9.00
   Reissue, no Trading Card 7.00
   Reissue, random Trading Card 9.00
Chewbacca (#12416) 8-back header card 9.00
   Reissue, no Trading Card 7.00
   Reissue, random Trading Card 9.00
Luke Skywalker (#12417) 8-back header card 9.00
   Reissue, no Trading Card 7.00
   Reissue, random Trading Card 9.00
Princess Leia (#12418) 8-back header card 15.00
   Reissue, no Trading Card 9.00
   Reissue, random Trading Card 9.00
Loose figures, each 2.50

Second Batch (1994) with matching *Star Wars* Galaxy card
Wicket the Ewok (#12452) 12.00
   Reissue, no Trading Card 8.00
   Reissue, random Trading Card 8.00
Han Solo (#12453) 12.00
   Reissue, no Trading Card 8.00
   Reissue, random Trading Card 8.00
Obi-Wan Kenobi (#12454) 10.00
   Reissue, no Trading Card 7.00
   Reissue, random Trading Card 7.00
The Emperor (#12455) 10.00
   Reissue, no Trading Card 7.00
   Reissue, random Trading Card 7.00
Loose figures, each 3.00

Tusken Raider Bend-Ems Figure (Just Toys 1995)

Third Batch (1995) with random *Star Wars* Galaxy I or II card on header card with Stand-Up Bubble

Admiral Ackbar (#12549) 11.00
Bib Fortuna (#12552) 11.00
Boba Fett (scarce) 40.00
Emperor's Royal Guard (#12551) (Boba Fett card) 11.00
Gamorrean Guard (#12548) 11.00
Lando Calrissian (#12550) 11.00
Luke Skywalker in X-wing Gear. 20.00
Tusken Raider (#12553) 11.00
Loose figures, each 3.00

Multi-packs

Kmart exclusive 8-pack includes Leia, Darth Vader, Wicket, Emperor,
    R2-D2, C3-PO, Stormtrooper and Luke (#12433) 35.00
4 Piece Gift Set: Stormtrooper, R2-D2, C-3PO,
    Darth Vader (#12492, 1993) no cards 25.00
4 Piece Gift Set: The Emperor, R2-D2, Luke Skywalker and Darth Vader,
    plus four trading cards (#12493, 1993) 25.00
4 Piece Gift Set: Ben (Obi-Wan) Kenobi, Princess Leia, Han Solo and C-3PO,
    plus four trading cards (#12494, 1993) 25.00
4 Piece Gift Set: Imperial Stormtrooper, Wicket, an Ewok, Yoda and Chewbacca,
    plus four trading cards (#12498, 1993) 25.00
Deluxe Collector Set, all 20 figures in Darth Vader bust case (#15021, 1995) . . 70.00
4 Piece Gift Set: Jabba's Palace, with cards and coin (#12558, 1995) 12.00
4 Piece Gift Set: Cantina, with cards and coin (#12557, 1995) 12.00
10 Piece Gift Set (I) R2-D2, Stormtrooper, Darth Vader, Admiral Ackbar,
    Chewbacca, Han, Leia, Luke, Bib Fortuna and Emperor's Royal Guard,
    plus trading cards and brass-colored coin (#12360, 1995) 45.00
10 Piece Gift Set (II) Yoda, Ewok, Tusken Raider, Emperor Palpatine, C-3PO, Lando,
    Boba Fett, Obi-Wan, Luke in X-wing uniform and Gamorrean Guard,
    plus trading cards and brass-colored coin (#12320, 1995) 45.00
Darth Vader bust Collector Case (#15018, 1994) 15.00

Bend-Ems Four-Piece Gift Set (Just Toys 1993)

PVC FIGURES
Applause (1995–99)

Applause started producing PVC figures in 1995, with its
Classic Collector set of six figures. The figures have been available
individually at comic shops and party stores. The figures all come on
a circular molded stand with a date on the bottom.

Boxed Set

Star Wars Classic Collectors Series (6 figures):
   with Bespin Display Platform (#46038, 1995) $20.00

3-1/2" figures, First Batch (1995)

Darth Vader (#46104) 5.00
Luke Skywalker (#46105) 3.00
Han Solo (#46106) 3.00
Chewbacca (#46107) 4.00
C-3PO (#46108) 3.00
R2-D2 (#46109) 3.00

Second Batch (1996)

Emperor Palpatine (#46214) 3.00
Princess Leia (#46216) 3.00
Stormtrooper (#46218) 3.00
Boba Fett (#46239) 3.00

Third Batch (1997)

Obi-Wan Kenobi as ghostly Jedi (#42676) 4.00
Lando Calrissian (#42675) 3.00
Greedo (#42677) 3.00
Yoda (#42678) 3.00
Wedge Antilles (#42707) 4.00
TIE Fighter Pilot (#42708) 3.00
Store Assortment Box, 10-3/4" x 15-1/4" x 10", listing all
   16 figures from 1995–97 (#42674) empty 5.00

Fourth Batch (1998)

Admiral Ackbar (#42946) 3.00
Bossk (#42947) 3.00
Snowtrooper (#42948) 3.00

Star Wars Classic Collector Series PVCs (Applause 1995)

Tusken Raider (#42949) 3.00
Obi-Wan Kenobi (#42965) 3.00

Gift Boxes
Han Solo, Chewbacca, Boba Fett, Darth Vader and Luke Skywalker (#42989) . 20.00

Episode I PVC Figures (1999)
Figurine Gift Set, four figures, including exclusive
  OOM-9 with Theed Hangar Backdrop (#43036) 10.00
Figurine Gift Set, including Anakin Skywalker, Jar Jar Binks,
  Queen Amidala and Destroyer Droid (#61580) 10.00
Anakin Skywalker (#43037) 3.00

Four PVC figures (Applause 1995–96)

Darth Maul (#43038) 3.00
Destroyer Droid (#43039) 3.00
Jar Jar Binks (#43040) 3.00
Obi-Wan Kenobi (#43041) 3.00
Queen Amidala (#43042) 3.00
Pit Droid (#43043) 3.00
Qui-Gon Jinn (#43045) 3.00

Jumbo Dioramas (1997)
Han Solo and Jabba the Hutt (#42691) 10.00
R2-D2 and C-3PO (#42690) 10.00

Read-Along Play Packs Cassette and 3 PVCs (Walt Disney Records 1997)
Star Wars, A New Hope (#02844) 10.00
Star Wars, The Empire Strikes Back (#02854) 10.00
Star Wars, Return of the Jedi (#02834) 10.00

Episode I PVC Figurine Gift Set (Applause 1999)

PVC SHIPS
Applause (1995–99)

Star Wars Danglers, in clear acetate box
Six different ships, each $4.00

Episode I Danglers (1999)
Six different ships, each 4.00

VINYL FIGURES
Suncoast Vinyl Dolls (1993)

Darth Vader $20.00
Luke Jedi Knight 20.00
Luke X-wing Pilot. 20.00
Han Solo. 20.00
Chewbacca. 20.00
R2-D2 . . . . 20.00
C3-PO 20.00
Leia in white gown 20.00

VINYL FIGURES
Applause (1995–98)

Most of the vinyl figures produced by Applause are sold loose, with only a folded wrist tag or card to identify the figure and contain the UPC code for scanning. They are not articulated, although sometimes the arms or waist allow some motion. Applause also issued boxed figures of Darth Vader and Luke Skywalker in X-wing gear, plus a series of boxed resin figurines and dioramas.

Princess Leia Slave Girl Vinyl Figure (Applause 1998)

9"–11" Figures, First Batch (1995)

Darth Vader, limited (#46039) $20.00
Luke Skywalker with Yoda, 9-1/4" (#46040) 15.00
Princess Leia with R2-D2, 8-1/2" (#46041) 15.00
Han Solo as Stormtrooper, 10" (#46042) 15.00
Chewbacca, with C-3PO, 11" (#46043) 15.00

Second Batch (1996)

Darth Vader, 2nd edition, removable helmet (#46234) 17.00
Boba Fett (#46238) 15.00
Princess Leia in poncho with removable helmet (#46041) 15.00
Emperor Palpatine (*Star Wars* Classic) 10-1/2"
   (#46240) with glow-in-the-dark hands 16.00
Tusken Raider, 11" (#46241) 15.00
Dash Rendar (Shadows of the Empire) 10-1/2" (#46243) 17.00
Prince Xizor (Shadows of the Empire) 11" (#46244) 17.00

Third Batch (1997)

TIE Fighter Pilot, 10" (#42688) 15.00
Wedge Antilles, 11" (#42689) 17.00
Greedo, 10" (#42670) 15.00
Lando Calrissian, skiff guard, 10" (#42671) 15.00
Obi-Wan Kenobi, 10" (#42672) 15.00
R2-D2 with Sensor Scope, 5-1/2" (#42673) 15.00

Fourth Batch (1998)

Luke in Jedi Training, glow-in-the-dark lightsaber
   and removable helmet, 9" (#42945) 15.00
C-3PO, 9-1/2" (#42955) 15.00
Princess Leia Slave Girl (#42968) 20.00
Emperor's Royal Guard 15.00

Queen Amidala Character Collectible (Applause 1999)

Figures in Large Box

Darth Vader, 12" (#61096). 35.00
Luke Skywalker, in X-wing Pilot Gear, 9" (#61091). 25.00

Episode I Mega Collectible Figures (Applause 1999) 13"
  with lightsabers that light up, boxed

Qui-Gon Jinn (#43023) 30.00
Darth Maul (#43021) 30.00
Obi-Wan Kenobi (#43022). 30.00

Episode I Character Collectibles (Applause 1999)

Qui-Gon Jinn, 10-1/2" with Glow-in-the-Dark Lightsabers (#43029) 15.00
Obi-Wan Kenobi, 10-1/2" with Glow-in-the-Dark Lightsabers (#43031) 15.00
Darth Maul, 10 1/2" with Glow-in-the-Dark Lightsabers (#43028). 20.00
Queen Amidala, 9", head turns (#43030) 17.00

Episode I Kid's Collectible Figures (Applause 1999)

Anakin Skywalker, 6-1/2" (#43024) 10.00
Jar Jar Binks, 7-1/2" (#43026) 10.00
Watto, 7" (#43027). 10.00
Darth Maul, 7" (#43025) 10.00

DIORAMAS AND FIGURINES

Resin Figurines (Applause 1995–97)

Darth Vader Limited Edition Resin Figurine, limited
  (#46048, 1995) light-up base $50.00
Luke Skywalker Limited Edition Resin Figurine, limited
  (#46049, 1995) light-up base 50.00
Bounty Hunters Resin Diorama, limited (#46196, 1996) 60.00
Jabba and Leia, with Salacious Crumb, limited (#46197, 1996) 60.00

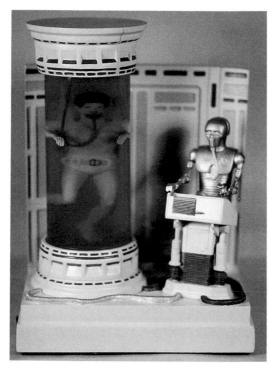

Luke Skywalker in Bacta Tank Sculpture (Applause 1998)

Shadows of the Empire limited (#46199, 1996). 60.00
Leia's Rescue Statuette (#42669, 1997) 40.00
Han Solo Release From Carbonite Statue, limited
   (#61064, 1997) Diamond Previews exclusive 110.00
Star Wars Rancor Statuette (#42735, 1997) 40.00
Star Wars Sandtrooper on Dewback cold-cast resin statuette
   (#42687, 1997) 75.00
Darth Vader in Meditation Chamber (#42978, 1998). 80.00
Wampa Attack Statuette (#42987, 1998). 75.00
Luke Skywalker in Bacta Tank Sculpture (#42988, 1998) 125.00

Episode I Dioramas & Sculptures (Applause 1999)
Duel of the Fates Diorama (#43113) with certificate 60.00
The Guardians of Peace Lighted Sculpture limited (#43119) 75.00
Queen Amidala Miniature Figurine, limited (#43117) 30.00
Qui-Gon Jinn Miniature Figurine, limited (#43118) 30.00
Darth Maul Miniature Figurine, limited (#43115) 30.00
Obi-Wan Kenobi Miniature Figurine, limited (#43116) 30.00

FIGURAL BANKS

Plastic (Adam Joseph 1983)
Darth Vader, 9" tall. $25.00
Emperor's Royal Guard, 9" tall 25.00
Gamorrean Guard, 9" tall, rare 50.00
R2-D2, 6" tall 30.00
Princess Kneesa, 6" tall, playing tambourine 15.00
Wicket, 6" tall, playing drum 15.00

Metal
Darth Vader Bust Metal Bank, 6" high (Leonard Silver Mfg. 1981) 65.00

Jar Jar Binks Figural Bank (Applause 1999)

Darth Vader Metal Bank, tin litho. box
    with combination dials (Metal Box Co. 1980) 50.00
Yoda Metal Bank, tin litho. box with combination dials (Metal Box Co. 1980) 50.00
The Empire Strikes Back Metal Bank, tin octagonal bank
    with photos of characters (Metal Box Co. 1980) 40.00

Episode I Figural Banks (Applause 1999)
Darth Maul on Sith Speeder Bank, 7" (#43032) 15.00
Jar Jar Binks Bank, 8" (#43033) 15.00

PLUSH FIGURES

Plush
Chewbacca (Regal) $60.00
Chewbacca, 20" tall (Kenner 1977) 35.00
R2-D2, 10" tall (Kenner 1977) 50.00
Ewoks (Kenner 1983)
    18" Zephee 40.00
    14" Wicket 30.00
    14" Princess Kneesa 30.00
    14" Paploo 40.00
    14" Latara 40.00

Episode I, Small Plush (Applause 1999)
Jar Jar Binks (#43072) 10.00
Watto (#43073) 10.00

Episode I, Medium Plush (Applause 1999)
R2-D2, 12" (#43071) 15.00
Watto, 14" (#43070) 15.00
Jar Jar Binks, 14" (#43069) 15.00

Max Rebo Star Wars Buddies Figure (Kenner 1997–2000)

STAR WARS BUDDIES
Kenner (1997–2000)

Buddies (Bean Bag)

C-3PO	$8.00
Chewbacca, original black bandolier strap	15.00
Chewbacca, new brown bandolier strap	8.00
Darth Vader	8.00
Figrin D'An	8.00
Gamorrean Guard	8.00
Jabba the Hutt	8.00
Jawa	10.00
Luke Skywalker	8.00
Max Rebo	12.00
Princess Leia	8.00
R2-D2	8.00
Salacious Crumb	10.00
Stormtrooper	8.00
Wampa	12.00
Wicket the Ewok	9.00
Yoda	20.00

Episode I Buddies (1999)

Darth Maul (#26248)	8.00
Jar Jar Binks (#26247)	7.00
Obi-Wan Kenobi (#26245)	6.00
Padmé Naberrie (#26244)	7.00
Qui-Gon Jinn (#26243)	5.00
Watto (#26249)	5.00

Complete Galaxy Endor, with Ewok (Kenner 1998)

COMPLETE GALAXY
Kenner (1998)

Each Complete Galaxy figure is a planet or moon attached to a base and flips open in the middle to reveal a scene and action figure. I guess Complete Galaxies make nice displays, but the only one I like is Endor, with the Ewok and glider.

Complete Galaxy Figures (1998)
Dagobah with **Yoda** (#69828) $10.00
Death Star with **Darth Vader** (#69829) 10.00

Second Batch
Endor with **Ewok** (#69869) 30.00
Tatooine with **Luke Skywalker** (#69826) 30.00

OTHER FIGURES

Episode I (Hasbro 1999)
Jabba Glob, Jabba the Hutt with jar of Gel (#63355) $10.00

Froot Loops with Han Solo Offer (Kellogg's 1996)

BREAKFAST FOOD, FAST FOOD, JUNK FOOD AND PIZZA

Over the years, *Star Wars* has had promotions with each of the four major food groups—fast, junk, breakfast and pizza—not to mention a pet food promotion in Australia. These promotions generate a variety of collectibles, from food containers to toys and mail-in premiums.

BREAKFAST FOOD

Every toy collector should start off with a hearty breakfast. In 1978, General Mills, which owned Kenner at the time, began promotions with various *Star Wars* Cheerios boxes. This was probably the nutritional high point of *Star Wars* food products until the 1997 Taco Bell promotion. From then on, the offers featured cereals like Boo Berry, Count Chocula and Lucky Charms. *Star Wars* moved to Kellogg's in 1984 and C-3PO got his own cereal. Finally, in 1996 Froot Loops had its highly successful Han Solo Stormtrooper action figure offer. Toucan Sam and R2-D2 were perfect together. The boxes are just as collectible as the premiums.

Listed prices are for complete and clean boxes. A complete box has all four top flaps, all four sides (no missing coupons) and all four bottom flaps. A box that has the top and bottom flaps opened is a "collapsed" box (but still complete). A "Flat" is a mint (usually a file copy) unused cereal box. A flat commands up to 40 percent more than the listed price.

General Mills Cereal Boxes

Cheerios, with *Star Wars* tumbler offer $35.00
Cheerios, 1978, *Star Wars* Poster in Pack, Space Scenes 30.00

Boo Berry, with trading card premium 25.00
Franken Berry, with trading card premium 25.00
Cocoa Puffs, with trading card premium 25.00
Chocolate Crazy Cow, with trading card premium 25.00
Strawberry Crazy Cow, with trading card premium 25.00
Trading Cards, 18 different (see Trading Cards chapter).

Franken Berry, with sticker premium 25.00
Count Chocula, with sticker premium 25.00
Trix, with sticker premium 25.00
Cocoa Puffs, with sticker premium 25.00
Lucky Charms, with sticker premium 25.00
Stickers, 16 different, each 2.00
Lucky Charms, with spaceship hang glider premium 25.00

Kellogg's Cereal Boxes

C-3PO Cereal (1984) with sticker trading card offer 20.00
C-3PO Cereal (1984) with mask on back, six different masks of C-3PO,
   Chewbacca, Darth Vader, Luke Skywalker, Stormtrooper or Yoda, each . . . 30.00
   Set, eight different C-3PO mask boxes 200.00
C-3PO Cereal (1984) with Rebel Rocket in pack, plus stickers 20.00
   Set, eight different boxes plus stickers 200.00

Froot Loops (1996) with Han Solo in Stormtrooper outfit mail-in offer 10.00
Apple Jacks (1996) with Dark Horse comic book mail-in offer 2.00
Corn Pops (1996) with *Star Wars* video offer 2.00
Raisin Bran (1996) with *Star Wars* video offer 2.00

FAST FOOD

The 1970s and 1980s promotions of choice with fast food restaurants were glasses and plastic cups. The most famous of these promotions were the Burger King/Coca-Cola four-glass sets sold for each of the three movies. Coca-Cola also produced a number of collector plastic cups, which were distributed in various fast-food chains, both national and regional.

Glassware

Star Wars Promotional Glasses (4 different glasses: Luke, Han Solo, Darth and R2-D2/C-3PO, Burger King/Coca-Cola 1977), each $15.00

    Set of 4 . . . . 60.00

Star Wars Glasses (Burger King/Coca-Cola 1977)

*Three The Empire Strikes Back and Three Return of
the Jedi Glasses (Burger King/Coca-Cola 1980–83)*

The Empire Strikes Back Promotional Glasses (4 different glasses: Luke, Lando,
R2-D2/C-3PO and Darth, Burger King/Coca-Cola 1980), each 12.00
Set of 4 . . . . 50.00
Return of the Jedi Promotional Glasses (4 different: Sand barge fight scene,
Jabba's palace, Ewok village, & Luke/Darth fighting,
(Burger King/Coca-Cola 1983), each 10.00
Set of 4 . . . . 40.00
Plastic cups, Mass. only, each 12.50
Set of 4 . . . . 50.00

Plastic Coca-Cola Cups 1970s–80s
Star Wars numbered 20-cup set, each 10.00
Set of 20 . . . . 175.00
Star Wars numbered eight-cup set
Large, "7–11" or "Coke" each 5.00
Set of eight large cups 30.00
Small, "Coke" each 5.00
Set of eight small cups 25.00
Star Wars unnumbered 1979 eight-cup set, each 5.00
Set of eight "Coke" cups 30.00
Return of the Jedi 12-cup set, each 5.00
Set of 12 "7-11" cups, large or small 50.00

The Empire Strikes Back movie theater plastic cup
(Coca-Cola 1980) depending on size, each 7.00
Return of the Jedi movie theater plastic cup
(Coca-Cola 1983) depending on size, each 6.00
Star Wars Trilogy Special Edition movie theater
plastic cup, featuring picture of AT-AT (Pepsi-Cola 1997) 2.00

Star Wars Classic Series PEZ Dispensers (PEZ 1997)

CANDY

Topps Candy Boxes (1980–83)
The Empire Strikes Back figural head candy containers
    (Topps 1980) box with 18 containers 40.00
    Set, including Stormtrooper, Boba Fett,
    Chewbacca, C-3PO and Darth Vader 12.50
The Empire Strikes Back figural head candy containers
    (Topps 1981) box with 18 containers, New Yoda series 40.00
    Set of six, Tauntaun, Bossk, Yoda, 2-1B 12.50
Return of the Jedi figural head candy containers
    (Topps 1983) box with 18 containers 50.00
    Set of six, Admiral Ackbar, Darth Vader, Ewok,
    Jabba The Hutt, Sy Snootles and Wicket 15.00

PEZ Dispensers (PEZ 1997–2004)
    Classic Figures Series, nine different, each 3.00
    Episode I Series, several different, each 2.00
    Attack of the Clones Series, several different, each 2.00

Star Wars Escape From Death Star game and
The Empire Strikes Back Hoth Ice Planet Adventure Game
(Kenner 1979–80)

GAMES

Kenner made the first *Star Wars* games, as well as a variety of jigsaw puzzles, bop bags, vans and, of course, action figures. Many of these were advertised in its various mini-catalogs that came in the boxes for the vehicles. Parker Bros. started making the games in about 1983 and continues to do so today. Kenner, like Parker Bros., is now part of Hasbro.

Original Kenner Games (1977–82)

Adventures of R2-D2, board game (Kenner 1977) *Star Wars* logo $25.00
Destroy Death Star game (Kenner 1979) *Star Wars* logo 30.00
Escape From Death Star board game (Kenner 1979) *Star Wars* logo 25.00
Hoth Ice Planet Adventure Game (Kenner 1980)
　　The Empire Strikes Back logo. 25.00
Yoda, The Jedi Master board game (Kenner 1981)
　　The Empire Strikes Back logo. 25.00

Parker Bros. Games (1982–98)

Star Wars (Parker Bros. 1982) box pictures Luke in X-wing gear 30.00
Wicket the Ewok (Parker Bros. 1983) 25.00
The Ewoks Save the Trees! (Parker Bros. 1983). 25.00
Battle at Sarlacc's Pit (Parker Bros. 1983). 30.00
Return of the Jedi Card Game (Parker Bros. 1983) 10.00
Star Wars Death Star Assault Game (Parker Bros. #40390, 1995) 20.00
Star Wars Monopoly Classic Trilogy Edition (Parker Bros. #40809, 1997) . . . 35.00
Ewok Card Games (several different, Parker Bros. 1984) 15.00
Star Wars Escape the Death Star Action Figure Game
　　with Luke Skywalker and Darth Vader figures (Parker Bros. #40905) 15.00

Star Wars Monopoly Game (Hasbro 1997)

Other Games

Star Wars Card Trick (Nick Trost 1978) 10.00
Top Trumps New Spacecraft (Waddington) 15.00
Yoda, the Jedi Master magic answer fortune-telling toy (Kenner 1981) 50.00

Star Wars Episode I Games (1999)

Naboo Fighter Target Game (Hasbro-Milton Bradley #40971) 20.00
Electronic Lightsaber Duel Game with Qui-Gon Jinn and
    Darth Maul figures (Hasbro-Milton Bradley #40991) 20.00
Jar Jar Binks 3-D Adventure Game (Hasbro #40997) 15.00
Simon Electronic Space Battle Game (Hasbro #40983) 35.00
Star Wars Episode I Monopoly (Parker Bros. #41018) 40.00
Clash of the Lightsaber's Card Game (Milton Bradley #40993) 13.00
Battle For Naboo 3-D Action Game (Hasbro #40979) 20.00

PUZZLES

The earliest puzzles came in blue- or purple-bordered boxes. Later the boxes were printed with black borders. Several puzzles are advertised in Kenner's mini-catalogs. They are among the earliest Kenner products and are not titled. The box contained the movie logo, the puzzle's picture and the number of pieces.

140-Piece Puzzles 14" x 18" (add $5.00 for blue box)

C-3PO and R2-D2 . . . . $10.00
Chewbacca and Han Solo 10.00
Purchase of the Droids 10.00
Luke and Han in trash compactor 10.00
Tusken Raider 10.00
Stormtroopers and Landspeeder 10.00

Star Wars 1,000-Piece Jigsaw Puzzle (Kenner 1978)

500-Piece Puzzles 15" x 18" (add $5.00 for blue box)
Ben Kenobi and Darth Vader dueling 12.00
Cantina Band 12.00
Luke and Leia 12.00
Luke on Tatooine 12.00
Jawas selling Droids 12.00
Space battle 12.00
Victory celebration 12.00
X-wing Fighter in hangar 12.00

1,000-Piece Puzzles 21-1/2" x 27-1/2"
Crew aboard the *Millennium Falcon* 15.00
Movie art poster, Hildebrandt Bros. art 15.00

1,500-Piece Puzzles 27" x 33"
Millennium Falcon in space 20.00
Stormtrooper in corridor 20.00

CraftMaster Jigsaw Puzzles (1983) *Return of the Jedi*
Battle of Endor, 170 pieces 12.00
B-wings, 170 pieces 12.00
Ewok leaders, 170 pieces 12.00
Jabba's friends, 70 pieces 10.00
Jabba's throne room, 70 pieces 10.00
Death Star, 70 pieces 10.00
Wicket and Friends, three different, each 5.00

Frame Tray Puzzles
Darth Vader Frame Tray 5.00
Gamorrean Guard Frame Tray 5.00
Jedi Characters Frame Tray 5.00

R2-D2 Puzz 3-D (Hasbro 1999)

Wicket The Ewok Frame Tray Puzzles

Ewoks on Hang Gliders Frame Tray 5.00
Ewok Village Frame Tray. 5.00
Leia and Wicket Frame Tray. 5.00
R2-D2 and Wicket Frame Tray 5.00
Wicket Frame Tray 5.00

Match Blocks Puzzles

Ewoks Match Block Puzzle 10.00
Luke and Jabba Match Block Puzzle 10.00

Jigsaw Puzzles (1995–98)

Star Wars, A New Hope, 550 piece, 18" x 24"
   (Milton Bradley #4498-1, 1996) 12.50
Star Wars, The Empire Strikes Back, 550 piece,
   18" x 24" (Milton Bradley #4498-2, 1996) 12.50
Star Wars, Return of the Jedi, 550 piece, 18" x 36"
   (Milton Bradley #4498-3) 12.50
The Empire Strikes Back, 1,500 piece, 28 3/4" x 36"
   (Springbok/Hallmark PZL9028, #45548, 1997) 17.00
Star Wars: A New Hope 500-piece puzzles (RoseArt #97033, 1997) 12.00
Star Wars: The Empire Strikes Back 500-piece
   puzzles (RoseArt #97033, 1997) 12.00
Star Wars: Return of the Jedi 500-piece puzzles
   (RoseArt #97033, 1997) 12.00
Star Wars: A New Hope Poster Illustration Puzzle,
   1,000 piece (RoseArt #08062, 1997) 7.50

3-D Puzzles (Milton Bradley)

Millennium Falcon Puzz 3-D (#04678, 1995) 35.00
Star Wars Puzz 3-D Imperial Star Destroyer (#04617, 1996) 35.00
Darth Vader 3-D Sculpture, 9-1/2" (#04737, 1997) 35.00

Episode One R2-D2-shaped 100-piece puzzle (Hasbro 1999)

R2-D2, Episode I Puzz 3-D battery power (#41094, 1999) 25.00
Jar Jar Binks Episode I 3-D Sculpture, 9" tall (#41099, 1999) 30.00

Episode I Jigsaw Puzzles (Hasbro 1999)
100-piece puzzles, four different, each 4.00
Mos Espa Podrace Puzzle, Glow-in-the-Dark 200-piece, 12" x 16" (#49034) . . 5.00
Jedi vs. Sith, Glow-in-the-Dark, 200-piece 5.00
Movie Teaser Poster Puzzle, 300-piece (#41229) 7.50
Bravo Squadron Assault, 750-piece, two-sided 10.00
Podrace Challenge, 750-piece, two-sided 10.00
Gungan Sub Escape, 750-piece, two-sided 10.00

Episode I, 50-Piece Mini-Puzzles, four different, each 3.00

ROLE PLAY GAMES

West End Games began producing *Star Wars* role-playing games in 1987. This was in the middle of the dark ages, when no new *Star Wars* action figures, novels or comics were being produced. During this time, West End Games was the only company keeping the *Star Wars* saga alive with anything like new storylines.

Role-playing games have their own section in most book stores. As such, their books and boxed sets are generally available. Politicians no longer consider them Satanic rituals or Communist plots. They even have to compete with CCGs (Customizable Card Games) for the game fanatics' attention. Lastly, their fanatics accumulate game modules, rule books and other items in order to actually play the games (gasp!), not just collect them. New and revised editions of rule books are much more useful than original editions. Consequently,

Star Wars Live-Action Adventures (West End Games)

most of these items, even in near-mint condition, are worth little more than their original price!

Boxed Games (West End Games) 9" x 11-1/2" boxes

Star Warriors Role-Playing Board Game (40201, 1987) $35.00
    Reprint: (1992) 20.00
Assault on Hoth, two-person board game (40203, 1988) 35.00
    Reprint: (1992) 20.00
Battle for Endor, board game (40206, 1989) 30.00
    Reprint: (1992) 20.00
Escape From the Death Star, board game (40207, 1990) 30.00
    Reprint: (1992) 20.00

Basic Game and Source books (8-1/2" x 11" hardcovers)
    Most available at, or near . . . . cover price

Adventure Modules
    Many different, each 10.00

Softcovers 1991-98
    Most available at, or near . . . . cover price

Guide Books (8-1/2" x 11" Trade Paperbacks)
    Many available, from . . . . 12.00 to 15.00
    Otherwise . . . . cover price

Supplements
    Many available, each . . . . 12.00 to 15.00

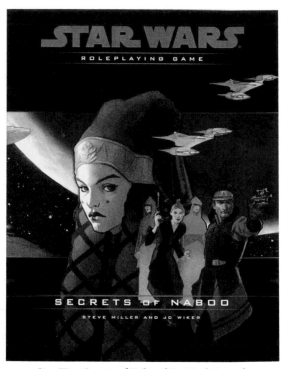

Star Wars Secrets of Naboo (West End Games)

GAMING MINIATURES
West End Games (1988–97)

In 1988, West End Games began producing 25 mm lead miniature figures to accompany its games. The figures are not heavily collected by nongamers. In 1993, West End Games started making three-figure blister packs. The company has made more than 50 different packs and several sets of ships to date.

Miniatures: 10-Figure packs (25 mm, in 4" x 8" boxes)

14 available, each . . . . $20.00 to 25.00

25 mm pewter, three-figure blister packs

Heroes 1 (40401, 1993) Luke, R2-D2 & C-3PO 9.00
Heroes 2 (40402, 1993) Han, Chewbacca and Leia 9.00
Imperial Troop 12-pack (50455, 1997) 20.00
Rebel Troop 12-pack (50456, 1997) 20.00
Many others available, from . . . . 5.00 to 6.00

Ships/Vehicles

Landspeeder (40501, 1994) 6.00
Imperial Speeder Bikes (40502, 1994) 6.00
Rebel Speeder Bikes (40503, 1994) 9.00
Storm Skimmer (40504, 1994) 9.00
AT-PT (40505, 1994) 9.00
Snowspeeder (40506, 1994) 9.00
Bantha with Rider (40507, 1995) 2-pack 9.00
Tauntaun Patrol (40508, 1996) 10.00

*Mos Eisley Cantina and The Rancor Pit
Adventure Set Miniature Packs (West End Games 1989–90)*

Miniatures Battles (Boxed)

Star Wars Miniatures Battle (40044, #264-7, 1995) 35.00

Star Wars Miniatures Rules, 2nd Edition (40090, 1994) 18.00

Star Wars Miniatures Battle, Starter Set (40210, 1995) 12 miniatures 35.00

2nd Edition (1996) 35.00

Vehicles Starter Set, with Rebel Snowspeeder,

two speeder bikes and book (40211, #285-X, 1996) 35.00

The Dark Stryder Campaign, books, cards, poster

(Games 40209, #254-X, 1995) 30.00

Darkstryder Deluxe Campaign Pack, boxed set (Games 40220, 1998) 39.00

Darkstryder: Endgame (40112, #287-6, 1996) 18.00

Lords of the Expanse, books, guides, maps (40215 #297-3, 1997) 30.00

NEW ROLE PLAY GAMES

Hasbro/Wizards of the Coast now produces *Star Wars* role play games. The Invasion of Theed game has been a popular collectible for nongamers because of the exclusive Wookiee action figure. Whether this results in more gaming remains to be seen.

New Role Playing Games (Hasbro/Wizards of the Coast)

Star Wars Invasion of Theed Adventure Game

Starter Box with exclusive Wookiee action figure on blister card

(2000) $30.00

Most source books and rule books . . . . cover price

Invasion of Theed Adventure Game (Hasbro)

CUSTOMIZABLE CARD GAMES

Customizable Card Games (CCGs) were one of the 1990's hottest items. There are many players around and lots of new product. Many of the playing cards are quite valuable. The primary reasons for this are scarcity and play value in the game. Scarcity is always a factor in value, but the other factor is usually some kind of intrinsic desirability or charisma in the item. As long as the game is played, scarce cards will be valuable. When the world moves on to the next game, they may not be quite so valuable. Then manufacturers will box up the unsold cards and sell the packs cheaply, as in the box pictured on the next page.

PREMIERE SET

This initial card set is based on characters and events from the first *Star Wars* movie. Decipher introduced it in December 1995 and was long awaited by Customizable Card Game enthusiasts. It was available in 60-card starter decks, with 324 cards in all, divided between light and dark sides. In this game, which is a struggle between the light and dark sides, each player wields a 60-card deck, either light or dark. The object is to reduce the opponents' original force of 60 to zero.

STAR WARS LIMITED

Complete Set: 324 cards $250.00

Collectible Card Game Packs, for sale cheap (Decipher 2002)

Star Wars Premiere Light Side Cards (Decipher 1995)

Starter Deck: 60 cards 9.00
Booster Pack: 15 cards 3.00
Common Card 0.15–0.40
Uncommon Card 1.00–2.50

STAR WARS UNLIMITED
Decipher Inc. (1996–98)

Complete Set: 324 cards $220.00
Starter Deck: 120 cards 10.00
Starter Deck: 90 cards 8.00
Booster Box 75.00
Booster Pack: 15 cards 3.00
Rare and uncommon cards are worth about 75 percent
of the same card in the "Limited Series."

Enhanced Premiere Expansion Set (Nov. 1998)
Set: Four unlimited expansion boosters and six new premium cards
Booster Box: 20 packs 120.00
Booster Pack: 11 cards 12.00

A NEW HOPE

Complete Set: 162 cards $100.00
Booster Pack: 15 cards 2.25

Revised *A New Hope* Expansion Set (1998)
Set: 162 cards 25.00
Booster Pack: 9 cards. 2.00

A New Hope Expansion Set pack (Decipher 1997)

STAR WARS SPECIAL EDITION
Decipher (Nov. 1998)

Complete Set: 324 cards $150.00
Starter Deck: 60 cards 11.00
Booster Pack: 9 cards (including one rare) 2.25

EXPANSION SETS
HOTH

Limited Editon Expansion Set (1996)

Complete Set: 162 cards $150.00
Booster Pack: 15 cards 2.25

Revised Hoth Expansion Set (1998)

Set: 162 cards 100.00
Booster Pack 1.75

DAGOBAH

This is the first set to be sold in packs of nine cards, rather than 15, and in boxes of 60 packs, rather than 36. Both ratios yield the same 540 cards per box.

Complete Set: 180 cards $30.00
Booster Pack: nine cards (including one rare) 2.25

Revised Dagobah Expansion Set (1999)

Booster Pack: nine cards. 2.00

Jawa Card from Cloud City Expansion Set (Decipher 1997)

CLOUD CITY

Limited Editon Expansion Set (1997)
Complete Set: 180 cards $175.00
Booster Pack: nine cards (including one rare) 2.50

Enhanced Cloud City (1999)
Set: 12 new cards
Booster Pack: 11 cards 2.00
Booster Pack: 39 cards 4.00

JABBA'S PALACE

Limited Editon Expansion Set (1998)
Complete Set: 180 cards $150.00
Booster Pack: nine cards (including one rare) 2.25

Enhanced Jabba's Palace (2000)
Set: 12 additional cards cards
Booster Pack: 11 cards 15.00

ENDOR

Limited Editon Expansion Set (1999)
Complete Set: 180 cards $150.00
Booster Pack: nine cards (including one rare) 2.25
Foil Set: 18 cards 175.00

DEATH STAR II

Limited Editon Expansion Set (2000)
Set: 182 cards 175.00
Booster Pack: 11 cards 2.25
Preconstructed Starter Deck: 60 cards 7.00

Death Star II Expansion Set card (Decipher 2000)

TATOOINE

Limited Editon Expansion Set (2001)
Complete Set: 120 cards 100.00
Booster Pack: 11 cards 3.00

CORUSCANT

Limited Editon Expansion Set (2001)
Complete Set: 180 cards 250.00
Booster Pack: 11 cards 3.00

THEED PALACE

Limited Editon Expansion Set (2001)
Complete Set: 120 cards 100.00
Booster Pack: 11 cards 3.00

ANTHOLOGY SETS

The first set includes two white-border 60-card starter decks, two black-border 15-card *A New Hope* expansion packs, two black-border 15-card Hoth expansion packs, a rules supplement, an 11-card Jedi Pack and six rare white-border cards previewing the *Star Wars Special Edition* expansion set. The second anthology set featured out-of-print Dagobah packs.

First Anthology (May 1997)
First Anthology Set in 15" x 13" x 6" box $20.00
First Anthology preview cards, Set of six 10.00

Reflections Pack (Decipher 2000)

Second Anthology (July 1998)
Second Anthology preview cards, Set of six 10.00
Second Anthology Set 35.00

Third Anthology (June 2000)
Third Anthology set, 174 cards 20.00
Third Anthology, six new cards 10.00

REFLECTIONS
Decipher (2000–2002)

Reflections I, Foil versions of 114 rares from previous sets (Jan. 2000)
Set: 114 foils. 400.00
Booster Pack: 18 cards 4.00

Reflections II, complete reissue set (Jan. 2001)
Set: 154 cards 350.00
Booster Pack: 18 cards 5.00
Darth Vader case card 20.00

Reflections III, complete reissue set (2002)
Booster Pack: 18 cards 5.00
Six Theed Palace previews 2.50

YOUNG JEDI
Decipher (1999–2001)

Young Jedi is based on Episode I. It is a separate game and is not compatible with other cards.

Young Jedi Menace of Darth Maul Pack (Decipher 1999)

THE MENACE OF DARTH MAUL

Set issued (1999)

Set: 140 cards $95.00
Foil Set: 18 cards 100.00
Booster Pack: 11 cards 2.75
Starter Deck: 60 cards 7.00
Enhanced Set: six new cards (Aug. 2000) 8.00
Enhanced Starter Deck 15.00

THE JEDI COUNCIL

Set issued (1999)

Set: 140 cards, plus 18 foils $85.00
Booster Pack: 11 cards 2.75
Starter Deck: 60 cards 7.00

BATTLE OF NABOO

Set issued (2000)

Set: 140 cards, plus 18 foils $85.00
Booster Pack: 11 cards 2.75
Starter Deck: 60 cards 15.00
Enhanced Set: 12 new cards 10.00

DUEL OF THE FATES

Set issued (2000)

Set: 60 cards 70.00
Booster Pack: 11 cards 2.75

BOONTA EVE PODRACE

Set Issued (2001)

Set: 60 cards 70.00
Booster Pack: 11 cards 2.75

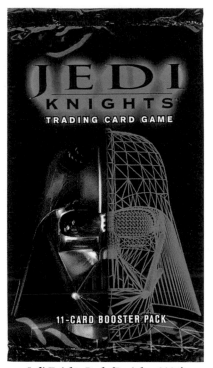

Jedi Knights Pack (Decipher 2001)

JEDI KNIGHTS
Trading Card Game
Decipher (2001)

Jedi Knights is a new trading card game featuring 3-D computer generated images. It is not compatible with other games.

Premier Set: 205 cards $125.00
Starter Box 95.00

SCUM AND VILLAINY

Set: 160 cards, plus 12 flip move cards. $125.00
Booster Pack: 11 cards 2.75
Booster Box - First Day: 36 packs 100.00
Promo cards, five different, each 2.00
Admiral Motti replacement card 10.00

MASTERS OF THE FORCE

Set: 140 cards $90.00
Booster Pack: 11 cards 2.00

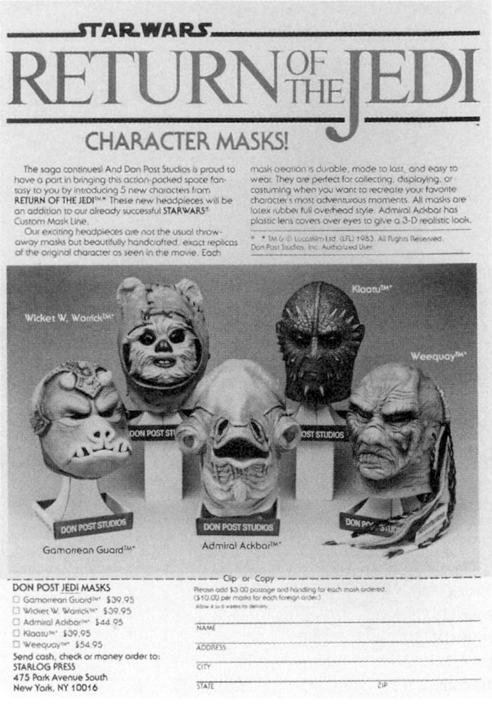

Advertisement for Masks (Don Post 1983)

MASKS, HELMETS AND COSTUMES

Mask and costume collecting extends far beyond *Star Wars*. Just about every famous or infamous person and fictional character has appeared on some type of Halloween costume over the years. Classic monsters, superheroes and science fiction characters have always been popular, and *Star Wars* provides a host of interesting mask and costume possibilities. Both masks and costumes appeared in 1977, months before there were any *Star Wars* action figures.

MASKS AND HELMETS

Don Post Studios has always made the high-end masks—those designed for adults and for display, rather than for a child's Halloween costume. Lately it has added hands and collector helmets to their line-up. It also produces deluxe replica helmets, which are listed in the *Statues* chapter.

MASKS

Masks (Don Post Studios 1977–98)

C-3PO latex mask (Don Post 1977) $100.00
    reissue (1978) 75.00
    reissue (late 1980s) 50.00
    reissue, 12" gold-tone heavy vinyl (1994) 45.00
Cantina Band Member rubber mask (Don Post 1980) 75.00
    reissue (1990s) 60.00
    reissue, 13" latex (1994) 45.00

Klaatu Mask (Don Post 1983)

Chewbacca rubber mask (1977) 250.00
    reissue (1978) 100.00
    reissue (1990) 75.00
    reissue, 11" multicolored hair (1990s) 50.00
Darth Vader Collector Helmet, plastic (1977) 200.00
    reissue (1978–82) 75.00
    reissue (1983) 50.00
    reissue (1994) 50.00
Stormtrooper Collector Helmet, plastic (1977) 90.00
    reissue (1978) 75.00
    reissue (late 1980s) 60.00
Tusken Raider rubber mask (late 1970s) 90.00
    reissue (late 1980s) 70.00
    reissue, 11" latex (1995) 35.00
Ugnaught mask (1980s) 75.00
Yoda rubber mask (1980s) 60.00
    reissue (1990s) 50.00
    reissue, 10" latex with hair (1994) 30.00
Admiral Ackbar rubber mask (1983) 75.00
    reissue (1990s) 60.00
    reissue, 13" latex (1994) 40.00
Gamorrean Guard rubber mask (1983) 75.00
    reissue, 11" (1995) 30.00
Klaatu rubber mask (1983) 75.00
    reissue (1990s) 60.00
    reissue, 12" latex with hood (1995) 35.00
Nien Nunb rubber mask, 11" (1996) 30.00
Weequay rubber mask (1983) 90.00
Wicket W. Warrick rubber mask (1983) 90.00
    reissue (1990) 75.00
    reissue, 10" hair and hood (1994) 40.00
Emperor Palpatine rubber mask 80.00
    reissue, 11" latex with cloth hood (1994) 45.00

Boba Fett Helmet (Don Post 1996)

Greedo, 11" latex (1997) 35.00
Prince Xizor, 12" latex and hair (1994) 35.00
Jawa 40.00

Episode I Masks (Don Post 1999)
Queen Amidala Theed, throne headdress (#82205) 50.00
Jar Jar Binks (#82206) 35.00
Darth Maul (#82208) 35.00
Sebulba (#82212) 40.00
Watto (#82213) 40.00
Ki-Adi-Mundi (#82214) 50.00
Even Piell (#82216) 50.00
Nute Gunray Deluxe (#82219) 75.00
Rune Haako Deluxe (#82220) 70.00
Jar Jar Binks Deluxe (#82302) 120.00
Sebulba Deluxe (#82303) 65.00

HANDS

Hands
Prince Xizor's Hands, 9" latex (1994) $30.00
Cantina Band Member's Hands, 10" latex (1994) 23.00
Greedo Hands (1994) 30.00
Admiral Ackbar Hands, 15" latex (1994) 30.00

HELMETS

Collector Helmets (Don Post 1996–98)
Boba Fett, 10" plastic (#82019, 1996) $60.00
Darth Vader, 13" plastic (#82001) 50.00
Emperor's Royal Guard, 18" (#82020, 1996) 85.00
Stormtrooper, 11" (#82002) 60.00
TIE Fighter, 11" (#82025, 1997) 75.00

Scout Trooper Helmet, 11" (#82024, 1997) 75.00
X-wing Fighter, 13" (#82026, 1997) 80.00

Episode I Collector Helmets (Don Post 1999)
Anakin's Podracer Helmet (#82200) 55.00
Naboo Starfighter Helmet (#82210) 40.00

Classic Action Helmets (Don Post 1997)
Darth Vader Classic Action Helmet, 15" (#82108) 180.00
Stormtrooper Classic Action Helmet, 13" (#82107) 160.00
TIE Fighter Classic Action Helmet, 15" (#82105) 150.00

Collectible Riddell Mini-Helmets, 45 percent scale, with display base
Darth Vader Mini-Helmet, three pieces 95.00
X-wing (Pilot) Mini-Helmet, moveable pieces 85.00
C-3PO Mini-Helmet, battery-powered eyes 80.00
Stormtrooper Mini-Helmet, with die-cast metal parts 85.00
Boba Fett Mini-Helmet, die-cast metal parts 85.00

COSTUMES

Ben Cooper was the most famous maker of collectible Halloween costumes in the 1970s and 1980s. All of the product the Cooper company made for kids. This means that old costumes in prime condition are hard to find.

Rubies currently makes Halloween costumes for the same market. Its current crop of classic *Star Wars* items may never receive much collector attention, since it must compete with Ben Cooper originals and with Don Post's higher quality.

Costume and Mask, boxed (Ben Cooper)
Darth Vader (#740, 1977–85)
   Star Wars $35.00
   The Empire Strikes Back 20.00
   Return of the Jedi 20.00
Luke Skywalker (#741, 1977–85)
   Star Wars 35.00
   The Empire Strikes Back 20.00
   Return of the Jedi 20.00
C-3PO (#742, 1977–85)
   Star Wars 35.00
   The Empire Strikes Back 20.00
   Return of the Jedi 20.00
Luke Skywalker, X-wing
   Star Wars 35.00
   The Empire Strikes Back 20.00
   Return of the Jedi 20.00
R2-D2 (#744,1977–85)
   Star Wars . . . . ; 35.00
   The Empire Strikes Back 20.00
   Return of the Jedi 20.00
Princess Leia (#745, 1977–85)
   Star Wars 35.00
   The Empire Strikes Back 20.00
   Return of the Jedi 20.00
Chewbacca (#746, 1977–85)
   Star Wars 35.00
   The Empire Strikes Back 20.00
   Return of the Jedi 20.00
Stormtrooper (#747, 1977–85)
   Star Wars 35.00
   The Empire Strikes Back 20.00
   Return of the Jedi 20.00

Darth Maul Mask (Rubies 1999)

Boba Fett (#748, 1977–85)
   Star Wars 35.00
   The Empire Strikes Back 20.00
   Return of the Jedi 20.00
Yoda Costume (#749, 1980–85)
   The Empire Strikes Back 30.00
   Return of the Jedi 30.00
Wicket, *Return of the Jedi* (#735, 1983–85) 25.00
Admiral Ackbar, *Return of the Jedi* (#736, 1983–85) 25.00
Gamorrean Guard, *Return of the Jedi* (#737, 1983–85). 25.00
Klaatu, *Return of the Jedi* (#738, 1983–85) 25.00

Costumes and Masks (1995–97)
Darth Vader polyester jumpsuit, bootcovers, cape
   and PVC mask (J.C. Penney 1997) 25.00
Chewbacca costume, includes jumpsuit, mask and sash (#15242, 1996) . . . 95.00
Chewbacca rubber mask (#C2867) 20.00
Darth Vader costume, includes jumpsuit,
   chestpiece, cape and mask (#15236, 1996) 75.00
Stormtrooper costume, includes jumpsuit,
   chestpiece and mask (#15243, 1996). 70.00
C-3PO Costume (#15237, 1997) 70.00
Yoda Costume (#15400, 1997) 50.00

Rubies Costumes
Darth Vader mask (#2865) 25.00
C-3PO hard mask (#2866) 30.00
Chewbacca mask (#2867) 25.00
Stormtrooper latex mask (#2868) 25.00
Yoda mask (#2869) 30.00
Darth Vader Costume Kit, cape, chest armor, mask
   and lightsaber (#17016, 1996), boxed 15.00

Darth Maul Deluxe Makeup Kit (Rubies 1999)

Darth Vader mask (#2993) 25.00
Chewbacca mask (#2994) 30.00
C-3PO mask (#2995) 25.00
Princess Leia wig 20.00

Episode I Costumes (Rubies 1999)
Darth Maul Costume Klt, with hooded cloak, belt,
    PVC mask & glo lightsaber (#17033) on card 18.00
Obi-Wan Kenobi Costume Kit (#17039) on card 18.00
Obi-Wan Kenobi Costume Kit (#17041) boxed 18.00
Qui-Gon Jinn Costume Kit (#17042) boxed 18.00

Episode I Adult Masks (Rubies 1999)
Darth Maul (#2509) 30.00
Jar Jar Binks and others, each 25.00

Episode I Costumes, sizes 3-4, 5-7, 8-10
Darth Maul 35.00
Anakin Skywalker. 35.00

Episode I Costumes, sizes 4-6, 8-10, 12-14
Jar Jar Binks, one-piece costume and mask 60.00
Anakin Skywalker, costume and helmet 60.00
Queen Amidala, costume and headpiece. 60.00
Qui-Gon Jinn, one-piece costume. 60.00
Obi-Wan Kenobi, one-piece costume 60.00

Makeup Kit
Queen Amidala Makeup Kit (Rubies #19661) 5.00
Darth Maul Deluxe Makeup Kit (Rubies #19658) 10.00
Jedi Hair Braid, 12". 5.00
Anakin Skywalker necklace 7.50

Death Star Escape, Micro Collection (Kenner 1982)

MICRO FIGURES AND VEHICLES

STAR WARS MICRO COLLECTION
Kenner (1982)

Kenner's Micro Collection consists of plastic playsets and plastic vehicles for use with 1-inch die-cast figures. The nine playsets could be bought individually or grouped into three "Worlds": Hoth Ice Planet, Bespin Cloud City and Death Star.

Action Playsets

Bespin Control Room (#69920) with two Luke figures
  and two Darth Vader figures (#256-001-004) $35.00
Bespin Freeze Chamber (#69930), includes eight
  figures (#460-009–017) 75.00
Bespin Gantry (#69910), includes two Luke figures
  and two Darth Vader figures (#258-001–004) 35.00
Bespin World: Bespin Control Room, Bespin Freeze
  Chamber and Bespin Gantry sets, includes
  16 figures in 12" x 8" x 7" box (#69940, 1982) 150.00
Death Star Compactor (#93300), includes eight figures (#517-014–021) 60.00
Death Star Escape (#69990), includes six figures (#583-018–023) 60.00
Death Star World: Death Star Compactor and Death Star Escape sets
  (#93310), includes 14 figures 125.00
Hoth Generator Attack (#93420) includes six figures (#668-001–006) 25.00
Hoth Ion Cannon (#69970) includes eight figures (#692-001–008) 35.00
Hoth Turret Defense (#69960) includes six figures (#463-010–015) 25.00
Hoth Wampa Cave (#69950) includes a Wampa
  and four figures (#269-001–004 & #269-009-A) 25.00
Hoth World: Hoth Generator Attack, Hoth Ion Cannon
  and Hoth Wampa Cave sets, includes 19 figures 125.00

Hoth Generator Attack Micro Collection (Kenner 1982)

Vehicles

Imperial TIE Fighter, includes pilot figure (#270-010) 75.00
X-wing Fighter (#69670) with pilot figure (#270-014) 65.00
Millennium Falcon (#70140), includes six figures
   (#733-001–006), Sears exclusive 400.00
Rebel Armored Snowspeeder, with working harpoon (#70150), includes
   pilot and harpooner figures (#261-015–016), J.C. Penney exclusive 200.00

Mail-In Figures

Build Your Armies, with three Rebel Soldiers (#088-001–003)
   and three Snowtroopers (#088-005–007) 25.00

MICRO MACHINES
Galoob (1993–98)

The Galoob *Star Wars* Micro Machines collection debuted in 1994 as part of its "Space" segment. At the time, *Star Wars* was the hottest collectible on the market, but very few new items had appeared. The first batch of Micro Machines contained a three-ship set for each of the three movies, and only list the first three series on the back (3-back). These were reissued when the next three items were released, and list all six series on the back (6-back).

"SPACE" VEHICLE SETS (1993–95)

First Batch (1993) on header card

   #1 *Star Wars*: *Millennium Falcon*; Imperial Star Destroyer;
   X-wing Starfighter (#65886) on 3-back card $15.00
   Reissue as *Star Wars: A New Hope*, 1994 copyright, generic logo, 6-back . . 7.00
   #2 *The Empire Strikes Back*: TIE Starfighter; Imperial AT-AT;
   Snowspeeder (#65887) on 3-back card. 15.00

Star Wars: A New Hope Space Vehicle Set #4 (Galoob 1993)

Reissue, 1994, generic logo, 6-back. 7.00

#3 Return of the Jedi: Imperial AT-ST (Chicken Walker);

Jabba's Desert Sail Barge; B-wing Starfighter (#65888) on 3-back card . . . 15.00

Reissue, 1994, generic logo, 6-back. 7.00

#4 Star Wars: A New Hope: Y-wing Starfighter; Jawa Sandcrawler;

Rebel Blockade Runner (#65897). 8.00

#5 The Empire Strikes Back: Imperial TIE Bomber, Boba Fett's *Slave I*;

Bespin Twin-Pod Cloud Car (#65898) 8.00

#6 Return of the Jedi: Speeder Bike with Rebel Pilot;

Imperial Shuttle *Tydirium*; A-wing Starfighter (#65899) 8.00

VEHICLE COLLECTOR SETS

Special Edition Vehicle Sets (1995) pewter finish, boxed

Star Wars: A New Hope, eight ships (#65851) $20.00

The Empire Strikes Back, eight ships (#65852) 20.00

Return of the Jedi, eight ships (#65853) 20.00

Gift Sets, boxed

Star Wars Collector's Gift Set, 14 vehicles, 12 figures, bronze finish,

with special Death Star Battle Station 2 (#64624, 1995) 30.00

Master Collector's Edition, 19 *Star Wars* vehicles, includes exclusive Super Star

Destroyer *Executor* (#64061) 20.00

VEHICLE SETS (1996–98)

First Batch (1996) on header card

I TIE Interceptor, Imperial Star Destroyer,

Rebel Blockade Runner (#66111). $7.00

II Landspeeder, *Millennium Falcon*, Jawa Sandcrawler (#66112) 7.00

III Darth Vader's TIE Fighter, Y-wing Starfighter,

X-wing Starfighter (#66113). 7.00

IV Imperial Probot, Imperial AT-AT, Snowspeeder (#66114) 7.00

V Rebel Transport, TIE Bomber, Imperial AT-ST (#66115) 7.00

Vehicle Set II (Galoob 1996)

VI Escort Frigate, Boba Fett's *Slave I*, Bespin Twin-Pod Cloud Car (#66116) 7.00
VII Mon Calamari Star Cruiser, Jabba's Desert Sail Barge,
Speeder Bike with Rebel Pilot (#66117) 7.00
VIII Speeder Bike with Imperial Pilot, Imperial Shuttle *Tydirium*,
TIE Starfighter (#66118) 7.00
IX Super Star Destroyer *Executor*, B-wing Starfighter,
A-wing Starfighter (#66119) 7.00
X Incom T-16 Skyhopper, Lars Family Landspeeder,
Death Star II (#66137) 7.00
XI Bespin Cloud City, Mon Calamari Rebel Cruiser,
Escape Pod (#66138) 7.00

Second Batch (1997)
XII A-wing Starfighter (Battle Damaged)
TIE Starfighter (Battle Damaged)
Y-wing Starfighter (Battle Damaged) (#65154) 7.00
XIII Red Squadron X-wing (Battle Damaged)
Green Squadron X-wing (Battle Damaged)
Blue Squadron X-wing (Battle Damaged) (#65155) 7.00

Third Batch (1998)
XIV Imperial Landing Craft, S-Swoop, Death Star (#65123) 7.00
XV Outrider, Tibanna Gas Refinery, V-35 Landspeeder (#65124) 7.00

SHADOWS OF THE EMPIRE VEHICLES

First Batch, with exclusive Micro Comic
I Stinger, IG-2000, Guri, Asp and Darth Vader (#66194) $6.00
II Virago, Swoop with Rider, Prince Xizor and
Emperor Palpatine (#66195) 6.00
III Outrider, Hound's Tooth, Dash Rendar,
LE-BO2 D9 and Luke Skywalker (#66196) 6.00

Shadows of the Empire Vehicles II (Galoob 1998)

EXCLUSIVE SETS

Star Wars Fan Club Star Destroyer vehicle, boxed $25.00

Star Wars Fan Club *Millennium Falcon* vehicle, boxed 30.00

Star Wars Toy Fair Three-pack, *Millennium Falcon*,
    Slave I, and Death Star, window box 25.00

Rebel Forces Gift Set (#65836, 1994) Target. 12.00

Imperial Forces Gift Set (#65837, 1994) Target. 12.00

Galaxy Battle Collector's Set, three ships and three
    figures each from the Rebel Alliance and the
    evil Empire (#64602, 1994) Kmart 9.00

11 Piece Collector's Gift Set, seven from the Rebel
    Alliance and four from the evil Empire (#65847, 1994) Kay-Bee 16.00

Master Collector's Edition 19 vehicle set (#64601, 1994) Toys "R" Us 30.00

Star Wars Special Rebel Forces Gift Set, Second Edition
    (#65856, 1995) Target 12.00

Star Wars Special Imperial Forces Gift Set, Second Edition
    (#65857, 1995) Target 12.00

Galaxy Battle Collector's Set, Second Edition (#64598,1995) 18.00

Collector's Gift Set, 27 piece, bronze color (#64624, 1995) 40.00

Classic Series I, X-wing Starfighter and Boba Fett's
    Slave I (#67085, 1996) J.C. Penney 15.00

Classic Series II, Imperial Shuttle and Imperial Emblem
    (#67806, 1996) FAO Schwarz. 15.00

Classic Series III, Darth Vader's TIE Fighter and
    Millennium Falcon (#67088, 1996) 15.00

The Balance Of Power, X-wing Fighter and TIE Fighter
    (#66091, 1996) 15.00

Rebel Forces vs. Imperial Forces Gift Set, eight pieces
    (#68042, 1996) Musicland. 15.00

Master Collector's 40 vehicle set (#68048, 1997) Toys "R" Us 40.00

Rebel Forces Gift Set Second Edition (Galoob 1995)

FIGURES
Galoob (1996–98)

The first *Star Wars* Micro Machine figure sets appeared in 1996, at the same time that the "Action Fleet" vehicles appeared. Each of those vehicles included a couple of small figures, and the figure sets fleshed out the line. The first ones came in packaging similar to the small vehicles listed previously, and later they were reissued on header cards that featured stripes.

First Batch (1996) nine figures, on header cards

I Imperial Stormtroopers (#66081)	$7.00
II Ewoks (#66082)	7.00
III Rebel Pilots (#66083)	7.00
IV Imperial Pilots (#66084)	7.00
V Jawas (#66096)	7.00
VI Imperial Officers (#66097)	7.00
VII Echo Base Troops (#66098)	7.00

Second Batch (1997)

VIII Tusken Raiders (#66109)	7.00
IX Rebel Fleet Troops (#66108)	7.00
X Imperial Naval Troopers (#66099)	7.00
XI Classic Characters (#66158)	10.00
Reissues, on stripe header card, each	7.00

Third Batch (1998)

XI Classic Characters, new poses	10.00
XII Endor Rebel Strike Team (#67112)	10.00
XIII Imperial Scout Troopers	10.00
XIV Bounty Hunters (#66114)	10.00

Rebel Pilots Figures (Galoob 1996)

Droids Collection (1997)

Droids, 16 articulated droids (#66090) 17.00

EPIC COLLECTIONS (1997)

Figures in a box (box looks like a paperback book)

Heir to the Empire (#66281) $3.50

Jedi Search (#66282) 3.50

The Truce at Bakura (#66283) 3.50

MINI-ACTION TRANSFORMING PLAYSETS

These are small heads on a header card. Each head opens to reveal a micro figure inside the head. They weren't much of a playset and only came with one figure, but there were three in each set.

Mini-Action Transforming Playsets (1997)
 Four different sets of three, each set $6.00

Mini-Action Boxed Set
Mini-Action 7-head set, includes Gamorrean Guard, Nien Nunb,
 Darth Vader, Jawa, Greedo, Admiral Ackbar and Princess Leia
 (#68038, 1996) with *Star Wars* Trilogy Widevision promo #4 . . . . 15.00

PLAYSETS
Galoob (1994–98)

 The two large playsets are elaborate and excellent collectibles. The small playsets are smaller than the Action Fleet playsets, some of which have similar names. Most of the reissues were available at very reasonable prices during the big *Star Wars* discount sale.

LARGE PLAYSETS

Millennium Falcon playset, opens into *Star Wars*
 command center (#65878, 1995) "Space" on package $38.00
 In early box, with 24 kt. promotion offer 45.00
Death Star, transforms into planet Tatooine and Mos Eisley spaceport
 (#75118, 1997) "Double Takes," stripes package 40.00

Heir to the Empire Epic Collection (Galoob 1997)

SMALL PLAYSETS

First Batch (1994) boxed

The Death Star playset (#65871) $11.00
Ice Planet Hoth playset (#65872) 11.00
Endor playset (#65873) 11.00
Reissues, in stripe design packaging 8.00

Second Batch

Planet Tatooine playset (#65858) 11.00
Planet Dagobah playset (#65859) 11.00
Reissues, in stripe design packaging 9.00

Third Batch (1998)

Cloud City playset (#65995) 11.00
Rebel Transport playset (#65996) 11.00

TRANSFORMING ACTION PLAYSETS

These are helmet- or head-shaped toys that transform into playsets. The reissues were available at very reasonable prices during the big *Star Wars* discount sale and make a nice-looking collection in a head-hunter sort of way. Later a few ships were added. The same concept was used for some Episode I heads.

First Batch, Helmet/Head shaped, boxed

C-3PO transforms into Mos Eisley Cantina (#65811) $15.00
Darth Vader transforms into Bespin Imperial outpost (#65812) 15.00
R2-D2 transforms into Jabba's Desert Palace (#65813) 15.00
Stormtrooper transforms into Death Star battle station (#65814) 15.00
Chewbacca transforms into Endor's forest moon (#65815) 15.00

Rebel Transport and Cloud City Playsets (Galoob 1998)

Boba Fett transforms into Bespin's Cloud City (#65816) 15.00
Luke Skywalker transforms into ice planet Hoth (#65817) 15.00
Royal Guard transforms into the Death Star II Battle Station (#65695) 15.00
TIE Fighter Pilot transforms into Imperial Academy (#65694) 15.00
Reissues, in stripe-design packaging, each 12.00

Second Batch (1998)
Yoda transforms into swamp planet Dagobah (#68063) 15.00
Jabba the Hutt transforms into Mos Eisley Spaceport (#68064) 15.00
Slave I transforms into planet Tatooine (#67095) 15.00
Star Destroyer transforms into Space Fortress (#67094) 15.00

Episode I Inside Action Sets (1999)
Battle Droid transforms into Trade Federation Droid Control Ship
    (#66552) 13.00
Jar Jar Binks transforms into Naboo (#66551) 13.00
Gungan Sub transforms into OTOH Gunga (#69554) 13.00

ADVENTURE GEAR/PLAYSET

Adventure Gear consists of weapons or gear that open into playsets and are similar to the Transforming Action playsets listed above, but don't look as nice on display. Adventure Gear Playsets are available quite cheaply at red-tag sales.

First Batch, boxed (1996)
Vader's Lightsaber opens into Death Star Trench,
    includes vehicle and three figures (#68031) 12.00
Luke's Binoculars open into Yavin Rebel Base,
    includes vehicle and three figures (#68031) 12.00
Reissues, in stripe-design packaging, each 10.00

Royal Guard Transforming Action Playset (Galoob 1998)

MICROMACHINE X-RAY FLEET
Galoob (1996–97)

X-Ray Fleet vehicles are the same size as Galoob's die-cast vehicles and considerably bigger than the regular Micro Machine size, but still a lot smaller than its Action Fleet ships. The outer hull of each X-Ray Fleet ship is clear plastic, allowing collectors to view the inner portions of each vehicle. This only really works if the inside portions correspond to the known insides of the ship, as seen in the movies. Some of the X-Ray Fleet correspond fairly well to the movie version, notably the Imperial AT-AT and AT-ST, but most are not so successful.

The *Star Wars* Trilogy Gift Set includes only one X-Ray Fleet ship, the Shuttle *Tydirium*. The other nine ships are the same size as the X-Ray Fleet (and Die-Cast ships) but are painted.

First Batch (1996) "Space" packaging
I Darth Vader's TIE Fighter and A-wing Starfighter (#67071) $7.00
II X-wing Starfighter and Imperial AT-AT (#67072) 7.00
III *Millennium Falcon* and Jawa Sandcrawler (#67073) 7.00
IV Boba Fett's *Slave I* and Y-wing Starfighter (#67074) 7.00

Second Batch (1997)
V TIE Bomber and B-wing Starfighter 20.00
VI TIE Fighter and Landspeeder. 20.00
VII Imperial AT-ST and Snowspeeder 20.00

Large Boxed Set
Star Wars Trilogy Gift Set, 10 larger, X-Ray vehicle-sized
   ships with display stands (#67079, 1996) 35.00

X-Ray Fleet Collection III (Galoob 1996)

ACTION FLEET VEHICLES
Galoob (1996–98)

Action Fleet vehicles are larger than Galoob's X-Ray Fleet and die-cast vehicles, but are smaller than Kenner's action figure vehicles. It has proven to be a popular size with both kids and collectors.

The first 2,500 pieces, from the production run of each of the first batch vehicles, were numbered with a special blue collector's sticker. The Rebel Snowspeeder was short packed in the assortment.

First Batch (Spring 1996)
Luke's X-wing Starfighter (#67031) $12.00
   With numbered collector sticker 20.00
Darth Vader's TIE Fighter (#67032) 12.00
   With numbered collector sticker 20.00
Imperial AT-AT (#67033) 12.00
   With numbered collector sticker 20.00
A-wing Starfighter (#67034) 12.00
   With numbered collector sticker 20.00
Imperial Shuttle *Tydirium* (#67035) 12.00
   With numbered collector sticker 20.00
Rebel Snowspeeder (#67036) 15.00
   With numbered collector sticker 20.00

Second Batch (1996)
Jawa Sandcrawler (#67039) 10.00
Y-wing Starfighter (#67040) 10.00
Slave I (#67041) 10.00
TIE Interceptor (#67058) 10.00

Third Batch (1997)
Rancor (#66989) 10.00
Virago (#66990) 10.00
X-wing Starfighter (#66991) 10.00
Y-wing Starfighter (#66992) 10.00
A-wing Starfighter (#66993) 10.00
TIE Fighter (#66995) 10.00
TIE Bomber (#67059) 10.00

*Imperial Shuttle Tydirium Action Fleet Vehicle
(Galoob 1996)*

Fourth Batch (Fall 1997)

Bespin Twin-Pod Cloud Car (#66996) 10.00
B-wing Starfighter (#66994) 10.00
X-wing Starfighter (#67023) 10.00
Y-wing Starfighter (#67024). 10.00
Rebel Snowspeeder (#67025) 10.00

Fifth Batch (Spring 1998)
Four different, each 10.00

Sixth Batch (Fall 1998)
Three different, each 10.00

Two-Pack, Kay-Bee exclusive (1995)
Luke's Landspeeder and Imperial AT-ST (#67077) 20.00

SERIES ALPHA (1997–99)
Concept Design Prototype and Final Design
Seven different, each 20.00

Episode I Series Alpha
Sith Infiltrator 20.00
Royal Starship 18.00
Naboo Fighter 15.00

CLASSIC DUELS (1997–98)
Toys "R" Us special (1997)
Millennium Falcon vs. TIE Interceptor (#68302) $20.00
X-wing Starfighter vs. TIE Fighter (#68301) 20.00

FLIGHT CONTROLLERS (1997–98)
These hold the included fighter, or one of the other flying vehicles in the Action Fleet line, and have lights, sounds and spring-loaded missile. Basically it's a handle that lets you mount the ship and use it in simulated battle.

First Batch (1997)
Rebel Flight Controller (#73417) $20.00
Imperial Flight Controller (#73418) 20.00

TIE Interceptor Action Fleet Vehicle (Galoob 1996)

Second Batch (1998)
Rebel Flight Controller with Y-wing Starfighter 20.00
Imperial Flight Controller with TIE Interceptor 20.00

BATTLE PACKS (1996–98)
18 different, each 8.00

PLAYSETS

These playsets are much larger than the Micro Machine playsets, some of which have the same name. They fold open for play and fold closed into a case (with attractive side graphics) for storage.

Playsets in box with slant side, Ralph McQuarrie art
Ice Planet Hoth (#67091) $30.00
The Death Star (#69092) 30.00
Yavin Rebel Base (#69093) 30.00

STAR WARS EPISODE I
MICRO MACHINES
Galoob (1999–2001)

Episode I Vehicle/Figure Collections (1999)
Ten different collections, each $5.00

Episode I Platform Action Sets (1999)
Six different, each 10.00
Deluxe Royal Starship Repair (#66561) 20.00
Deluxe Theed Palace Assault (#66562) 20.00

ACTION FLEET TURBO PODRACERS

Episode I Turbo Podracers (1999)
Gasgano's Podracer (#68148) $13.00
Ody Mandrell's Podracer (#68149) 13.00

ACTION FLEET PLAYSETS

Episode I Action Fleet Playsets (1999)
Gian Speeder and Theed Palace, Sneak Preview $20.00

AT-AT Series Alpha Figure (Galoob 1998)

Warman's *Star Wars* Field Guide

Podracer Hangar Bay (#68156) 15.00
Mos Espa Market (#68157) 15.00
Trade Federation MTT/Naboo Battlefield (#66566) 20.00
Naboo Hangar–Final Conflict (#68177) 15.00

Episode I Action Fleet Mini Scenes (1999)
Five different, each 5.00

ACTION FLEET VEHICLES

Episode I Action Fleet Vehicles (1999)
Naboo Starfighter (#65131) $10.00
Trade Federation MTT (#68132) 12.00
Sebulba's Podracer (#68133) 10.00
Republic Cruiser (#68134) 12.00
Trade Federation Droid Fighter (#68135) 10.00
Gungan Sub (#68136) 10.00
Flash Speeder (#68137) 12.00
Trade Federation Landing Ship (#68138) 15.00
Anakin's Podracer (#68139). 10.00
Mars Guo's Podracer (#68140) 15.00

Episode I, Electronic Action Fleet
Electronic Fambaa (#68161) 20.00
Electronic Trade Federation Tank (#68162). 20.00

PODRACING

Episode I Podracing (Galoob 1999)
Electronic Boonta Eve Challenge Track Set (#66570) $40.00
Podracer Launchers (#66547) 12.00

Anakin's Podracer Action Fleet (Galoob 1999)

MICRO MACHINES

Trilogy Series (Hasbro 2002)

Solar Sailer (#46848) 11.00
AT-TE 11.00
Naboo N-1 Starfighter 11.00

Electronic Fambaa and Trade Federation Tank (2000)

The Empire Strikes Back Lunch Box (King Seeley 1980)

MISCELLANEOUS

There are many other types of *Star Wars* collectibles. A few other items that don't fit in other sections of this book are covered in this chapter.

ELECTRONIC TOYS

Radio-Controlled
Radio Controlled R2-D2, 8", *Star Wars* logo (Kenner #38430, 1979) $175.00
    Loose 75.00

LUNCH BOXES

Classic Lunch Boxes (King Seeley-Thermos)
Star Wars, space battle on front, Tatooine scene
    on reverse, Droids thermos (1977), metal box 60.00
    Thermos 20.00
Star Wars, red with Darth and Droids pictured on front,
    Droids thermos (1978), plastic box 40.00
    Thermos 15.00
The Empire Strikes Back, *Millennium Falcon* on front,
    Luke, Yoda and R2-D2 on back, Yoda thermos (1980), metal box 45.00
    Thermos 15.00
The Empire Strikes Back, Dagobah scene on lid,
    Hoth battle on back, Yoda thermos (1980), metal box 45.00
    Thermos 15.00
The Empire Strikes Back, red, Chewbacca, Han, Leia and Luke
    on lid, Yoda thermos (King Seeley-Thermos 1980), plastic box 30.00
    Thermos 15.00

Millennium Falcon Ornament (Hallmark 1996)

The Empire Strikes Back, photo cover with logo
    and inset pictures, Droid sand logo on thermos (1980), plastic box 30.00
    Thermos 15.00
Return of the Jedi, Luke in Jabba's Palace on lid
    and space scene on back, Ewok thermos (1983), metal box 40.00
    Thermos 15.00
Return of the Jedi, red with Wicket and R2-D2 on front,
    Ewok thermos (1983), plastic box 25.00
    Thermos 10.00

ORNAMENTS

Christmas Ornaments (Hallmark 1996–2004)
Millennium Falcon ornament (#07474, 1996) $60.00
Darth Vader hanging ornament (#07531, 1997) 30.00
Yoda hanging ornament (#06355, 1997) 35.00
C-3PO and R2-D2 set of ornaments (#04265, 1997) 25.00
Luke Skywalker hanging ornament (#05484, 1997) 30.00
Star Wars Vehicles, three miniatures (#04024, 1997) 45.00
X-wing Starfighter, light-up (#07596 1998) 35.00
Other ornaments, each. . . . . original price

STAR WARS STUFF

Star Wars items were produced in dozens of categories from soap
to stamps, school supplies to silverware, and clothing to toothbrushes.
Not many people collect these things seriously, but dealers still sell
them at shows. Often they are displayed in a box labelled "Star Wars
Stuff" and priced at $3 to $5 each—a fair price for everything except
the odd item with some intrinsic worth.

R2-D2 Model Kit (MPC 1977)

MODEL KITS

MPC was Kenner's model kit company. Early kits have MPC's logo. When the Ertl company bought MPC in about 1990, the logo was changed to MPC/Ertl. Still later, the logo was changed to AMT/Ertl, which is what it remains today. The original models have been reissued, and this availability has reduced the collectors' price of the originals.

Star Wars Characters (MPC 1977–79)

The Authentic C-3PO (See-Threepio) $25.00
    Reissue, 6" x 10" box 20.00
C-3PO (MPC #1935, 1984) *Return of the Jedi* box 15.00
The Authentic R2-D2 (Artoo-Detoo) 25.00
    Reissue, 6" x 10" box 20.00
R2-D2 (MPC #1934, 1984) *Return of the Jedi* box 15.00
Darth Vader model kit, 11 1/2" tall 45.00
Darth Vader Bust Action model kit, snap-together 60.00

Space Ships (MPC 1977–79)

The Authentic Darth Vader TIE Fighter 35.00
    Reissue, 14" x 8" *Star Wars* box 25.00
The Authentic Luke Skywalker X-wing Fighter 35.00
    Reissue, 14" x 8" *Star Wars* box 25.00
Han Solo's *Millennium Falcon* with lights 120.00

The Empire Strikes Back Ships (MPC 1980–82)

Star Destroyer, 15" long 45.00
Luke Skywalker's Snowspeeder 40.00
AT-AT 40.00
Millennium Falcon, no lights 40.00

X-wing Fighter Snap Kit (MPC 1983) and
Star Destroyer (MPC 1983)

X-wing Fighter 25.00
Boba Fett's *Slave I* 35.00

Return of the Jedi Ships (MPC 1983)
AT-AT model kit 25.00
Shuttle *Tydirium* model kit 30.00
Speeder Bike Vehicle model kit 22.00

Snap Kits (MPC 1983) *Return of the Jedi box*
AT-ST, scout walker 30.00
A-wing Fighter 15.00
B-wing Fighter 15.00
TIE Interceptor 20.00
X-wing Fighter 15.00
Y-wing Fighter 15.00

Dioramas (MPC 1981–83)
Rebel Base Diorama Snap, *The Empire Strikes Back* 45.00
Battle on Ice Planet Hoth, *The Empire Strikes Back* 35.00
Encounter with Yoda on Dagobah, *The Empire Strikes Back* box 35.00
Jabba the Hutt Throne Room, *Return of the Jedi* box 40.00

Mirr-A-Kits (MPC 1984) *Return of the Jedi*
AT-ST 15.00
Shuttle *Tydirium* 15.00
Speeder Bike 15.00
TIE Interceptor 15.00
Y-wing 15.00
X-wing 15.00

Structors Action Walking models, wind-up motor
AT-AT model kit (MPC/Structors #1902, 1984) 30.00
    AT-AT (AMT/Ertl #6036, 1998) 10.00

Encounter with Yoda on Dagobah (AMT/Ertl 1996) and
X-wing Fighter Plus Pack (AMT/Ertl 1990)

AT-ST model kit, 4-1/2" high (MPC/Structors #1903, 1984)
  Return of the Jedi box 25.00
  Scout AT-ST (AMT/Ertl #6029, 1998) 10.00
C-3PO model kit (MPC/Structors #1901, 1984) 25.00

Vans: Snap together, with glow-in-the-dark decals
Artoo-Detoo Van model kit (MPC #3211, 1979) 30.00
Darth Vader Van model kit (MPC #3209, 1979) 35.00
Luke Skywalker Van model kit (MPC #3210, 1979) 35.00

MPC/ERTL and AMT/ERTL (1990–98)
Figures
Darth Vader, 12" tall, glow-in-the-dark lightsaber (#8154, 1992),
  14" x 8-1/2" *Star Wars* box 15.00
  Reissue: AMT/Ertl 12.50
Darth Vader Model Kit (AMT/Ertl #8784, 1996) 25.00
Luke Skywalker Model Kit (AMT/Ertl #8783, 1995) 25.00
Han Solo Model Kit (AMT/Ertl #8785, 1995) 25.00
Prince Xizor Model Kit (AMT/Ertl #8256, 1996),
  Shadows of the Empire box 25.00
Emperor Palpatine (AMT/Ertl #8258, 1996),
  Shadows of the Empire box 25.00

Action Scenes
Rebel Base Action Scene (MPC/Ertl and AMT/Ertl #8735, 1993),
  The Empire Strikes Back box 15.00
Jabba's Throne Room Model (AMT/Ertl #8262, 1996) 13.50
Encounter with Yoda Model (AMT/Ertl #8263, 1996) 13.50
Battle on Hoth Action Scene, with 11-1/2" x 17-1/2"
  vacu-formed base (AMT/Ertl #8743, 1995) 13.50

B-wing Fighter, Limited Edition (AMT/Ertl 1995)

Flight Displays

TIE Fighter Flight Display (AMT/Ertl #8275, 1996) 20.00
Speeder Bike Flight Display (AMT/Ertl #6352, 1997) 20.00
X-wing Flight Display (AMT/Ertl #8788, 1995) 19.50

Limited Editions

X-wing Limited Edition (AMT/Ertl #8769, 1995) 31.50
TIE Interceptor Limited Edition (AMT/Ertl #8770, 1995) 31.50
B-wing Limited Edition Model (AMT/Ertl #8780, 1995) 25.00

Ships

Shuttle *Tydirium* (MPC/Ertl and AMT/Ertl #8733, 1992)
    18-3/4" x 12-3/4" *Return of the Jedi* box 15.00
Speeder Bike (MPC/Ertl and AMT/Ertl #8928, 1990)
    14" x 8" *Return of the Jedi* box 10.00
Luke Skywalker's Snowspeeder (MPC/Ertl and AMT/Ertl #8914, 1990)
    10" x 7" *The Empire Strikes Back* box 15.00
Star Destroyer (MPC/Ertl and AMT/Ertl #8915, 1990)
    20" x 10" *The Empire Strikes Back* box 15.00
Darth Vader TIE Fighter (MPC/Ertl and AMT/Ertl #8916, 1990)
    4" x 10-1/4" *Star Wars* box 12.00
Millennium Falcon (MPC/Ertl and AMT/Ertl #8917, 1990)
    19-3/4" x 14-1/2" *Return of the Jedi* box 20.00
X-wing Fighter (MPC/Ertl and AMT/Ertl #8918, 1990)
    14" x 8" *Return of the Jedi* box 12.00
AT-AT (MPC/Ertl and AMT/Ertl #8919, 1990)
    14" x 8" *Return of the Jedi* box 15.00
Star Wars-Shadows of the Empire-Virago model
    (AMT/Ertl #8377, 1997) 15.00
TIE Fighter Plus Pack, with glue, paint and paintbrush
    (AMT/Ertl #8432, 1997) 16.00
Slave 1 (AMT/Ertl #8768, 1995) 13.50
Fiber Optic Star Destroyer Model (AMT/Ertl #8782, 1995)
    The Empire Strikes Back box 50.00
Millennium Falcon cutaway model (AMT/Ertl #8789, 1996). 27.00

Snap Kits

AT-ST, snap together (AMT/Ertl #8734, 1992)
    10" x 7" *Return of the Jedi* box 9.00
TIE Interceptor, snap together (AMT/Ertl #8931, 1990)
    10" x 7" *Return of the Jedi* box 10.00

Princess Leia Organa Vinyl Model (Polydata 1995)

X-wing Fighter, snap together (AMT/Ertl #8932, 1990)
   10" x 7" *Return of the Jedi* box 11.00
A-wing Fighter, snap together (AMT/Ertl #8933, 1990)
   10" x 7" *Return of the Jedi* box 10.00
Y-wing Fighter, snap together (AMT/Ertl #8934, 1990)
   Return of the Jedi box 10.00
Return of the Jedi 3-piece Gift Set: B-wing Fighter, X-wing Fighter,
   TIE Interceptor, (MPC/Ertl and AMT/Ertl #8912, 1992) 14-1/4" x 10" box . . 20.00

VINYL MODEL KITS

Vinyl Model Kits, (Polydata) 1/6 Scale
Luke Skywalker pre-painted model (1995) $35.00
Obi-Wan Kenobi pre-painted model (1995) 35.00
Tusken Raider pre-painted model (1995) 35.00
Princess Leia pre-painted model (1995) 35.00
Chewbacca pre-painted model (1996) 35.00
Lando Calrissian pre-painted model (1997) 35.00
Boba Fett pre-painted vinyl model kit (1997) 35.00

Vinyl Model Kits, (Screamin') 1/4 Scale
Luke Skywalker Vinyl Model (1996) 65.00
Darth Vader Vinyl Model (1992) 65.00
Yoda Vinyl Model (1992) 60.00
Han Solo Vinyl Model (1993) 65.00
C-3PO Vinyl Model (1993) 65.00
Stormtrooper (1993) 65.00
Chewbacca Vinyl Model (1994) 68.00
Boba Fett Vinyl Model (1994) 70.00
Tusken Raider Vinyl Model (1995) 68.00

Tusken Raider Vinyl Model (Screamin' 1995)

STEEL MODELS

Millennium Falcon - Star Wars Steel Tec Kit (Remco #7140, 1995) $25.00
X-wing Fighter *Star Wars* Steel Tec Kit (Remco #7141, 1995) 25.00

FLYING MODELS

Original *Star Wars* Flying Rocket Model Kits
R2-D2 (Estes #1298, 1979) $25.00
T.I.E.(Estes #1299, 1979) 30.00
X-wing Fighter (Estes #1302, 1979) 30.00
Proton Torpedo, with Launching Kit, Darth Vader
  picture box (Estes #1420, 1979). 50.00
X-wing Fighter with Launching Kit (Estes 1979) 50.00

LEGO SYSTEM
Lego (1999–2004)

Lego has made a lot of *Star Wars* models in the last few years.
Unlike the action figures, they have not been available at deep
discounts.

Episode I Model (1999–2001)
Lightsaber Duel, 50 pieces (#07101) $8.00
Droid Fighter, 62 pieces (#07111) 8.00
Gungan Patrol, 77 pieces (#07115) 10.00
Naboo Swamp, 81 pieces (#07121) 12.00
Flash Speeder, 105 pieces (#07124). 10.00
Battle Droid Carrier, 133 pieces (#07126) 13.00
Anakin's Podracer, 134 pieces (#07131) 15.00

TIE Fighter (Lego 2000)

Naboo Fighter, 174 pieces (#07141) 20.00
Sith Infiltrator, 243 pieces (#07151) 30.00
Trade Federation AAT, 158 pieces (#07155) 20.00
Gungan Sub, 375 pieces (#07161) 35.00
Mos Espa Podrace, 894 pieces (#07171) 80.00
Trade Federation MTT, 470 pieces (#07184) 45.00
Watto's Junkyard, 446 pieces (#07186) 40.00

Star Wars Model (1999–2004)
Desert Skiff, 53 pieces (#07104) 9.00
Droid Escape, 44 pieces (#07106) 9.00
Land Speeder, 47 pieces (#07110) 9.00
Tusken Raider Encounter, 50 pieces (#07113) 10.00
Twin Pod Cloud Car, 117 pieces (#7119) 10.00
AT-ST, 107 pieces (#07127) 10.00
Speeder Bikes, 90 pieces (#07128) 10.00
Snowspeeder, 212 pieces (#07130) 25.00
A-wing Fighter, 123 pieces (#07134) 18.00
Ewok Attack with Biker Scout, 119 pieces (#07139) 13.00
X-wing Fighter, 263 pieces (#07140) 30.00
Slave I, 165 pieces (#07144) 25.00
TIE Fighter, 169 pieces (#07146) 20.00
TIE Fighter and Y-wing Fighter (#07150) 45.00
Imperial Shuttle, 234 pieces (#07166) 35.00
B-wing at Rebel Control Center (#07180) 40.00

Ultimate Collector's Series
TIE Interceptor, 703 pieces (#07181) 80.00
Millennium Falcon, 659 pieces (#07190) 80.00
X-wing, 1,304 pieces (#07191) 150.00
Yoda, 1,075 pieces (#07194) 100.00

Lego Droid Escape and Naboo Fighter (2000–02)

Episode I Lego Technic

Pit Droid, 217 pieces (#08000) 25.00
Battle Droid, 328 pieces (#08001) 30.00
Destroyer Droid, 553 pieces (#08002) 50.00
C-3PO, 339 pieces (#08007) 40.00
Stormtrooper, 361 pieces (#08008) 40.00
R2-D2, 242 pieces (#08009) 20.00
Darth Vader, 397 pieces (#08010) 40.00

Episode I Lego MindStorms

Droid Developer Kit, 657 pieces (#9748) 75.00
Dark Side Developers Kit (#9754) 75.00

Exclusives

Darth Maul Bust, 1,860 pieces (#10018) 17" tall 120.00
Rebel Blockade Runner, 1,748 pieces (#10019) 200.00
Cloud City, 698 pieces (#10023) 100.00
Naboo Starfighter, 187 pieces (#10026) 40.00
Rebel Snowspeeder, 1,457 pieces (#10029) 130.00
Imperial Star Destroyer, 3,104 pieces (#10030) 300.00

Toy Fair Giveaway (1999)

Star Wars music box "Building a New Galaxy in 1999,"
    scarce, market price not established 1,000.00
Star Wars logo, yellow Lego piece 10.00

Episode II (2002–04)

Geonosian Fighter, 169 pieces (#04478) 20.00
Jedi Starfighter, 138 pieces (#07143) 20.00
Jango Fett's *Slave I*, 158 pieces (#07153) 50.00
Super Battle Droid, 381 pieces (#08012) 35.00
Recent releases, each . . . . current retail price

Star Wars 1990 Calendar (Cedco 1989)

PAPER COLLECTIBLES

CALENDARS

Calendars were only made for a few years when the movies first appeared. Since 1995, calendars have been sold every year, and you can bet this will continue. Calendars appear in about July of the year before the year printed on the calendar. By December they are available at discount, and by January they are discounted heavily. If you intend to collect them, wait to get them at half price and don't unseal them.

Star Wars Calendars (Ballantine Books 1977–84)

1978 *Star Wars* Calendar, Sealed	$30.00
Open	15.00
1979 *Star Wars* Calendar, Sealed	20.00
Open	10.00
1980 *Star Wars* Calendar, Sealed	20.00
Open	10.00
1981 *The Empire Strikes Back* Calendar, Sealed	25.00
Open	10.00
1984 *Return of the Jedi* Calendar, Sealed	15.00
Open	10.00
1984 Ewok Calendar, with stickers, Sealed	15.00
Open, complete with all stickers	10.00

Calendars (1990s)

Star Wars 1990 Calendar (Cedco), Sealed	10.00
Star Wars 1991 Calendar (Cedco), Sealed	10.00
Star Wars 1991 Lucasfilm Calendar (Abrams), Sealed	25.00

Ewoks Figures (many not issued) from 1986 Kenner Catalog

Star Wars movies or other calendars (1995–2004)

Sealed . . . . cover price

Open . . . . half cover price

CATALOGS

Kenner issued two kinds of catalogs that covered *Star Wars* toys. The best known are the small pocket or consumer catalogs included in most of the vehicle packages. The larger retailer catalogs were given to the stores to get them to order *Star Wars* toys.

Every toy company with a *Star Wars* license produces a catalog, but most collector interest focuses on Kenner. The Kenner Fall 1977 *Star Wars* catalog features the Early Bird Certificate Package and naturally predates it, since the retailer must buy the toy before it gets in the toy store for the consumer to purchase. This makes it the very first Kenner collectible, but hardly the first *Star Wars* collectible.

One of Kenner's more interesting *Star Wars* catalogs is from the 1986 Toy Fair. This is the last one to contain *Star Wars* merchandise until the mid-1990s revival of the line. The 1986 catalog covers the Droids and Ewoks lines and includes pictures of a number of figures that were never actually released.

Consumer Mini Catalogs

Star Wars 1977, logo cover, list 12 figures $20.00

Star Wars, X-wing cover, eight new figures (1978–79) 15.00

Star Wars, Death Star and X-wing cover (1979) 10.00

The Empire Strikes Back (1980–81), any 10.00

Return of the Jedi (1983–84), any 10.00

The Empire Strikes Back Lobby Card (1980)

Retailer Catalogs (Kenner)

"Star Wars Toys and Games Available Fall 1977" Catalog,
   featuring the Early Bird Certificate Package. 75.00

Star Wars 1978 Catalog, featuring the first nine figures. 50.00

Star Wars 1979 Catalog, featuring the Boba Fett
   rocket-firing backpack 35.00

Star Wars Collector Series 1984 Catalog. 30.00

Kenner 1986 Toy Fair Catalog. 25.00

LOBBY CARDS

Lobby cards are large prints containing scenes from a movie, or pictures of the stars, which as the name implies, were designed for displaying in movie theater lobbies. They are 11" x 14" or 8" x 10" and were made in sets of eight different cards.

Star Wars
Set of eight lobby cards, 11" x 14" (1977) $125.00
Set of eight photo cards, 8" x 10" (1977) 100.00

The Empire Strikes Back
Set of eight lobby cards, 11" x 14" (1980) 90.00
Set of eight photo cards, 8" x 10" (1980) 75.00

Return of the Jedi
Set of eight lobby cards, 11" x 14" (1983) 75.00
Set of eight photo cards, 8" x 10" (1983) 60.00

MAGAZINES

Several magazines have been devoted exclusively, or almost exclusively, to *Star Wars*. Surprisingly, some were started more than a decade after the last movie had come and gone. Magazines covering collectibles, general interest and humor are covered immediately following those that exclusively featured *Star Wars*.

Lucasfilm Fan Club #12 (1990)

BANTHA TRACKS
Lucasfilm

#1 to #4, each	$15.00
Combined reissue #1–#4	10.00
#5 to #9	6.00
Later issues, each	5.00

LUCASFILM FAN CLUB MAGAZINE
The Fan Club (1987–94)

# 1 Anthony Daniels interview, 14 pgs. (1987)	$10.00
# 2 through #10, each	5.00
#11 *The Empire Strikes Back* 10th Anniv.	8.00
#12 through #18, each	5.00
#19 *Return of the Jedi* 10th Anniv., 30 pgs.	10.00
#20 34 pgs.	10.00
#21 36 pgs. (1994)	10.00
#22 TIE Fighter video game	5.00

Becomes:

STAR WARS INSIDER
The Star Wars Fan Club (1994–98)

#23 56 pgs., Obi-Wan photo cover (1994)	$9.00
#24 Ralph McQuarrie cover, 60 pgs. (1995)	10.00
#25 James Earl Jones interview, 72 pgs.	5.00
#26 George Lucas interview, 80 pgs.	6.00
#27 Luke and Landspeeder cover, 80 pgs. (1996)	8.00
#28 Peter Mayhew interview, 64 pgs.	5.00
#29 Shadows of the Empire, 64 pgs.	5.00
#30 Han and Jabba foldout cover, 64 pgs.	5.00

Official Poster Monthly #3 (Paradise Press 1978)

#31 Expanded *Star Wars* Universe, 68 pgs. 5.00
#32 84 pgs. (1997) 5.00
Later issues 5.00

OFFICIAL POSTER MONTHLY

Star Wars

#1 Stormtrooper cover $10.00
#2 Darth Vader/Luke Skywalker cover 8.00
#3 Han Solo cover 6.00
#4 through #8, each 5.00
#9 Luke and Leia circus cover. 8.00
#10 Darth Vader cover 5.00
#11 through #18, each 10.00

The Empire Strikes Back

#1 . . . . .6.00
#2 through #5, each 5 00

Return of the Jedi

#1 through #4, each 5.00

STAR WARS GALAXY MAGAZINE
Topps (1994–97)

#1 Fall 1994, *Star Wars* Widevision SWP3 card $7.50
Later issues, many with promo trading cards, each 5.00
Becomes:

Star Wars Galaxy #9 (Topps 1995)

STAR WARS GALAXY COLLECTOR
Topps (1998)

Most issues, each 5.00
Boba Fett one-shot special (April 1998) 6.00

MAGAZINES: COLLECTIBLES

Many collector magazines have run *Star Wars* covers. Many of
these collector magazines came with *Star Wars* promos polybagged
with the magazine. Magazines with their original promos can be
worth a lot more money, depending on the collectibility of the item,
but they can often be found, bagged and complete at reduced prices in
comics shops or at shows. Most promo cards, along with their source,
are listed in the *Trading Cards* chapter. Use this as your guide when
bargain hunting.

Most collectibles magazines, *Star Wars* cover, but without promos . . . $5.00 or less

MAGAZINES: GENERAL

Mass-market Collectible #3 is the May 30, 1977, issue of *Time*
magazine, which appeared a few days before the movie opened and
featured a two-page spread praising the movie as the best picture of
the year. The value of old magazines generally depends on the cover
photo or painting. The *Star Wars* movies have generated hundreds,
perhaps thousands, of magazine covers. When something is popular,
everybody wants it on their cover.

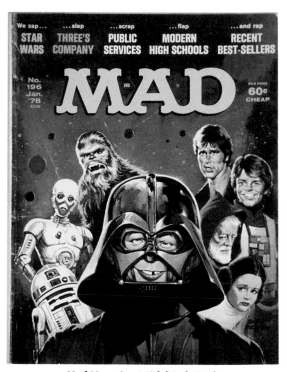

Mad Magazine #196 (Mad 1978)

Generally, the covers are photos from the movie or photos of the stars. Often the photos are promotional releases provided by Lucasfilms, but magazines like to get exclusive photos if they can.

Cinefantastique
Vol. 6 No. 4, The Making of *Star Wars* $20.00
Vol. 7 No. 1, The Making of *Star Wars* 20.00

Mad **Magazine**
#196, Jan. 1978, Alfred E. Neuman as Darth Vader 10.00
#203, Dec. 1978, The Mad *Star Wars* musical 9.00
#220, Jan. 1981, Alfred E. Neuman as Yoda 7.00
#242, Oct. 1983, Unmasks the *Return of the Jedi* 7.00

People **Magazine**
July 18, 1977, C-3PO cover 10.00
Aug. 14, 1978, Carrie Fisher cover 10.00

Starlog **(Starlog Group)**
Issue #7, X-wing and TIE Fighter 35.00
Issue #13, David Prowse 10.00
Issue #14, SF Matte painting cover 10.00
Issue #21, Mark Hamill 10.00
Issue #31, *The Empire Strikes Back* 10.00
Issue #35, Billy Dee Williams 10.00
Issue #99, C-3PO and R2-D2 . . . . .8.00
Issue #236, *Star Wars* 20th Anniversary 6.00
Issue #237, George Lucas 6.00

Time **Magazine (Time Warner)**
May 30, 1977 . . . . 20.00

*The Empire Strikes Back
32-Figure Store Display (Kenner 1981)*

May 19, 1980, Darth Vader cover 10.00

Most general magazines, *Star Wars* cover . . . . $5.00 or less

STORE DISPLAYS

Point of Purchase displays and store signs are designed to attract customers' attention, so they are colorful. They display the product just as nicely in your room as they did in the store. And, best of all, they are items that were never intended to be sold to the general public in the first place, so not everybody has one.

Over the years a lot of store displays have been produced and many more are to come. Size and artwork are important components of their collectible value, along with the importance of the product they promote. Displays for Kenner's action figures rank at the top.

Since the displays are placed in stores, it helps to work in one if you want to collect them. Undoubtedly many displays are thrown away at the end of the promotion; however, thousands of stores sell action figures. Each store gets a generous supply, so this tends to keep the price within reason. Flat signs and displays look nice when framed and make a handsome addition to a collection.

Star Wars Action Figure sign (1978–80), depending on size $100–250
The Empire Strikes Back Action Figure sign (1980–1982),
  depending on size 75–125
Return of the Jedi Action Figure sign (1983–1984),
  depending on size 40–90

Star Wars Blueprints (Ballantine 1977)

The most valuable store display is quite recent. In the fall of 1997, many Toys "R" Us stores received a hanging four-foot plastic *Millennium Falcon* that looked just like a scaled-up version of the toy. Only 500 were made, and they were given away in a drawing conducted by Rosie O'Donnell. The contest entry forms estimated the value of each at $500, but I think $2,500 is closer. The store display for the contest is a nice consolation collectible. It shows the *Falcon* in a reversed picture.

PORTFOLIOS AND BLUEPRINTS

The Empire Strikes Back promo art portfolio. $40.00
Star Wars Intergalactic Passport & Stickers (Ballantine 1983) 10.00
Star Wars Blueprints, in vinyl pouch (Ballantine 1977). 15.00
   Reprint: $6.95 (Ballantine 1992) .7.00
Star Wars Portfolio by Ralph McQuarrie, 11" x 14"
   color paintings, originally $7.95 (Ballantine 1977) 20.00
The Empire Strikes Back Portfolio by Ralph McQuarrie,
   Ballantine Books (1980) 15.00
Return of the Jedi Portfolio by Ralph McQuarrie,
   Ballantine Books (1983) 15.00
Star Wars Power of the Force Planetary Map, set,
   issued as a mail-in 20.00
Star Wars/The Empire Strikes Back Portfolio (1994) 12.00
Star Wars Trilogy Print Portfolio Set (Zanart 1996) 12.00
Star Wars Post-Art Portfolio (Classico 1995) 15.00
Star Wars Trilogy Movie Card Portfolio (Zanart 1994) 14.00

PRESS KITS

Press Kits
   Original *Star Wars* kit (1977) $150.00
   Star Wars kit (1978) 100.00
   Holiday special kit (1978) 175.00
   NPR Presents kit (1979) 35.00
   The Empire Strikes Back kit (1980) 60.00
   Introducing Yoda kit (1980). 35.00
   NPR Playhouse kit (1981) 30.00
   Return of the Jedi kit (1983) 30.00

*Return of the Jedi Official Collector's Edition
(Paradise Press 1983)*

PROGRAMS

Star Wars Movie Program (1977) limited quantity, offered in 1994 . . . . . . $75.00
The Empire Strikes Back Official Collector's Edition (Paradise Press) 15.00
The Return of the Jedi Official Collector's Edition (Paradise Press) 10.00

PROOFS

A few header card proofs are made for every action figure so design staff, company executives and others can check the graphics, weigh the sales appeal of the package and generally bless the product. Everybody wants to participate to justify their jobs, so changes are frequent, and often the proof is not quite like the final package. This makes proofs interesting collectibles. The most valuable proofs are for those items that never actually hit the production line, or in which the design was changed in some significant way. After that, the value of proofs varies with the value of the final figure.

ACTION FIGURE CARD PROOFS

The most famous *Star Wars* change was the retitling of the third movie from *Revenge of the Jedi* to *Return of the Jedi*. No product was actually released with a *Revenge of the Jedi* package, but the original name is mentioned on a number of packages. Also, a few magazines and action-figure card proofs have the *Revenge of the Jedi* logo. They are the most highly sought card proofs, since they are as close as one can come to an actual *Revenge of the Jedi* product. Minor character proofs sell for about $150 each, and major characters up to $250 apiece.

Boba Fett Revenge of the Jedi Proof Card

Empire Strikes Back Laser Pistol (Kenner 1980)

ROLE PLAY TOYS

Role play toys include weapons, communicators, armor, utility belts and similar items that are full size, or sized for a kid to play with. They are hardly a new idea. Every movie and TV Western hero had cap guns, hats, boots and all manner of full-sized licensed products.

Electronic Heavy Blaster (Kenner 1996)

With so little product, collector interest in the few classic items is quite high. As yet, there has been little collector interest in the 1990s items, and they can all be acquired for about their original retail prices. The only exception is the Boba Fett Armor Set, which has been scarce and expensive.

CLASSIC WEAPONS

Classic Lightsabers

Star Wars Lightsaber, inflatable, 35" long, light-up
(Kenner #38040, 1997), boxed $90.00

Loose 40.00
Droids Battery-Operated Lightsaber (Green)
  (Kenner 1984) 100.00
  Loose 50.00
Droids Battery-Operated Lightsaber (Red) (Kenner 1984) 200.00
  Loose 80.00

Classic Pistols and Rifles
Three-Position Laser Rifle, folding stock, secret on/off button, two-speed
  laser sound, battery-powered, (1978), in *Star Wars* package 250.00
  Loose, with *Star Wars* logo. 75.00
  Reissue as Electronic Laser Rifle (1980) in
  The Empire Strikes Back package 250.00
  Loose, with *The Empire Strikes Back* logo 75.00
Laser Pistol replica of Han Solo's laser pistol with
  secret on/off button, battery-powered (1978)
  Original *Star Wars* package 125.00
  Loose, with *Star Wars* logo. 25.00
  Reissue *The Empire Strikes Back* package. 100.00
  Loose, with *The Empire Strikes Back* logo. 20.00
  Reissue *Return of the Jedi* package. 75.00
  Loose, with *Return of the Jedi* logo. 20.00
Biker Scout Laser Pistol, battery-powered (Kenner #71520, 1983)
  Return of the Jedi package 75.00
  Loose 25.00

NEW WEAPONS

New Lightsabers (1995–98)
Electronic Luke Skywalker Lightsaber (1996) 50.00
Electronic Darth Vader Lightsaber (1996), red box 60.00
  Reissue, green box 50.00

Boba Fett's Armor (Hasbro 1998)

Loose . . . . half of boxed/carded price

Other New Weapons
Chewbacca's Bowcaster (Kenner #27734, 1997) 18.00
Electronic Heavy Blaster BlasTech DL-44 (Kenner #27737, 1996)
   in orange box 20.00
Electronic Blaster Rifle BlasTech E-11 (Kenner #27738, 1996)
   white, in orange box 20.00
   Reissue, striped, in green box 15.00
Star Wars Electronic Blaster Laser Rifle, 18-1/2" long,

battery-powered Stormtrooper weapon 17.00
Star Wars Endor Blaster Pistol (Kenner #27737, 1998) 14.50
Star Wars Commando Blaster Laser Rifle (Kenner #27738, 1998) 20.00
Loose . . . . half of boxed/carded price

EPISODE I WEAPONS

Episode I Lightsabers (Hasbro 1999)
Electronic Darth Maul Double-Bladed Lightsaber (#84103) 30.00
Darth Maul Double-Bladed Lightsaber (#84527) 20.00
Electronic Qui-Gon Jinn Lightsaber (#84102) 20.00
Electronic Obi-Wan Kenobi Lightsaber (#84907) 20.00
Qui-Gon Jinn's Lightsaber (#26264) loose 10.00

Other Episode I Weapons (Hasbro 1999)
Electronic Tatooine Blaster Pistol (#57133) 20.00
Electronic Battle Droid Blaster Rifle (#26237) 20.00
Naboo Foam Firing Blaster (Hasbro #57127) 15.00

COSTUME LIGHTSABERS

New Costume Lightsabers (Rubies 1995–2004)
Star Wars Lightsaber, battery-operated, any color 9.00
Loose, any color 4.00

ACCESSORIES

New Accessories
Luke Skywalker's Utility Belt (Kenner #27735, Aug. 1997) in green box 18.00
Loose 9.00
Boba Fett Armor Set, includes chest shield, blaster, two arm gauntlets
and face shield (Kenner #27796, 1998) 50.00
Loose 25.00

Rancor Creature (Illusive Originals 1996)

STATUES — MAQUETTES — BUSTS — FINE REPLICAS

Few, if any, collectors can afford to buy all these expensive items—usually they buy one (or a few), which then forms the centerpiece of their collection. Although expensive collectibles hold their value, they are hard to sell quickly. Since almost no one is trying to collect all of them from a series, there is not much extra demand for the first one produced, or any particularly scarce one. As long as there are collectors willing to buy, the companies will produce new items.

MAQUETTES

Yoda Maquette, 26", mounted on black wood base,
limited to 9,500 (Illusive Originals 1995) $950.00
Boba Fett Maquette, 15" tall, mounted on black wood base,
limited to 10,000 (Illusive Originals) 300.00
Admiral Ackbar Maquette, 11" tall, mounted on black wood base,
limited to 10,000 (Illusive Originals) 150.00
Jabba the Hutt Maquette, 27" long, mounted on black wood base,
limited to 5,000 (Illusive Originals) 300.00
Chewbacca Maquette, 17" tall bust, mounted on black wood base,
limited to 7,500 (Illusive Originals) 300.00
Han Solo in Carbonite Prop Replica, 7' tall, cast in fiberglass
(Illusive Originals) 2,000.00
Darth Vader Reveals Anakin Skywalker Bust,
three-piece mask/helmet opens (Illusive Originals 1998) 1,500.00

Cinemacast Darth Vader Statue (Cinemacast 1995)

Rancor Creature Maquette, 21" x 7" x 24",
   limited to 9,500 (Illusive Originals) 600.00

STATUES

Cinemacast Darth Vader statue, 15 1/2" cold cast
   porcelain, limited to 10,000 (1995). $400.00
Boba Fett Bronze Statue, sculpted by Randy Bowen,
   12-1/2" tall, weighs 18 lbs., mounted
   on black Spanish marble, with certificate of
   authenticity (Dark Horse Comics, March 1997). 3,000.00
Rancor Bronze Statue, sculpted by Randy Bowen,
   15" tall, weighs 25 lbs., mounted on black
   Spanish marble, limited edition of 50 numbered
   copies, with certificate of authenticity
   (Dark Horse Comics, 1998) 3,500.00
Darth Vader Bronze Statue, sculpted by Randy Bowen,
   14" tall, 1/6 scale, limited edition with
   certificate of authenticity
   (Dark Horse Comics, May 1999) 3,500.00
Chewbacca Bronze Statue, sculpted by A. Wasil,
   19-1/2" tall, weighs 38 lbs., mounted on polished
   granite, limited edition of 50
   (Dark Horse Comics, Aug. 2000) 3,600.00
Darth Vader Nutcracker, 18" tall, FAO Schwarz exclusive,
   limited to 5,000 pieces (Steinbach). 225.00
Luke and Leia pewter statue, FAO Schwarz exclusive,
   limited to 1,000 pieces 450.00

Obi-Wan Kenobi Lightsaber (Icons 1998)

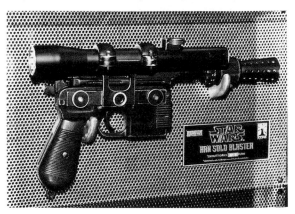

Han Solo Blaster Replica (Icons 1998)

REPLICAS

Icons Authentic Replicas

Authentic Darth Vader Lightsaber, die-cast metal
and plastic prop replica, with numbered plaque,
certificate of authenticity and Plexiglas
display case, limited to 10,000 (Icons 1996) $850.00

James Earl Jones Signature Edition 1,000.00

Authentic Obi-Wan Kenobi Lightsaber, die-cast
metal and plastic prop replica, with numbered
plaque, certificate of authenticity and Plexiglas
display case, limited to 10,000 (Icons) 950.00

Authentic Luke Skywalker Lightsaber, die-cast
metal and plastic prop replica, with numbered
plaque, certificate of authenticity and Plexiglas
display case, limited to 10,000 (Icons) 750.00

Mark Hamill Signature Edition 900.00

Han Solo Blaster replica with display case and plaque (Icons 1998) 600.00

TIE Fighter replica miniature, injected polyurethane
with weathered appearance, numbered plaque,
certificate of authenticity, Plexiglas display case,
limited to 1,977 (Icons) 1,500.00

X-wing Fighter replica miniature, injected polyurethane
with weathered appearance, numbered plaque,
certificate of authenticity and Plexiglas display case,
limited to 1,977 (Icons 1996) 1,500.00

Mark Hamill Signature Edition, 100 made 1,750.00

Emperor Palpatine Bust Sculpture (Legends in 3-D 1997)

DELUXE REPLICA HELMETS

Don Post Studios, cast from original movie prop

Deluxe Stormtrooper Helmet, 13" fiberglass helmet
with lining (#82102) numbered edition of 1,000 . . . . $750.00

Deluxe Scout Trooper Helmet, 13" fiberglass
(#82114) numbered edition of 500 . . . . 950.00

Deluxe X-wing Fighter Helmet, 13" fiberglass
helmet with lining (#82116) limited edition of 750 . . . . 950.00

Deluxe TIE Fighter Helmet, 15" fiberglass helmet
with lining (#82115) limited edition of 500 . . . . 1,200.00

Deluxe Darth Vader Helmet, 15" black fiberglass (#82100) 1,000.00

Deluxe Boba Fett Helmet, 15" fiberglass (#82101) 950.00

PORCELAIN BUSTS AND STATUES

Cold Cast Busts (Legends in Three Dimensions)
sculpted by Greg Aronowitz, limited to 3,000, box art by Drew Struzan

Emperor Palpatine bust sculpture (1997) $100.00

Greedo bust sculpture (1998) 125.00

Boba Fett bust sculpture (1998) 150.00

Cantina Band Member (1999) 125.00

Gamorrean Guard bust sculpture (1999) 200.00

Tusken Raider bust sculpture (1999) 150.00

Attakus Collection Porcelain Statues (*Star Wars* Fan Club)

Yoda 200.00

Han in Carbonite 235.00

R2-D2 . . . . 215.00

Boba Fett 300.00

Star Wars Official Chess Set (Danbury Mint 1995)

Darth Maul 270.00
Slave Leia 270.00

LIFE-SIZE REPLICA STATUES

Don Post Studios Statues
Boba Fett Life-Size Replica Statue, 6' 1/2" fiberglass,
    cast from original props (#82023) $5,000.00
Stormtrooper Replica Statue, 6' fiberglass,
    cast from original props (#82022),
    limited to 500 pieces 4,500.00
Deluxe C-3PO Replica (#82031) 15,000.00
Deluxe R2-D2 Replica (#82030) 8,000.00

Rubies Figure
Darth Vader Full-Size Display Figure (Rubies 1997) 4,500.00

OTHER FINE COLLECTIBLES

Star Wars Official Pewter Chess Set, 15" x 15" x 3" board,
    plus 32 pewter figures on bases,
    sold at $19.95 per figure (Danbury Mint 1995) $650.00
Life-Size Ewok Plush Figure, 30" tall in sitting position,
    12 lbs., 3,200 made, PepsiCo promo
    (Douglas Toys 1997) 500.00
Millennium Falcon Hanging Display from Toys "R" Us Stores,
    large 6' ship given away in charity raffle on
    The Rosie O'Donnell Show, with shipping box 2,500.00

Star Wars: Series 1 Card; Series 2 Sticker;
Series 3 Card (Topps 1977)

STAR WARS
Topps (1977)

Topps was the major producer of movie tie-in cards in the 1960s, 1970s and 1980s. The standard it created and followed with just about every movie set was 66 (or 88) cards, plus 11 (or 22) stickers. The cards and stickers came in colorful wax wrappers, and all three came in boxes of 36 packs. Stickers came one to a pack, making a sticker set harder to assemble than a card set. Some stickers were even rumored to have been, (gasp!), peeled off and stuck to something, further reducing the number in circulation. Consequently, stickers are worth about $2 each, while the cards go for less.

Series 1, blue border with stars

Set: 66 cards/11 stickers	$75.00
Pack: 7 cards + 1 sticker	8.00
Box: 36 packs	200.00

Series 2, red border

Set: 66 cards/11 stickers	45.00
Pack	5.00
Box: 36 packs	110.00

Series 3, yellow border

Set: 66 cards/11 stickers	50.00
Pack	5.00
Box: 36 packs	120.00

Series 4, green border

Set: 66 cards/11 stickers	45.00

Two Wonder Bread and Two Burger King Cards
(1977, 1980)

Pack 4.00
Box: 36 packs 100.00

Series 5, brown/orange border
Set: 66 cards/11 stickers 40.00
Pack 4.00
Box: 36 packs 100.00

OTHER EARLY *STAR WARS* CARDS

Several other types of *Star Wars* cards, stickers and wrappers appeared in the late 1970s and early 1980s. The Wonder Bread series of 16 cards were packaged one per loaf of bread. General Mills cereals produced two series of stickers, and Kellogg's created peel-away sticker cards. Meanwhile, Topps made sugar-free bubble gum with distinctive wrappers and inside photos. Burger King gave out three-card strips, while Hershey candy bars could be purchased in six-packs with a tray card.

STAR WARS

Set: 16 cards (Wonder Bread 1977). $25.00

STAR WARS
SUGAR-FREE GUM WRAPPERS

Set: 56 wrappers (Topps 1978) $75.00

STAR WARS

Set: 18 different large cards (General Mills 1978) $50.00
Card: each 3.00

The Empire Strikes Back Series 1 Box (Topps 1980)

STAR WARS AND
THE EMPIRE STRIKES BACK
"Everybody Wins Trading Cards"

Set: 12 different strips (Burger King 1980) $30.00
Set: 36 cards, cut 25.00

THE EMPIRE STRIKES BACK
Topps (1980)

While Topps made only three series of *The Empire Strikes Back* cards, more cards and stickers were printed than for the previous movie. As before, stickers are more valuable than cards because each pack contained only one sticker.

Series 1, grey and red border
Set: 132 cards/33 stickers $60.00
Pack: 12 cards. 4.00
Box: 36 packs 75.00

Series 2, grey and blue border
Set: 132 cards/33 stickers 50.00
Pack 4.00
Box: 36 packs 60.00

Series 3, green and yellow border
Set: 88 cards/22 stickers 25.00
Pack 4.00
Box: 36 packs 55.00

Star Wars Galaxy One Promo Cards (Topps 1993)

RETURN OF THE JEDI
Topps (1983)

There were only two series of *Return of the Jedi* cards and only about half as many total cards as in the previous two series. Stickers are again more valuable, and each comes with two different backgrounds.

Series 1, red border
Set: 132 cards/33 stickers $25.00
Pack: 10 cards, 1 sticker 2.00
Box: 36 packs 40.00

Series 2, blue border
Set: 88 cards/22 stickers 20.00
Pack: 10 cards, 1 sticker 2.00
Box: 36 packs 35.00

STAR WARS GALAXY
Topps (1993–95, Art)

Star Wars Galaxy cards were the first new set of *Star Wars* cards in 10 years and the first to use art rather than pictures from the movies. This first *Star Wars* Galaxy set is also an important element in the *Star Wars* marketing revival. New novels and comics started in 1991, but very few other collectibles were being produced. This card series was heavily marketed and gave a good boost to the *Star Wars* revival.

Star Wars Galaxy Three First Day Cards (Topps 1995)

The *Millennium Falcon* factory set was one of the best publisher/editor freebies Topps ever gave away. Thanks again, Topps, for sending me one.

Set: 140 cards $15.00
Pack: 8 cards 1.50
Box: 36 packs 35.00
Millennium Falcon factory foil-stamped set,
   plus holo-foil cards, in plastic ship model 75.00
Etched-Foil cards, six different, each 8.00
Autographed cards 30.00
Six-card uncut-sheet (one per case) 30.00
Promo Cards, 7 different, each . . . . .5.00 to 10.00

STAR WARS GALAXY TWO

Set: 135 cards (#141-#275) $15.00
Pack: 8 cards 1.25
Box: 36 packs 30.00
Factory tin set, with #00 card 50.00
Etched-Foil cards, six different, each 7.00
Uncut etched-foil sheet 70.00
Autographed card (2000) 40.00
Six-card uncut sheet (one per case) 30.00
Promo cards, P1 through P6, each 10.00
SWG1 promo 8.00
Biker Scout/Ewok (Jim Starlin art) from *Triton #3*
   variant card #266, Ewok with knife 15.00

Star Wars MasterVisions Card (Topps 1995)

STAR WARS GALAXY THREE

Set: 90 cards: #276–#365 and #L1–#L12 . . . . $15.00

Pack: 5 cards, 1 first day issue card and 1 insert card 1.00

Box: 36 packs 30.00

First day set: 90 cards 50.00

First day card, each. 1.00

Etched-Foil Cards, six different, each. 6.00

Uncut etched-foil panorama sheet 60.00

Agents of the Empire Clear Zone, six different, each 8.00

Promo Cards

P2 Snowtroopers, convention giveaway 10.00

P3 through P8 (except P5), each 5.00

P5 error promo 25.00

STAR WARS GALAXY—BEND-EMS
Topps (1993–95, Art)

Most of Just Toys' Bend-Em figures came with trading cards from 1993 to 1995. The cards are variant *Star Wars* Galaxy cards, which are lettered on the back instead of numbered. The earliest cards and figures matched, but the later ones were random, making it that much harder to complete a set of cards. Consequently, later cards are worth more than earlier cards. There are 28 cards in the set, plus three mail-in cards. The cards may very well be more collectible (and more valuable) than the figures.

Just Toys Bend-Ems variants (Joe Smith art)

0 Darth Vader mail-in card (Ken Steacy art) $15.00

00 Darth Vader mail-in card (Ralph McQuarrie art). 15.00

Two Star Wars Finest Chromium Cards, and
Two Shadows of the Empire Cards (Topps 1996)

Checklist card, variation, mentions Series 2. . . . . 15.00
Cards A through M, each. 3.00
Cards M through X, each 5.00

***Star Wars* Galaxy Series 2 cards**
Cards Y through BB, each 5.00

STAR WARS MASTERVISIONS
Topps (1995)

Topps MasterVisions cards are large enough to be called wall art and are UV-coated, foil-stamped and printed on premium 24-point stock. The series features full-bleed artwork by Ralph McQuarrie, Dave Dorman, The Hildebrandts, Boris Vallejo, Ken Steacy, Drew Struzan, Hugh Fleming, Michael Whelan and more.

Boxed Set: 36 cards 6-3/4" x 10-3/4". $30.00
Card 1.00

Promos
No # 2.50
P2 promo (*Star Wars Galaxy* Mag. #5) 2.50

STAR WARS FINEST
Topps (1996)

This is an all-chromium set, subtitled "The character guide to the *Star Wars* universe." The cards features text written by Andy Mangels and consist of 10 nine-card subsets by different artists.

Set: 90 Chromium cards $30.00

Star Wars Widevision Cards (Topps 1995)

Pack: 5 cards 2.50
Box: 36 packs 55.00
Topps Matrix Chase Cards, four different, each 10.00
Embossed Chase Cards, six different, F1 to F6, each 10.00
Topps Finest Refractor (1:12) 90 different, each 5.00
Refractor Set: 90 cards 400.00
MasterVisions Matrix redemption (1:360) 75.00
MasterVisions Matrix mail-in 75.00
Promos, SWF1 through SWF3, each 4.00
Refractor promo 40.00
Oversize chromium promo 15.00

STAR WARS:
SHADOWS OF THE EMPIRE
Topps (1996)

Shadows of the Empire cards are based on the novel, comic book and video game "multimedia extravaganza" of the same name.

Set: 90 cards (#1 through #72 and #82 through #100) $15.00
Pack: 9 cards 1.50
Box: 36 packs 45.00
Etched foil, gold gilt (1:9) six different, each 7.00
Foil Embossed (1:18) four different, each 10.00
Redemption card (1:200) 60.00
Autographed MasterVisions mail-in redemption 50.00
Promos, SOTE1 through SOTE7, each 3.00

Trilogy Special Edition Cards (Topps 1977)

STAR WARS WIDEVISION
Topps (1995–97)

With Widevision cards, Topps returned to movie images. This time the pictures had high quality and the same aspect ratio as the films (like the letterbox videotape version). The images were transferred directly from the original film master, not a second-generation version. Production was limited to 4,000 cases.

Widevision versions of the other two movies followed and, in 1997, the Special Edition was covered in turn.

Set: 120 cards, 4-1/2". $40.00
Pack: 10 cards. 5.00
Box: packs 90.00
Topps Finest, C1 through C10, each 15.00

Promo Cards
SWP0 . . . . 15.00
SWP1 and SWP4, each 5.00
SWP2, SWP3, SWP5, SWP6, each 10.00
Promos from Classic Edition 4-Pack action figures
K01 through K04, each 8.00

THE EMPIRE STRIKES BACK

Set: 144 cards $25.00
Pack: 9 cards 2.75
Two different packs
Box: 24 packs 40.00
Chromium cards (1:12) C1 through C10, each 10.00
Movie Poster Set (1:24) six different, each 8.00

Star Wars Widevision 3-D Cards (Topps 1997)

Promos, P1 through P4, P6 . . . . 10.00
P5 Stormtroopers and Han Solo in Carbonite. 30.00

RETURN OF THE JEDI

Set: 144 cards $20.00
Pack: 9 cards 2.50
Box: 24 packs 60.00
Topps Finest Chromium, C/1 through C/10, each 10.00
Mini-Posters (one per box) six different, each. 10.00
3-D (one per case) Admiral Ackbar 50.00
Redemption card 30.00
Promo Cards, #0, P1 through P5, each. 4.00
P6 Han Solo, Luke and Chewbacca 50.00

TRILOGY SPECIAL EDITION

Set. 72 cards (Hobby) $25.00
Box: 36 packs 75.00
Lasercut Set (1:9) 6 different, each 9.00
Holograms (1:18) 2 different, each 12.00

Set: 72 cards (Retail). $15.00
Pack: 9 cards 2.00
Box: 36 packs 40.00
Lasercut Set, 6 different, each 9.00
Spec. Ed. 3-D card (one per box) X-wings departing 15.00

Promos

P0 Lasercut 10.00
P1 through P3, P7 & P8, each 5.00
P4 through P6, each 10.00

Episode I Widevision Packs (Topps 1999)

STAR WARS WIDEVISION 3-D

This card set contains all new images from the first movie and uses an exclusive, multilevel 3-D digital imagery technology. The technology is quite impressive, but also expensive.

Set: 63 cards	$90.00
Pack: 3 cards	4.00
Box: 36 packs	120.00
Chase Card 1m 3-D Motion card	30.00

Promos

2m	10.00
3Di 1	10.00
3Di 2	25.00
P1	10.00
P2	50.00

STAR WARS VEHICLES
Topps (July 1997)

The *Star Wars* Vehicle cards feature 50 comic art cards by Top Cow Studios, plus 22 cards with movie photos featuring ships.

Set: 72 cards	$20.00
Pack: 5 cards	2.00
Box: 36 packs	45.00
Cutaway, C1 through C4, each	8.00
3-D cards, two different, each	20.00
Redemption card (1:360) for uncut pair of 3-D cards	50.00
Mail-in card	40.00

Two Episode I Promo Cards:
One Front (top), One Back (bottom) (Topps 1999)

Promos

P1 Speeder Bikes	10.00
P2 Shuttle *Tydirium*	15.00
P1 Speeder Bikes, refractor	50.00
P2 Shuttle *Tydirium,* refractor	85.00

STAR WARS CHROME ARCHIVES
Topps (1999)

These cards appeared in February 1999. Topps took cards from the three classic series and reissued them in an all-chrome format. They turned out very well and the set has been popular.

Set: 90 chromium cards	$35.00
Pack: 5 cards	4.00
Box: 36 packs	80.00
Double-Sided Chrome Insert (1:12) nine different, each	8.00
Clear Chrome (1:18) four different, each	15.00
Promos P1 and P2, each	4.00

STAR WARS EPISODE I WIDEVISION
Topps (1999)

Series One (Hobby Edition)

Set: 80 cards	$12.00
Pack: 8 cards	1.00
Box: 36 packs	30.00
Expansion Set: 40 cards	30.00
Expansion Card	1.00
Chromium Inserts (1:12) eight different, each	8.00
Promos, three different, each	2.00

Star Wars Evolution cards (Topps 2001)

Series One (Retail Edition)
Set: 80 cards and 16 stickers 10.00
Pack: 8 cards 2.00
Box: 36 packs 45.00
Stickers (1:2) 16 different, each 1.00
Foil Inserts (1:8) 10 different, each .5.00
Mega Chromes five different, each 10.00
Collectors Tin set: 8 cards 20.00
Hallmark Promos, H1–H3, each 3.00

Series Two (Hobby Edition)
Set: 80 cards. 15.00
Pack: 8 cards 1.75
Box: 36 packs 35.00
Embossed Foil Inserts (1:12) six different, each 5.00
Chrome Inserts (1:18) four different, each 10.00
Oversize Promos, 4" x 7 1/2"
OS-1 Dueling with Darth Maul 2.00
OS-2 A Time to Rejoice. 2.00

STAR WARS EPISODE I 3-D
Topps (2000)

Set: 46 cards. $65.00
Pack: 2 cards 3.00
Box: 36 packs 85.00
Multi-Motions Chase Cards, two different, each 10.00
P1 Promo, Naboo Hangar 5.00

STAR WARS EVOLUTION
Topps (2001)

Set: 90 cards, all foil $15.00
Pack: 8 cards 2.00
Box: 36 packs 60.00
Checklists: C1 to C3 . . . . 5.00
Autographed Card Inserts (one per box) 30.00
Evolution A, 1A to 12A (1:6) 8.00
Evolution B, 1B to 8B (1:12) 12.00
Promos P1, P2 . . . . .1.00
P3 Nien Nunb 20.00
P4 Anakin Skywalker 10.00

ATTACK OF THE CLONES
Topps (2002)

Set: 100 Cards $15.00
Pack: 7 cards 2.00
Box: 36 packs 60.00
Silver Foil Cards (1:2), each 3.00
Prismatic Foil Cards (1:6), each 8.00
Panoramic Foldouts, each 3.00
Promos, six different 3.00

ATTACK OF THE CLONES WIDEVISION
Topps (2003)

Set: 80 cards $12.00
Pack 1.50
Box: 36 packs 45.00

CLONE WARS
Topps (2004)

Set: 90 cards. $15.00
Pack 1.00
Box: 36 packs 40.00
Battle Motion inserts, each 5.00
Die-Cut Stickers, each 5.00

Darth Vader TIE Fighter (Kenner 1979)

VEHICLES, CREATURES, PLAYSETS AND ACCESSORIES

The 3-3/4" size of *Star Wars* figures allowed the production of vehicles large enough to accommodate several figures, so the larger vehicles became virtual playsets for the figures. Actual playsets, creatures and accessories extended this environment.

CLASSIC VEHICLES
Kenner (1978–86)

Vehicles were released over the period of all three movies, and many can be found in boxes from one, two or all three of the movies.

STAR WARS VEHICLES

Star Wars Vehicles (1978–79)

Landspeeder (#38020, 1978) *Star Wars* box	$75.00
Star Wars Collector Series Landspeeder (1983)	35.00
Loose, with all parts	20.00
X-wing Fighter (#38030, 1978) *Star Wars* box	125.00
Reissue in *The Empire Strikes Back* box	200.00
Loose, with all parts	45.00
Imperial TIE Fighter (#38040, 1978) *Star Wars* box	135.00
Reissue in *The Empire Strikes Back* box	200.00
Loose, with all parts	45.00
Darth Vader TIE Fighter (#39100, 1979)	
Star Wars box	125.00
Star Wars box with Battle Scene	500.00

Star Wars Collector Series Landspeeder (Kenner 1983)
The Empire Strikes Back Slave I (Kenner 1982)

Star Wars Collector's Series (1983). 60.00
Loose, with all parts 40.00
Loose, with all parts, with Battle Scene. 150.00
Millennium Falcon Spaceship (#39110, 1979)
Original *Star Wars* box. 325.00
Reissue in *The Empire Strikes Back* box. 225.00
Reissue in *Return of the Jedi* box. 175.00
Star Wars Collector Series (1983). 125.00
Loose, with all parts 80.00
Radio-Controlled Jawa Sandcrawler (#39270,1979)
Original *Star Wars* box. 600.00
Reissue in *The Empire Strikes Back* box. 650.00
Loose, with all parts 250.00
Imperial Troop Transporter (#39290, 1979)
Original *Star Wars* box. 100.00
Reissue in *The Empire Strikes Back* box. 115.00
Loose, with all parts 45.00

Exclusive Vehicles (1979–80)
Sonic-Controlled Landspeeder with R2-D2 shaped clicker,
   J.C. Penney exclusive (#38540, 1979)
Original *Star Wars* box. 600.00
Loose, with all parts 200.00
Imperial Cruiser, similar to Imperial Troop Transporter,
   Sears exclusive (#93351, 1980)
Original *The Empire Strikes Back* box. 125.00
Loose, with all parts 40.00

THE EMPIRE STRIKES BACK VEHICLES

The Empire Strikes Back Vehicles (1980–82)
Darth Vader's Star Destroyer (#39850, 1980)
Original *The Empire Strikes Back* box. $150.00

The Empire Strikes Back AT-AT (Kenner 1981)

Loose, with all parts 40.00
Twin-Pod Cloud Car (#39860, 1980)
   Original *The Empire Strikes Back* box 100.00
   Reissue in *The Empire Strikes Back* box with
   Bespin Security Guard (white) figure. 125.00
   Loose, with all parts, no figure 40.00
AT-AT All-Terrain Armored Transport (#38810, 1981)
   Original *The Empire Strikes Back* box 250.00
   Reissue in *Return of the Jedi* box. 275.00
   Loose, with all parts 110.00
Rebel Armored Snowspeeder (#39610, 1982)
   Original *The Empire Strikes Back* box 125.00
   Reissue in *The Empire Strikes Back* box with
   Rebel Soldier (Hoth Battle Gear) figure 175.00
   Loose, with all parts 40.00
Slave I, Boba Fett's Spaceship, including
   Frozen Han Solo figure (#39690, 1982)
   Original *The Empire Strikes Back* box 175.00
   Reissue in *The Empire Strikes Back* box with
   Battle Scene Setting. 275.00
   Loose, with all parts 40.00
Rebel Transport, 20" long, including five Hoth Backpacks and
   four Asteroid gas masks (#69740, 1982)
   Original *The Empire Strikes Back* box 150.00
   Loose, with all parts 35.00
"Battle Damaged" X-wing Fighter (#69780, 1981)
   Original *The Empire Strikes Back* box 275.00
   Reissue in *Return of the Jedi* box. 150.00
   Loose, with all parts 35.00
Scout Walker (#69800, 1982)
   Original *The Empire Strikes Back* box 80.00
   Reissue in *Return of the Jedi* box. 60.00

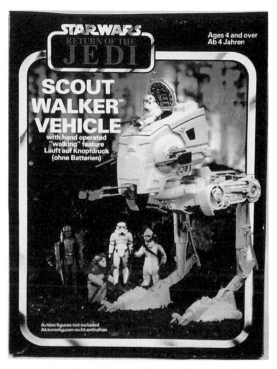

Return of the Jedi Scout Walker (Kenner 1983)

Loose, with all parts 25.00
Imperial TIE Fighter (Battle Damaged) in blue with
   "damage" decals (#71490, 1983)
   Original *The Empire Strikes Back* box 150.00
   Reissue in *Return of the Jedi* box 125.00
   Loose, with all parts 40.00

RETURN OF THE JEDI VEHICLES

Return of the Jedi Vehicles (1983–84)

Speeder Bike 8" long (#70500, 1983)
   Original *Return of the Jedi* box $30.00
   Reissue in Power of the Force box 20.00
   Loose, with all parts 15.00
Y-wing Fighter (#70510, 1983)
   Original *Return of the Jedi* box 120.00
   Loose, with all parts 60.00
B-wing Fighter (#71370, 1984)
   Original *Return of the Jedi* box 125.00
   Loose, with all parts 60.00
TIE Interceptor (#71390, 1984)
   Original *Return of the Jedi* box 150.00
   Loose, with all parts 75.00
Imperial Shuttle (#93650)
   Original *Return of the Jedi* box 450.00
   Loose, with all parts 225.00

POWER OF THE FORCE VEHICLES

Power of the Force Vehicles (1984–85)

Tatooine Skiff (#71540, 1985)
   Original Power of the Force box $500.00
   Loose, with all parts 250.00

Electronic X-wing Fighter (Kenner 1995)

DROIDS VEHICLES

Droids Vehicles (1985)
A-wing Fighter, with planetary map (#93700)
    Original Droids box $600.00
    Loose, with all parts 300.00
ATL Interceptor Vehicle (#93900) Original Droids box 35.00
    Loose, with all parts 15.00
Side Gunner with Planetary Map (#94010)
    Original Droids box 50.00
    Loose, with all parts 15.00

NEW VEHICLES
Kenner/Hasbro (1995–2002)

Kenner (now Hasbro) has produced new Power of the Force vehicles right along with the new action figures, and its boxes have followed the same color sequence—first red, then green, with a few purple boxes for Shadows of the Empire vehicles, then a different green design, and so on. There have been box variations as well, and many can be identified by the packaging variation number found near the bar code on most boxes.

(NEW) POWER OF THE FORCE VEHICLES

Power of the Force Vehicles, red boxes (1995–96)
Landspeeder (#69770, 1995) $12.00
    Loose, with all parts 6.00
TIE Fighter (#69775, 1995) 20.00
    Loose, with all parts 10.00

A-wing Fighter and A-wing Pilot (Kenner 1997)

Imperial AT-ST (Scout Walker) (#69776, 1995) 50.00
   Loose, with all parts 15.00
Electronic X-wing Fighter (#69780, 1995) 25.00
   Loose, with all parts 15.00
Electronic Rebel Snowspeeder (#69585, 1996) 35.00
   Loose, with all parts 15.00
Electronic *Millennium Falcon* (see Playsets)

Power of the Force Vehicles, green boxes (1996–97)

Luke's T-16 Skyhopper (#69663, 1996) 25.00
   Loose, with all parts 10.00
Cruise Missile Trooper (#69653, 1997) 15.00
   Loose, with all parts 7.00
Darth Vader's TIE Fighter (#69662, 1997) 35.00
   Loose, with all parts 12.00

Power of the Force Vehicles with figures (1997–98)

A-wing Fighter with **A-wing Pilot** figure (#69732, 1997) 30.00
Electronic Imperial AT-AT Walker with **AT-AT Commander**
   and AT-AT Driver (#69733, 1997) [.00]
   graphic covers bottom of figures' photo 100.00
   Variation [.00] decal over graphic 100.00
   Variation [.01] full photo shown 90.00
Loose, with all parts and figure(s), each . . . . half boxed price

Second Batch, new green box (Hasbro 1999–2000)

Tatooine Skiff with **Jedi Knight Luke Skywalker**
   (#26458) Target exclusive 50.00
Y-wing Fighter with **Rebel Alliance Pilot** 30.00
Loose, with all parts and figure(s), each . . . . half boxed price

Shadows of the Empire Boba Fett's Slave I (Kenner 1996)

SHADOWS OF THE EMPIRE VEHICLES

Shadows of the Empire Vehicles, purple boxes (1996)

Boba Fett's *Slave I*, including **Han Solo in Carbonite** (#69565, 1996) $30.00

    Reissue in Power of the Force green box 25.00

Dash Rendar's Outrider (#69593, 1996) 45.00

    Reissue (#69814) in Power of the Force box 30.00

Swoop vehicle with **Swoop Trooper** figure, (#69591, 1996)

    Shadows of the Empire box 15.00

Loose, with all parts and figure(s), each. . . . . half boxed price

SPEEDER BIKES

Speeder Bike Vehicles with figures

Imperial Speeder Bike with **Biker Scout Stormtrooper**

    (#69765, 1996) red Power of the Force box $25.00

Speeder Bike with **Luke Skywalker** in Endor Gear

    (#69651, 1997) green Power of the Force box

    [.00] two white gloves in front photo 20.00

    Variation [.01] wearing one black glove 15.00

Speeder Bike with **Princess Leia Organa** in Endor

    Gear (#69727, 1997) green Power of the Force box

    [.00] with rocks in side photos 25.00

    Variation [.01] moss airbrushed over rocks 15.00

Power Racing Speeder Bike with **Scout Trooper**

    (#60588, 1998) green Power of the Force box 15.00

Loose, with all parts and figure(s), each. . . . . half boxed price

EXPANDED UNIVERSE VEHICLES

Expanded Universe Vehicles (1998)

Cloud Car with exclusive **Cloud Car Pilot** figure,

    from *The Art of Star Wars* (#69786) $15.00

Episode I Electronic Naboo Fighter (Hasbro 1999)

Airspeeder with exclusive **Airspeeder Pilot** figure,
  from *The Art of Star Wars* (#69774) 15.00
Speeder Bike with **Rebel Speeder Bike Pilot**
  figure (#69772, 1998) 15.00
Loose, with all parts and figure(s), each. . . . . half boxed price

ELECTRONIC POWER F/X VEHICLE

Electronic Power F/X Vehicle (1998) green box
Electronic Power F/X Luke Skywalker Red Five X-wing Fighter,
  plus non-removable lever-activated Luke Skywalker
  and R2-D2 (#69784) [.00] $75.00
  Reissue [.01] 75.00
  Loose, with all parts 35.00

EPISODE I VEHICLES

Large Vehicles
Royal Starship (see Playsets)
Electronic Naboo Fighter (#84099, 1999)
  [.02] "with Lights and Sounds" $25.00
  [.03] "with Real Movie Lights and Sounds" 20.00
Trade Federation Tank (#84101) 30.00
Loose, with all parts and figure(s), each. . . . . half boxed price

Midsize Vehicles
Trade Federation Droid Fighters (#84171, 1999) 20.00
  Loose, with all parts 10.00

Podracer Vehicles with figure (1999)
Anakin Skywalker's Podracer with **Anakin Skywalker** (#84097) 20.00
Sebulba's Podracer with **Sebulba** (#84098) 25.00
Loose, with all parts and figure(s), each. . . . . half boxed price

Imperial AT-ST & Speeder Bike (Hasbro 2002)

Small Vehicles

Flash Speeder (#84191) 15.00
STAP and **Battle Droid** (#84139) 15.00
Sith Speeder and **Darth Maul** (#84141) 20.00
Loose, with all parts and figure(s), each. . . . . half boxed price

Episode I "Invasion Force" small vehicles

Armored Scout Tank and **Battle Droid** (#84367) [0000] 25.00
　　Reissue: [.0100]. 15.00
Gungan Assault Cannon with **Jar Jar** (#84368) 15.00
Gungan Scout Sub with **Obi-Wan Kenobi** (#84397) 25.00
Sith Attack Speeder with **Darth Maul** (#84399) 25.00
Loose, with all parts and figure(s), each. . . . . half boxed price

Episode I Exclusive Vehicles

Famba with Shield Generator and **Gungan Warrior**
　　(#84369) FAO Schwarz exclusive 100.00
　　Loose, with all parts and figure 60.00
Ammo Wagon and Falumpaset with
　　nonremovable Gungan Warrior (#84358) Wal-Mart 25.00
　　Loose, with all parts 15.00

POWER OF THE JEDI VEHICLES

Power of the Jedi Vehicles (Hasbro 2001–02)

B-wing Fighter with **Sullustan Pilot** (#26481)
　　Target exclusive $25.00
Imperial AT-ST and Speeder bike with **Paploo** (#32468)
　　Toys "R" Us exclusive 30.00
TIE Interceptor with **Imperial Pilot** figure (#32457)
　　Toys "R" Us exclusive. 30.00
Luke Skywalker's Snowspeeder with **Dack Ralter**
　　and Luke Skywalker figure (#26483) 40.00

Attack of the Clones: Zam Wesell Speeder (Hasbro 2002)
Red Leader's X-wing Fighter (Hasbro 2004)

TIE Bomber, with **Imperial Pilot** figure (#26479)
  Wal-Mart exclusive 25.00
Loose, with all parts and figure(s), each. . . . . half boxed price

ATTACK OF THE CLONES VEHICLES

Attack of the Clones vehicles (2002–03)
Anakin Skywalker Speeder (#84871) $15.00
Anakin Skywalker Swoop Bike 10.00
Imperial Dogfight TIE Fighter 30.00
Obi-Wan Kenobi's Jedi Starfighter (#84869) 25.00
Republic Gunship (#84874) 20.00
Jango Fett's Slave I (#84873) 25.00
Darth Tyranus Speeder Bike 10.00
Zam Wesell Speeder (#84888) 15.00
Loose, with all parts and figure(s), each. . . . . half boxed price

Attack of the Clones exclusive vehicles (2002–03)
Dagobah X-wing (Toys "R" Us) 40.00
A-wing, green (Target) 30.00
Imperial Shuttle (FAO Schwarz) 100.00
Obi-Wan Kenobi's Jedi Starfighter (#84810) 25.00
Loose, with all parts and figure(s), each. . . . . half boxed price

CLONE WARS VEHICLES

Clone Wars, blue-stripe window box
Trade Federation Armored Attack Tank (AAT) (#84941) $20.00
Anakin Skywalker's Jedi Starfighter (#84847). 20.00
Homing Spider Droid. 20.00
Geonosian Starfighter (#84976) 22.00
Loose, with all parts and figure(s), each. . . . . half boxed price

Hoth Wampa (Kenner 1984)

TRILOGY VEHICLES

Trilogy Vehicles in blue window box (2004)

A-wing Fighter, with pilot (#26750) $30.00
Imperial Dogfight TIE Fighter with Imperial pilot (#26702) 30.00
Red Leader's X-wing Fighter (#32152) 30.00
Loose, with all parts and figure(s), each . . . . half boxed price

ORIGINAL TRILOGY VEHICLES

Original Trilogy Vehicles, black box

Slave I with Boba Fett figure (Target exclusive) (#34512) $20.00
Jawa Sandcrawler with figures (#26795) Previews Exclusive 40.00
Millennium Falcon (#85234) 50.00
TIE Fighter (#85247) 20.00
X-wing Fighter (#85426) 20.00
Darth Vader TIE Fighter (#32564) 30.00
Loose, with all parts and figure(s), each . . . . half boxed price

SHIPS
Kenner (1997–98)

Ships differ from "vehicles" because ships are not scaled to fit action figures, but vehicles are. Obviously Kenner couldn't make a Star Destroyer the same scale as its other vehicles—it would be over 100 feet long!

Collector Fleet in try-me box (Kenner 1997–98)

Electronic Rebel Blockade Runner (#27844) $25.00
Electronic Star Destroyer (#27835) 25.00
Electronic Super Star Destroyer *Executor* (#27914) 30.00

Ronto and Jawa figure (Kenner 1997)

CLASSIC CREATURES
Kenner (1979–84)

Classic Creatures

Patrol Dewback (#39240, 1979)

    Original *Star Wars* box $75.00

    Reissue in *The Empire Strikes Back* box 250.00

    Star Wars Collector Series Patrol Dewback (1983) 50.00

    Loose, with all parts 25.00

Tauntaun (#39820, 1980)

    Original *The Empire Strikes Back* box 75.00

    Loose, with all parts 25.00

Tauntaun with Open Belly Rescue Feature

    (#93340,1982) *The Empire Strikes Back* box 75.00

    Loose, with all parts 25.00

Wampa, Snow Creature from Hoth (#69560, 1982)

    Original *The Empire Strikes Back* box picturing Rebel Commander 60.00

    Reissue as Hoth Wampa in *The Empire Strikes Back* box

    picturing Luke Skywalker Hoth Gear 35.00

    Reissue in *Return of the Jedi* box 40.00

    Loose, with all parts 20.00

Jabba the Hutt Action Playset, including **Jabba** and

    Salacious Crumb molded figure (#70490, 1983)

    Original *Return of the Jedi* box 60.00

    Reissue in *Return of the Jedi* box (Sears) 40.00

    Loose, with all parts 30.00

Rancor Monster (1984)

    Original *Return of the Jedi* box 75.00

    Reissue in Power of the Force box 60.00

    Loose, with all parts 30.00

Dewback and Sandtrooper;
Rancor and Luke (Kenner 1998)

NEW CREATURES
Kenner (1997–2002)

The first three creature and figure combinations are based on the new footage from the first movie. Deluxe creatures came out in 1998. Only action-figure scale creatures (3-3/4") are listed here. All doll scale creatures (12") are listed in the *Dolls and Figures* chapter.

"Special Edition" Creature and Figure Combos (1997)

Ronto and Jawa in green Power of the Force box, with
    exclusive Jawa figure (#69728) $18.00
    Loose, with all parts and figure 8.00

Dewback and **Sandtrooper** in green Power of the Force box (#69743)
    [.00] Galactic Empire and Unaffiliated logos on front 18.00
    Variation, [.01] Galactic Empire logo only. 15.00
    Loose, with all parts and figure 8.00

Jabba the Hutt and **Han Solo** in green Power of the Force box (#69742)
    [.00] Galactic Empire and Rebel Alliance logos,
    Han pictured to Jabba's right 35.00
    Variation [.01] Han pictured to Jabba's left 18.00
    Variation [.02] Unaffiliated and Rebel Alliance logos, Han pictured on left   18.00
    Loose, with all parts and figure 8.00

Second Batch (1998)

Tauntaun with **Han Solo in Hoth Gear** (#84107) 85.00
    Loose, with all parts and figure 30.00

Luke Skywalker and Tauntaun (#69729) 25.00
    Loose, with all parts and figure 10.00

Wampa and **Luke Skywalker (Hoth Gear)** (#69768) 45.00
    Loose, with all parts and figure 10.00

Acklay Creature (Hasbro 2002)
Creature Cantina Playset (Kenner 1979)

Deluxe Creatures and Figure (1998)

Rancor and Luke Skywalker, with **Jedi Luke** (#69771) 40.00
   Loose, with all parts and figure 15.00
Bantha and Tusken Raider, with **Tusken Raider**
   with Gaderffii Stick (#69769) 40.00
   Loose, with all parts and figure 15.00

EPISODE I CREATURES

    The first two Episode I creatures were overproduced like all of the early Episode I action figures. Jabba with the two-headed announcer, and Eopie with Qui-Gon Jinn came out later and are very scarce. On the other hand, Jabba the Hutt was available in quantity—on a header card with a can of slime and some frogs to eat—as "Jabba Glob." This is listed in the *Dolls and Figures* chapter.

Episode I Creature & Figure (1999–2001)

Kaadu and **Jar Jar Binks** (#84094) $15.00
   Loose, with all parts and figure 8.00
Opee and **Qui-Gon Jinn** (#84096) warning on sticker 15.00
   Loose, with all parts and figure 7.00
Jabba the Hutt with **Two-Headed Announcer** (#84167) 30.00
   Loose, with all parts and figure 15.00
Eopie and **Qui-Gon Jinn** (#84354) 75.00
   Loose, with all parts and figure 35.00
Femba with Gungan Warrior, (see Exclusive Vehicles)

ATTACK OF THE CLONES CREATURES

Creatures (2002) boxed

Reek $20.00
Acklay 25.00

Death Star Space Station Playset (Kenner 1979)

CLASSIC PLAYSETS
Kenner (1979–85)

With all the classic playsets Kenner produced in the 1980s, you would think it would have reissued some in the 1990s. So far, however, it has not done so.

STAR WARS PLAYSETS

Star Wars Playsets (1979)
Death Star Space Station, three-story playset
  (#38050) Original *Star Wars* box $225.00
  Loose, with all parts 60.00
Creature Cantina Action Playset (#39120)
  Original *Star Wars* box 125.00
  Loose, with all parts 40.00
Land of the Jawas Action Playset (#39130)
  Original *Star Wars* box 160.00
  Reissue in *The Empire Strikes Back* box 225.00
  Loose, with all parts 60.00
Droid Factory (#39150, 1979) *Star Wars* box 125.00
  Reissue in *The Empire Strikes Back* box 175.00
  Loose, with all parts 50.00

THE EMPIRE STRIKES BACK PLAYSETS

The Empire Strikes Back Playsets (1980–82)
Imperial Attack Base, Hoth scene (#39830, 1980)
  Original *The Empire Strikes Back* box $125.00
  Loose, with all parts 30.00
Hoth Ice Planet Adventure Set (1980)
  Original *The Empire Strikes Back* box 150.00

Ewok Village Action Playset (Kenner 1983)

Reissue with **Imperial Stormtrooper**
(**Hoth Battle Gear**) figure 225.00
  Loose, with all parts, no figure 50.00
Dagobah Action Playset (#38820, 1981)
  Original *The Empire Strikes Back* box 100.00
  Loose, with all parts 40.00
Turret and Probot Playset (#38330, 1981)
  Original *The Empire Strikes Back* box 150.00
  Loose, with all parts 60.00
Rebel Command Center Adventure Set, with **R2-D2**, **Luke Skywalker**
  and **AT-AT Commander** figures (#69481, 1981)
  Original *The Empire Strikes Back* box 275.00
  Loose, with all parts 120.00

RETURN OF THE JEDI PLAYSET

Return of the Jedi Playset (1983)
Ewok Village Action Playset (#70520, 1983)
  Original *Return of the Jedi* box $125.00
  Loose, with all parts 50.00

EWOK PLAYSET

Ewok Playset (1984)
Ewok Family Hut, 12" high plus four nonposeable figures (Kenner Preschool, 1984)
  Original *Ewoks* box $50.00
  Loose, with all parts 15.00

Exclusive Playsets
Cantina Adventure Set (Sears promotional set) with Greedo, Hammerhead,
  blue Snaggletooth and Walrus Man (#38861, 1979) *Star Wars* box 700.00
  Loose, with all parts 300.00
Cloud City Playset (Sears exclusive) with Han Solo in Bespin outfit,
  Ugnaught, Lobot and Dengar, and Boba Fett (#38781, 1981)

Electronic Naboo Royal Starship (Hasbro 1999)

Original *The Empire Strikes Back* box 450.00
Loose, with all parts 175.00
The Jabba the Hutt Dungeon Action Playset Variation #1, with Klaatu, Nikto and
    8D8 in red box, Sears exclusive (#71381, 1983)
Original *Return of the Jedi* box 130.00
Loose, with all parts 60.00
    Variation #2, with FV-9D9, Amanaman and Barada in green box,
    Sears exclusive (#59262, 1984)
Original *Return of the Jedi* box 350.00
Loose, with all parts 250.00

NEW PLAYSETS
Kenner/Hasbro (1995–2001)

The Electronic *Millennium Falcon* is pretty much the same as
the Classic vehicle of the same name. This was the only new playset
for the first few years An "Imperial Scanning Crew" figure was
included with the reissued *Millennium Falcon* carry case, but the
only secret compartments to scan are in this playset/vehicle.

Power of the Force Playset, red box
Electronic *Millennium Falcon* playset/vehicle, with
    "4 Real Movie Sounds" (#69785, July 1995). $65.00
Loose, with all parts 25.00

EPISODE I PLAYSETS

The premiere Episode I playset is the Naboo Royal Starship. Like
so many other Episode I items, it was eventually available at deep
discount. It has a number of interesting features, but the one that

Vehicle Maintenance Energizer (Kenner 1983)

intrigued me the most was the Queen's throne. There is no Queen Amidala figure that bends at the knees, so even if you could get the queen to sit in it in one of her fancy dresses, her legs would stick straight out!

Episode I Starship Playset
Electronic Naboo Royal Starship Blockade Cruiser/ Playset
(#84146) with **red R2 unit** $75.00
  Loose, with all parts and figure 45.00

Episode I Playset
Theed Generator Complex with **Battle Droid** (#26222) 20.00
  Loose, with all parts and figure 10.00

Episode I Power F/X Playset
Motorized Theed Hangar Playset with **Qui-Gon Jinn (Power Spin)**
and **Battle Droid (cut in half)** (#84173) 30.00
  Loose, with all parts and figure 15.00

POWER OF THE JEDI PLAYSET

Power of the Jedi Playset (2001–02)
Carbon-Freezing Chamber with **Bespin Security Guard** $40.00
  Loose, with all parts and figure 20.00

ATTACK OF THE CLONES PLAYSET

Geonosis Battle Arena $30.00

Radar Laser Cannon (Kenner 1983)

CLASSIC ACCESSORIES
Kenner (1981–84)

Some of the accessories listed in this section were called "playsets" or "one-figure vehicles" on their boxes. Their small size places them in this category.

Accessories

Vehicle Maintenance Energizer (#93430, 1983)
 Original *The Empire Strikes Back* box $20.00
 Reissue in *Return of the Jedi* box 15.00
 Loose, with all parts 9.00

Radar Laser Cannon (#93440, 1983)
 Original *The Empire Strikes Back* box 20.00
 Reissue in *Return of the Jedi* box 15.00
 Loose, with all parts 9.00

Tri Pod Laser Cannon (#93450, 1983)
 Original *The Empire Strikes Back* box 20.00
 Reissue in *Return of the Jedi* box 15.00
 Loose, with all parts 9.00

Ewok Assault Catapult (#71070, 1984)
 Original *Return of the Jedi* box 18.00
 Loose, with all parts 8.00

Ewok Combat Glider (#93510, 1984)
 Original *Return of the Jedi* box 18.00
 Loose, with all parts 8.00

Ewok Battle Wagon, with *Star Wars* Planetary Map
 (#93690, 1984) Power of the Force box 300.00
 Loose, with all parts 125.00

Imperial Sniper Vehicle (1984)
 Original Power of the Force box 100.00

INT-4 and MLC-3 Mini-Rigs (Kenner 1981)

Loose, with all parts 40.00
Security Scout (1984)
Original Power of the Force box. 100.00
Loose, with all parts 50.00
One-Man Sand Skimmer (1984)
Original Power of the Force box. 80.00
Loose, with all parts 30.00
Ewok Fire Cart (Kenner Preschool, 1984)
Original Ewoks box 40.00
Loose, with all parts 15.00
Ewok Woodland Wagon (Kenner Preschool, 1985)
Original Ewoks box 75.00
Loose, with all parts 20.00

MINI-RIGS

Mini-Rigs were one-man "crawling, climbing, flying" action figure accessories that were too small to be part of the regular vehicle lineup. They came in a box with a hanging flap, and the best graphics are on the back of the package.

None of these mini-rigs ever appeared in the three movies, but a few showed up in the animated *Droids* series. These days, Hasbro packages such items with a figure and sells them as "Deluxe" figures.

Mini Rig 1-Figure Vehicles, 6" x 4-1/2" boxes (1981-83)

MTV-7 Multi-Terrain Vehicle (#40010, 1981)
Original *The Empire Strikes Back* box $35.00
Reissue in *The Empire Strikes Back* box with **AT-AT Driver** figure . . . 60.00
Reissue in *Return of the Jedi* box. 25.00
Loose, with all parts, without figure 9.00
MLC-3 Mobile Laser Cannon (#40020, 1981)
Original *The Empire Strikes Back* box 35.00

Endor Attack Accessory (Kenner 1997)

Reissue in *The Empire Strikes Back* box
with **Rebel Commander** figure 60.00
Reissue in *Return of the Jedi* box 25.00
Loose, with all parts, without figure 9.00

PDT-8 Personnel Deployment Transport (#40070, 1981)
Original *The Empire Strikes Back* box 30.00
Reissue in *The Empire Strikes Back* box with **2-1B** figure 60.00
Reissue in *Return of the Jedi* box 15.00
Loose, with all parts, without figure 9.00

INT-4 Interceptor (#69750, 1982)
Original *The Empire Strikes Back* box 30.00
Reissue in *The Empire Strikes Back* box
with **AT-AT Commander** figure 60.00
Reissue in *Return of the Jedi* box 15.00
Loose, with all parts, without figure 9.00

CAP-2 Captivator (#69760, 1982)
Original *The Empire Strikes Back* box 25.00
Reissue in *The Empire Strikes Back* box with **Bossk** figure 60.00
Reissue in *Return of the Jedi* box 20.00
Loose, with all parts 9.00

AST-5 Armored Sentinel Transport (#70880, 1983)
Original *Return of the Jedi* box 15.00
Loose, with all parts 7.00

ISP-6 (Imperial Shuttle Pod) (#70890, 1983)
Original *Return of the Jedi* box 25.00
Loose, with all parts 9.00

Desert Sail Skiff (#93520, 1984) mini-rig
Original *Return of the Jedi* box 15.00
Loose, with all parts 10.00

Endor Forest Ranger (#93610, 1984) mini-rig
Original *Return of the Jedi* box 15.00
Loose, with all parts 10.00

Electronic Gungan Catapult Accessory Set (Hasbro 1999)

NEW ACCESSORIES
Kenner (1996–2002)

New Power of the Force Accessories are more like mini-playsets than anything else. Some of the larger weapons that might have been issued as accessories were instead sold with figures on header cards as "Deluxe Figures." In Episode I, Hasbro changed tactics and issued packages of small weapons and equipment as accessory sets, along with larger light-up weapons.

NEW POWER OF THE FORCE ACCESSORIES

First Batch (1996) red box

Detention Block Rescue (#27598) $15.00
Death Star Escape (#27599) 15.00

Second Batch (1997) green box

Hoth Battle (#27858) 20.00
Endor Attack (#27859) 20.00

EPISODE I ACCESSORY SETS

Episode I Accessory Sets (1999–2001)

Naboo Accessory Set (#26208) $6.00
Tatooine Accessory Set (#26209) 6.00
Underwater Accessory Set (#26211) 6.00
Sith Accessory Set (#26210) 6.00
Tatooine Disguise (#26215) 10.00
Rappel Line Attack (#26212) 10.00

Podracer Fuel Station (#26214) 10.00
Hyperdrive Repair Kit (#26213). 10.00

Electronic Episode I Accessories
Electronic Flash Cannon Accessory Set (#26217) 15.00
Electronic Gungan Catapult Accessory Set (#26218) 15.00

VANS AND RACERS
Various (1978–80)

A less authentic toy than a *Star Wars* van would be hard to
design. Not only are there no cars or vans in the movies, there aren't
even any roads.

Star Wars Van Set, two toy vans, plus 12 barrels, four pylons
  and two T-Sticks (Kenner #90170, 1978). $150.00
Darth Vader SSP (Super Sonic Power) Van, black,
  gyro powered (Kenner #90160, 1978) 50.00
Star Wars Heroes SSP (Super Sonic Power) Van,
  gyro powered (Kenner #90160, 1978) 50.00
Star Wars Duel at Death Star Racing Set,
  19" x 20" box (Fundimensions 1978) 200.00

WALL ART

Wall art includes just about every kind of picture, poster or other item designed to be framed and/or hung on a wall. Calendars are covered in the *Paper Collectibles* chapter.

CHROMART

ChromArt prints are 8" x 10" in an 11" x 14" matte. They are made with acrylic, foil and etching to create an illusion of depth. The images come from CD-ROM game boxes and videotape boxes, but the enhancements make them quite striking.

ChromArt Prints (Zanart Entertainment 1994)
SW-C1 through C20, each $12.00

Second Series
Ten different, each 13.00

Third Series
Eight different, each 12.00

Fourth Series
Six different, each 20.00

LITHOGRAPHS

Many *Star Wars* limited-edition lithographs were created by well-known science fiction and *Star Wars* artist Ralph McQuarrie. They

Star Wars ChromArt Print (Zanart)

are 18" x 12", framed and matted. Many other prominent *Star Wars* artists have also produced lithographs, including Boris Vallejo, Drew Struzan, the Bros. Hildebrandt and Dave Dorman.

Star Wars, A New Hope (Ralph McQuarrie art) framed

The Cantina on Mos Eisley (Willitts Designs) $150.00
Millennium Falcon (Willitts Designs) 180.00
Rebel Attack on the Death Star (Willitts Designs) 200.00
Rebel Ceremony (Willitts Designs) 150.00

The Empire Strikes Back (Ralph McQuarrie art) framed

Rebel Patrol of Echo Base (Willitts Designs) 150.00
Luke Skywalker and Darth Vader (Willitts Designs) 150.00
Battle of Hoth (Willitts Designs) 150.00
Cloud City of Bespin (Willitts Designs) 150.00

Return of the Jedi (Ralph McQuarrie art) framed

Jabba the Hutt (Willitts Designs) 175.00
The Rancor Pit (Willitts Designs) 175.00
Speeder Bike Chase (Willitts Designs) 175.00
Death Star Main Reactor (Willitts Designs) 175.00

Other Lithographs (Various artists)

Star Wars 15th Anniversary Serigraph, by Melanie Taylor Kent (1992) . . . 1,750.00
Star Wars Lithograph by Ken Steacy, 17" x 24"
    signed and numbered (Gifted Images 1994) 600.00
In a Galaxy Far, Far Away, limited, signed lithograph by Michael
    David Ward 175.00
Luke Skywalker Limited Edition Lithograph by Al Williamson (1996) 300.00
Darth Vader Limited Edition Lithograph by Al Williamson (1996) 300.00

Star Wars Style D Poster (Lucasfilm 1977)

Star Wars R2-D2 Remarked Lithograph by the
Bros. Hildebrandt, signed, 24" x 18" 175.00
Star Wars Luke and Yoda Lithograph by Boris Vallejo, signed and
numbered 600.00

Star Wars, Special Edition Lithographs by Dave Dorman
Star Wars Dewback Patrol Lithograph (1997) 75.00
Star Wars Battle of Hoth Lithograph (1997) 75.00
Star Wars Tales of the Jedi, Freedon Nadd Uprising 75.00
Star Wars Star's End Lithograph (1997) 75.00
Star Wars Princess Leia (Boushh) Lithograph (1997) 75.00
Star Wars Throne Room of Jabba (1997) 75.00

POSTERS

There are many types of posters, from those sold in toy stores to those that come in magazines and as fast-food giveaways, but the most valuable by far are the theater posters that were issued to promote the movies. These had no initial price because they were sent to movie theaters or given away at shows. Their value is entirely collector driven. A considerable number of general movie poster collectors compete with *Star Wars* collectors for these posters, keeping the prices high. Posters are most valuable when they are rolled, not folded, and should never be placed on a wall with thumbtacks. Unfortunately, valuable posters can be reproduced and sold as if original. Collectors should buy with care from reputable dealers.

POSTERS–THEATRICAL

Star Wars
Advance A One-sheet, "A long time ago..." $275.00

The Empire Strikes Back Re-Release Poster (Lucasfilm 1981)

Star Wars advance, second version. 175.00
Style A One-sheet, Tommy Jung art. 175.00
Star Wars, style A, with record promo 175.00
Star Wars advance, style B 150.00
Star Wars, style C 150.00
Style D One-sheet (Circus poster). 350.00
Anniversary One-sheet (1978) theater giveaway 600.00
'79 Re-release One-sheet, "It's Back!" 100.00
'81 Re-release One-sheet. 60.00
'82 Re-release One-Sheet 50.00

The Empire Strikes Back
Advance One-sheet 200.00
Style A One-sheet (Love Story), Rodger Kastel art 200.00
Style B One-sheet, Tommy Jung art. 75.00
'81 Re-release One-sheet, Tommy Jung art 50.00
'82 Re-release One-sheet, Tommy Jung art 40.00

Revenge of the Jedi
Advance *Revenge of the Jedi* One-sheet, 41" x 27"
   with release date 400.00
Variation, no release date 450.00

Return of the Jedi
Style A One-sheet 35.00
Style B One-sheet 50.00
Return of the Jedi, 1985 reissue 30.00

Star Wars Trilogy Special Edition, One-sheets (1997)
Advance One-sheet 50.00
Version B *Star Wars: A New Hope*, Drew Struzan art 40.00
Version C *The Empire Strikes Back*, Drew Struzan art. 40.00
Version D *Return of the Jedi*, Drew Struzan art 40.00

Return of the Jedi Style B (Lucasfilm 1983)

Episode I *The Phantom Menace*, One-sheets (1999)

Advance One-sheet 75.00
The Phantom Menace 50.00

POSTERS–SPECIAL EVENTS

The Art of *Star Wars*, Center for the Arts. $50.00
Caravan of Courage 60.00
Immunization Poster 10.00
Star Tours Poster 5.00
Public Radio Drama poster 150.00
Vintage Action Figures Photo poster 15.00

POSTERS–COMMERCIAL

Star Wars 10th Anniversary Poster, 27" x 41" (1987)
   signed by Drew Struzan, limited to 200 . . . . 100.00
Star Wars 15th Anniversary Poster
   by Melanie Taylor Kent, 20" x 30" (1992) 25.00
Star Wars 15th Anniversary Movie Poster,
   by Greg and Tim Hildebrandt, deluxe, signed edition 50.00
Return of the Jedi 10th Anniversary Advance Poster,
   deluxe version, gold-foil border 50.00
Star Wars Checklist Poster, 27" x 40" (Killian Enterprises 1995) full color
   reproductions of all movie one-sheet posters and variants 20.00
Star Wars Cutaway *Millennium Falcon* Poster (1997) 20.00
Star Wars Cutaway *Millennium Falcon* deluxe poster,
   signed and numbered, certificate of authenticity (1997) 40.00
Star Wars Cutaway X-wing/TIE Fighter poster (1997) 20.00
Star Wars Cutaway X-wing/TIE Fighter deluxe poster,
   signed and numbered, certificate of authenticity (1997) 40.00
AT-AT and Snowspeeder Cutaway Poster,
   36" x 24" black and white 20.00

Star Wars Public Radio Drama Poster

Deluxe, signed and numbered 40.00
Most other commercial posters . . . . 15.00 or less

Food Premiums
Burger Chef Premium posters (1978), four different, each 10.00
General Mills Premium posters (1978), four different, each 10.00
Procter & Gamble Premium posters (1978), three different, each 10.00
Most other food premium posters . . . . Less than 10.00

LIGHTED POSTERS

Star Wars Neon Movie Poster (Neonetics 1993), framed $200.00
Darth Vader Neon Framed Picture (Neonetics 1995) 225.00
Star Wars Millennium Falcon Neon Framed Picture (Neonetics 1994) 225.00
Star Wars Millennium Falcon LED Framed Picture (Neonetics 1994) 140.00

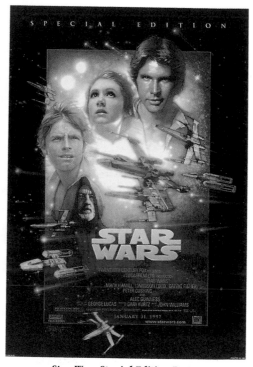

Star Wars Special Edition Poster

Index

Star Wars Trilogy DVD Collection Figures (Hasbro 2004)

Index

Warman's *Star Wars* Field Guide

Classic Jabba the Hutt and Friends (Kenner 1980–83)

Index

The Ultimate Reference for Star Wars Collectors

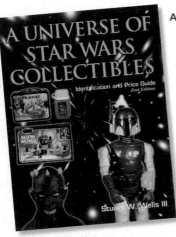

**A Universe of Star Wars® Collectibles
Identification and Price Guide
2nd Edition
by Stuart W. Wells III**

You'll find prices for more than 8,500 items and more than 700 photographs of some of the hottest collectibles, such as trading cards, books, action figures, clothing, games, vehicles, wall art, comics, and more! Covering items made from 1976-2002, this book also includes sections on Episode I: The Phantom Menace and Episode II: Attack of the Clones.

Softcover • 8-1/4 x 10-7/8 • 288 pages • 700+ color photos

Item# SWPG2 • $29.95